THE
TRAVELING
FEAST

THE
TRAVELING
FEAST

ON THE ROAD AND AT THE TABLE WITH
MY HEROES

RICK BASS

LITTLE, BROWN AND COMPANY
NEW YORK BOSTON LONDON

Little, Brown and Company
Hachette Book Group
1290 Avenue of the Americas, New York, NY 10104
littlebrown.com

First Edition: June 2018

Little, Brown and Company is a division of Hachette Book Group, Inc. The Little, Brown name and logo are trademarks of Hachette Book Group, Inc.

The publisher is not responsible for websites (or their content) that are not owned by the publisher.

The Hachette Speakers Bureau provides a wide range of authors for speaking events. To find out more, go to hachettespeakersbureau.com or call (866) 376-6591.

Portions of this book have previously appeared, often in different form, in the *Black Warrior Review*, the *Georgia Review*, *Mountain*, and *Narrative*.

ISBN 978-0-316-38123-9
LCCN 2018933125

10 9 8 7 6 5 4 3 2 1

LSC-C

Printed in the United States of America

For my father,
early mentor,
heroic geologist,
beloved storyteller,
and so much else

CONTENTS

Contents

THE
TRAVELING
FEAST

Prologue

The radio operator didn't like me. She worked the switch-board down in town for my shortwave, which was how people got in touch with me back in the late 1980s. There was no electricity up here then, no telephones, no nothing. Friends dialed the dispatcher's number, and she rang me up on the radio. She was a severe churchgoing lady, severe even by standards in western Montana.

The radio wasn't like a telephone call. People back in New York, or wherever they were calling from, thought that it was, because they were on a telephone. But out here, on the Canadian border, up in the trees and mountains, it was like a live talk show. Everybody in western Montana could hear our conversation, which was broadcast over the radio, and during the short winter days, the long winter nights, when entertainment

3

was scarce, that was what a good number of the folks up here ended up doing—monitoring one another's shortwave calls to hear all the dirt.

The radio dispatcher didn't like me because my callers were often drunk and used coarse language. I was too shy to tell them, my callers, that they were on the air, and besides, with many of my friends—so wild!—this would only have inspired them to further profanity. I merely quivered and winced, imagining the church-lady operator listening, imagining my neighbors listening, imagining, in bouts of winter paranoia, the FBI and the FCC listening, taking notes.

Why my friends told me these things in the first place, I didn't know. I hadn't asked to hear them—neither had the church lady—but since I was too shy to tell them "Please, stop it," the operator and I listened to the editor Gordon Lish use the f-word like water. "Bass," he said, calling to tell me about some new development, as enthusiastic as a twister, "you've got to read this, it's fanfuckingtastic, you've fucking got to fucking read this fucking book."

The church lady didn't even clear her throat. I trembled at some of the things she had to listen to, and wouldn't have blamed her for holding them against me, but I never dreamed of saying anything to any of the callers. All my life I'd been shy, and I wasn't about to change that.

Before my move to the remote Yaak Valley in Montana, I had lived in Mississippi. One summer there I attempted to become Eudora Welty's yard man. It was one of the many summers when I was writing, but had not published anything, and did not believe I ever would. I am sad to say this was not when I was a teenager; this was when I was a grown man: twenty-four, maybe twenty-five years old.

I just wanted to be close to her, was the thing. It seemed like the perfect world. I could be close to her, but I wouldn't have to say anything. I could just stagger around in the Jackson heat, shirtless, in her front yard, and perspire: trimming the hedges, mowing the lawn, sweeping the sidewalks and the driveway like some sort of yard savage. Standing guard is what I imagined it would feel like, protecting her, but more important, just being around her.

Why? I hesitate even to try to explain what the work of Eudora Welty, the best American writer never to win the Nobel Prize, has meant to me. Unlike Faulkner, her Mississippi neighbor, the flamboyant curmudgeon and drinker who wrote overbrimming, high-octane prose (Barry Hannah once called him, semi-endearingly, Old Blabbermouth) and who traveled the world, Miss Welty stayed for ninety-two years in her Jackson home on Pinehurst Street—the same house in which she had been born—writing, writing. "I am a writer who came from a sheltered life," she says in her memoir, *One Writer's Beginnings*. "A sheltered life can be a daring life as well. For all serious daring starts from within."

It was the music of her prose that moved me: the rhythm, the cadence, the lyricism. Two of what I consider the greatest similes ever written both belong to her: her description of a bird dog's pink panting tongue being the color of a faded rose, and the sound of cicadas in the early evening being like that of grain being poured into a metal bucket. In the former, I love how she compares the monstrous—there's nothing nastier than a bird dog's slobbering old tongue—to the sublime, the archetypal poetry of the rose. And the latter works its way far down into the subconscious, because even though the two sounds are not alike, both are elemental components of the Southern experience, and hearing each stirs a similar home-register in the brain.

My admiration extended beyond her writing. I had seen Miss Welty buying a frozen pizza at the Jitney Jungle one time and had even been impressed by the way she looked at each one before selecting the one she wanted, rather than taking the first one she saw. I figured I could learn things just by being bold enough to breathe some of the same air, but without ever mentioning to her that I was a writer; or rather, that I was trying to be one.

Perhaps I should not be telling this.

I bought a lawn mower and typed up a prospectus, listing my services: mowing, trimming, sweeping, etc. To increase my chances of employment, I gave price quotes that were crippling to any would-be competitors—two dollars per lawn, no matter the size. I went from door to door, putting these notices in the mailboxes, in the door slots. I would only embarrass myself further if I tried to tell you what it felt like, standing on Miss Welty's porch with my little notice.

I didn't gain Miss Welty's employ. The closest neighbor who hired me was a man who lived two houses down, but that was all right—it was closer than I'd ever been before, and I could breathe the air as I mowed laps around that delighted man's yard; that man who, for two dollars a week, was sure he was getting the better end of the bargain. But I knew better. I never complained about the stupefying heat, or about the humidity, and I kept a close eye on the yard two houses down the street. I was getting to breathe that air.

I haven't mentioned I had a real job back then, as a petroleum geologist, an executive's job with an office and a telephone and all that nonsense. Often people from the office would drive by in their rich cars and see me out there, laboring. It didn't bother me at all, though my savage yard work in that neighborhood was the beginning of my downfall in that office, with those office people and their rich cars, which is another story, and one I bring up only to illustrate my point, that shy men, or shy women, cannot live among people, nor should they try.

That summer I was nowhere near the writer I wanted to be, and I decided if I couldn't write, at least I could cut lawns, and do it well, and I suppose I wanted to show that to a real writer. The logic of it escapes me now, but I remember believing that lawn cutting would cure all the awkwardness I was experiencing with my writing.

Shyness can be a deadly thing.

About the worst case I ever heard of (besides mine) was from a writing student at the University of Montana named Jake, who related the following story to me. One time Jake and his friend Brian were fishing and drinking just outside the town where Tom McGuane lived. The sun was high and butter-yellow, a lovely June day. Tall grasses waved on the hillside where they sat taking a break from fishing, and drinking vodka. Along bounded a dog, up through the tall grass, wanting to play—McGuane's dog, Sadie, as it happened. She was a pointer, as I imagine it, polka-dotted, like a Dalmatian.

McGuane was one of Jake's gods. So what does he do, in his breathless shyness, in his drunkenness, in the beauty of the day? Jake, whom McGuane did not know from boo, took a sheet of paper from his notebook and scrawled his address on it. Giggling, he wrote, *Tom—loved your last novel. Let's have lunch—Jake*, and then withdrew from his rucksack a story manuscript he had with him and tucked this, along with the note, under the dog's collar.

It was a great joke, very funny, and he had Brian laughing, but before Jake could call the joke off and take the manuscript back, the McGuanes drove past in their new blue pickup on the gravel road above the river, the whole family, and the dog took off after them like something fired from a cannon.

Mortified, Jake jumped to his feet, wobbly-legged and drunkstaggering, and chased Sadie across the field toward the McGuanes' not-too-distant ranch. The truck stopped at a gate, and McGuane got out to open it, and his little daughter looked back and saw Sadie racing toward them; and then, surprisingly, not so far back, Jake, his legs churning, arms pumping. The McGuane family watched as Jake caught Sadie, bulldogged her down in the tall summer grass, wrestled the note and manuscript from her collar, then fled for the cottonwoods along the broad river.

That's how it is. You wait and you wait, and you work and you work, hoping to be a writer, a real writer—not as good as the ones you most admire, but good enough to maybe one day go up to them and say hello—but it very rarely works out that way. And if you've got this wretched shyness, you almost always seem to find yourself doing something foolish: rolling around wrestling a dog, or spending hot afternoons cutting lawns for free, when you should be inside writing. It's much better just to go off into the woods and not ever be seen again.

Protect yourself from yourself, stay cool, and do your work. You can be the party animal in the next life.

When you're shy, and a writer, it's not the same as being shy and, say, a mechanic. If you're a writer, people know you're watching them. It's like you've lost all your anonymity. You can't even stand in a crowd and be quiet, because they know what you're up to and then if that crowd happens to be other writers, well, that's the absolute worst.

One summer, Jim Harrison called me up on the radio and wanted my wife, Elizabeth, and me to meet him and the poet Dan Gerber in Livingston, at Jim's daughter and son-in-law's place, for dinner—a legendary Harrison-cooked meal, chicken and ribs and beans and turnip greens, in honor of our Southernness, Jim said. It was the first time I'd ever spoken to him— we had mutual friends at Lemuria Books, in Mississippi—and I had to brace myself to keep from falling over.

I had read his novella "Legends of the Fall," set in northern Montana, before I moved there, and it's the one story that metamorphosed me from a reader to a writer. I was struck by the powerful emotions beneath the surface that sometimes emerged like animals into the light of day; by the compression of story, in which the saga of a hundred years occurs within a hundred pages; and by the lush, painterly images: yellow cottonwood leaves pasting themselves on streamside boulders; an old man in a buffalo robe embracing his sons before they ride off to war, the breath of his farewell rising like smoke in a barn; a grieving soldier cutting out the heart of his war-killed brother and sealing it in wax to ferry back to Montana.

I'd been writing before I read this novella, working in Mississippi, where I made maps of underground treasure and wrote during my lunch breaks—*awful* stuff, among the worst prose ever written. At Lemuria, they kept trying to hand-sell me the book of the Harrison novellas. I kept turning it down, believing them to be rough he-man outdoor sagas, tales of blood and matted fur. Finally they just gave me the book, and it changed my life. When I read it, the slow sleeping atoms in my blood began, with that one awakening, to realign into crystalline forms that were unfamiliar to me. I followed them, no questions asked. I wrote a short story called "Where the Sea Used to Be" and sent it off to the *Paris Review*, where a young slush-pile reader, James Linville, handed it on to his boss, George Plimpton, and they decided to publish it, my first acceptance.

I still remember the letter: "I really liked it," James wrote to me. "It reminded me of 'Legends of the Fall.'"

It was nearly a day's drive from where Elizabeth and I lived to where Jim wanted us to meet him. We drove seventy-five miles an hour all the way. It was as if we were driving into battle—there was that sense of finality to it.

The weekend was perfect. We stayed at their house and slept on the back porch by a rushing stream with wind in the trees above, and stars and crickets. Jim and Jamie, his daughter, spent the whole afternoon preparing the meal, and the only thing the rest of us had to do was sit around and be awed. Dan, who is also a Buddhist priest, gave me one of his books and sat by himself on a boulder in a field at the base of the mountains as dusk fell, wearing pressed trousers and a clean white shirt. He came back in after dark and showed Elizabeth and me how to rub white yarrow, which was growing all over the yard, along our arms and faces to keep mosquitoes away and to smell good. Jim's agent and his wife, Bob and Kathy Dattila, were there—Kathy, like Elizabeth, is from Mississippi—and there were stories, stories. Kathy and Elizabeth lay together in the big hammock, and there was plenty to drink. Coyotes bayed in the distance. Jamie's husband, Steve, a lawyer, cooked the chicken, sprinkled water on the spattering coals. I wanted not to be shy, not this one evening, but couldn't help it. All I could do was watch and drink and eat and enjoy all the stories. It seemed to me that I lived in the woods and made up stories, but these people had actually gone out and lived *lives*.

There was one magical moment, after we thought everyone else had gone to bed. Elizabeth and I were outside, drinking, and in the kitchen window, we saw Jim and Jamie framed in the light, father and daughter, standing side by side at the twin sinks, working with concentration and talking to each other: Harrison's big balding tanned head and Jamie's slender schoolgirl-looking one, glasses on the end of her nose, dwarfed by Jim's massiveness, both of them happy in that yellow square of light, with Elizabeth and me on the outside, unseen, and the noise of that creek rushing past us.

When you are shy like this, you feel a million miles away from anything. You want to come closer, but cannot bear to bring yourself in. When you are a million miles out, though, you can see things, and you're free just to stand there and watch, and things that are sometimes ordinary to everyone else seem to your shy mind, in the last outpost, beautiful. You feel like falling over on your back, upturned, like a turtle.

Some years later, George Plimpton offered to punch me in the nose.

In the interim, after my defection from Mississippi to Montana, I had graduated from would-be yard man for Eudora Welty and become a bona fide writer, having published a collection of stories and a couple of books of essays. When George made his offer, we were standing in his office discussing a story of mine he was going to publish in the *Paris Review*, "The Legend of Pig-Eye," about a boxer in the Deep South. I wanted to tweak it a bit further, and told him that I was thinking about fighting a guy at Gleason's Gym in New York for the experience.

He grew very somber. "Don't get in the ring," he said. "Whatever you do, don't get in the ring. Those guys are serious. They'll hurt you. They would love to hurt a writer. Don't get in the ring," he repeated, so insistent that I wondered if he were receiving some kind of vision in which I was killed.

He pulled down a copy of *Shadow Box*, in which he had boxed Archie Moore, at that time the light heavyweight champion of the world, and toured with Muhammad Ali. Plimpton's eyes took on an interested look, and he moved between me and the doorway.

"If I hit you in the nose, though," he said, "you'd become part of a hoary genealogy." He began limbering his right arm, rolling his shoulder a little, flexing and unflexing his fingers. "When I was fighting Archie Moore, he broke my nose, and he had his nose busted by Ali, who had his nose punched by Joe Frazier, who had *his* nose punched by..." Plimpton recited, with pride, the chain of busted noses, of which I could become the most recent inductee—the tradition of it going way back before even Jack Dempsey's time.

I made some lame excuse toward leaving. Plimpton lingered

in the doorway, and the offer was made once more, with even more conviction—but finally he took the half-step aside that would let me leave his office without becoming part of boxing history. I have always wondered what it would have been like, and if I should have allowed him to reach out and tag me with that long right.

In some ways it might have been George Plimpton himself who put the idea for this book in my mind. Beginning with my fifty-fifth year, and having written nearly thirty books and however many hundreds of magazine articles, I decided to take a break from writing and go on an extended pilgrimage. I set out traveling the country (and in one case Europe) to visit writers who were mostly a generation older than I am, the ones who helped me become a writer trained outside a university. Sometimes they helped me by reading what I'd written, and commenting on it. Other times they were simply friends. Still others were mentors without my ever having met them: blazing trails through the dark forest. Some of them, then, I would have known for decades; others I would be meeting for the first time.

Along the way, I would bring a couple of my best students, the ones I believe in most, both a generation younger than I, in an attempt to provide them a makeshift apprenticeship in the time-honored fashion of artists and artisans, of the same sort my mentors had given me.

The plan was to cook a great meal for all of my heroes, one by one, and tell them thank you while they were still living, rather than that other thing writers usually do, speaking kindly of one another in the sterility of the obituary—which, however floral or nice, is never heard by the deceased. There was no sugarcoating the venture: a number of these heroes were on the way out. Quite a few were in their seventies or eighties. Indeed, in the end the project did take on an elegiac cast, with the departure first of Peter Matthiessen, then of John Berger, and last of Denis Johnson, all of them gone too soon, and in Denis's case much too soon.

Though occasionally others tagged along, like my younger daughter, Lowry, an aspiring writer herself, I made the majority of these trips with one of two mentees: Erin Halcomb (aka "the Left-handed Sawyer," a Westerner, who is an outdoorswoman and a live-trapper for the Forest Service and a writer of nonfiction, and, like me, an activist); and Cristina Perachio (an Easterner who'd never been west of the Mississippi; a former chef and food critic, and a short-story writer). I had met each of these writers at summer workshops, one in Montana and one in Maine.

What constitutes a fit between artist and mentor? It is not necessarily style, or even sensibility, though sensibility gets closer to describing it. *Aesthetic* might be the best. If a shared aesthetic exists, the mentor can come to view the mentee as another of his projects: a shaping and sculpting, and a carrying forward of the mentor's aesthetic.

In the end, however, is that age-old cliché, although it is the younger writers who are changed more it is also true that the mentor finds himself modified by the teaching. I had thought I would be able to stay on the perimeter of that venerable tradition, remaining a hermit in the Yaak Valley, working only on my art, because there is another tradition of the reclusive, solitary artist, deep in thought in a mountain hermitage, serving first and always the Muse. But as I eventually learned, that is only one-third of an artist's core. The other two parts are community, and relationships to other people—the one-on-one.

So off we went. Together we undertook this pilgrimage of gratitude and generosity. For the most part, the old writers we visited were the ones who had welcomed me nearly thirty years ago, back when I was an unpublished writer they took the time to read, to believe in, and to correspond with. Through them, I wanted to pass on to Erin and Cristina the excellence of not just the craft of writing, but the craft of living.

Over the course of a few years, I said thank you to my heroes by preparing a ceremonial meal for each of them. It mattered hugely to thank as many of them as possible while they were still alive, and it matters hugely to me that their gifts and powers not be diminished or forgotten by the generations behind me. I hoped to share that beauty across the membrane of time.

Occasionally, my mentees and I visited writers who were not that much older than I am—accomplished peers, essentially— to cook and eat and discuss the influence these older greats have had on younger writers; what they appreciate about, and have gleaned from, the aging greats. But the heart of this book is the Old Ones, from whom we learn the habits and being of greatness. We were curious about their loves, and their tastes: whom they read, whom they were influenced by, what they have found helpful in their long careers.

Sometimes I missed them by a hairbreadth. My dear friend the Texas writer John Graves died as I was starting this project, before I could cook for him and his wife of fifty-plus years, Jane. And some writers declined. I couldn't blame them. I myself wouldn't have said yes to the request. Strangers, in my house, trying to probe the secret, creative part of my soul and brain—and in my *kitchen*?

Sometimes I couldn't quite make it to their kitchens. With the great and ever-peripatetic Bill Kittredge, the dean of Western literature, the closest I was able to come was for Erin, her husband Pat, and me to buy him a burger at the James Bar in Missoula. In another time, another universe, we would have gone out to see him at the homestead of his partner, the writer Annick Smith, on the Big Blackfoot River, and grilled corn and ribs and sat around with them in the summer sun at a picnic table with a red checkered tablecloth. "Devouring Time," wrote Shakespeare, "blunt thou the lion's paws." And yet I also believe that time is the essence, the fuel, of beauty.

I anticipated that over the arc of the book, a recipe for greatness—in art and in life—might present itself. A guide to navigating the shoals of midlife and aging. Because there was another thing: I was recently separated, in the long and often agonizing journey of a divorce. Through that gauntlet I was lonely, and sometimes raw.

At one point in my life, it seemed I knew what it was like to get everything you wanted—everything you'd hoped for, and a little more. I fell in love with the most beautiful young woman in Mississippi, ended up marrying her. I wanted to become a writer, and became a writer, self-taught. I fell in love with a wild mountain valley in Montana and sought to protect its farthest places as wilderness, and got lucky in that regard, too. I wanted two daughters, and that dream happened as well: Mary Katherine, in 1992, and Lowry, in 1995. It seemed back then all I had to do was move toward the dream of whatever

I wanted, and I could get to where I was going. Mercy or grace—the undeserved dispensation of favor—remains one of the great mysteries in our lives. Who gets what luck and when, and why? "Why me?" any of us might and probably should ask, in the most grateful sense, every day.

One of the hardest lessons, in middle life? That even fortune's favorite sons or daughters can't have it all forever. Some things have to go away. The dissolution of my marriage was neither my idea nor my wish. But in the end it was not my call. I have carried that rawness in me, and do yet, years later.

Because of that bittersweetness, it was hard for me to witness these writers who have pulled off the miracle of giving their all to art and yet also maintaining long and successful—by all accounts even happy—marriages. Or who are happy now, having made it through the gate of hard times and survived, then prospered. Couples like Bill and Annick, or Tom and Laurie McGuane. Barry Lopez and Debra Gwartney. Those visits were hard on me. Denis and Cindy Johnson. David Sedaris and Hugh Hamrick. After those meals, I would bleed harder. And would keep moving, always moving.

That Elizabeth and I burned too hot is irrefutable. Cinders, sparks, embers, shavings of light falling from our hands and feet. In some respects, there was never a cooling period, and for that, the marriage was wonderful, which made its destruction a tragedy. When it was over, I ran.

I say it was wonderful, but of course it was not all wonderful. In time, though, I hope I will forget the hurt, and remember only the good. The woods where we lived were so amazing. I remember a camping trip deep in the wilderness, high in the mountains, when a summer thunderstorm blew up and I retreated to the tent. The rain came in waves, my green tent glowing in that afternoon light, until I heard hooves galloping our way, followed by terrified bleating and thumping. Then something tripped over the tent, a stampede, and the shadow of another animal leapt over the sunlit dome.

I shouted, to drive away the animal—a bear?—and when I unzipped the tent and peered out, two mountain goats stood panting at the edge of the five-hundred-foot cliff beside which I was camped. Unzipping the other door of the tent, I saw, up in the rocks, two mountain lions in sunlight as yellow as butter, prowling, pacing, their long tails twitching. Goats on one side, lions on the other, and me in the middle.

We lived in magical country. The goats looked first at me, then at the lions, and turned and disappeared over the cliff. Once the goats were gone, the lions also looked at me, twitched their tails again, then turned and vanished in the other direction, passing back into a labyrinth of boulders as if into a dream.

She and I were always sewn tighter together by the woods' magic and carried it with us further into our life, where on a winter day we stared out the window of our cabin at a mercuric silver–black vortex of otters diving in and out of a hole in the ice, pulling out one small silver trout after another and crunching them with relish—and it seemed their play was the coil of all the world's turning, and that the world was saying to us, "Be with this person for as long as you are living."

We would lie together, feet to feet, in the big hammock by the pond at the cabin where Mary Katherine was born, reading in the late afternoon, the early evening. In the fall the little shorebirds hopped from algae pad to algae pad. The view of the blue mountains downvalley gave the soothing impression that they, and everything else we wanted, went on forever.

Despite the pain involved in a divorce, it seems that in most marriages, as long as there was no abuse or trauma involved, you'd rather have had the experience than not. But I'm still not sure what to do with the leftovers. Do you share them? Or do you simply leave them behind and move on until, finally, you feel strong enough to stop and look around, to wonder at all that went past? Until the pain lessens, and you are glad for the sweet missing chunks that have ceased to be wounds and are instead just pieces that are not coming back. It seems impossible to endure at first, but after a long time I think you'd rather be haunted than not.

The way the haunting cries of pileated woodpeckers drift on the wind in the fall, as seasonal a marker as the opening and closing of a gate. There are a thousand such gates up here in this valley where we made our stand, raised our children, fought the dark forces of corporations in the timber wars, grew a little garden, and where season after season the wilderness scribed its way as if with subtle shadows across a stone sundial, lovely shadows that were specific only to our two lives, then our three lives, then our four.

It never stops—the remembering. Sometimes a moment will loosen vanished memories from the hardening matrix of my mind. It's as if cooling magma sets up slowly inside me, and glinting crystals form within that matrix. Recently I was walking through a lodgepole forest with my friend Doug Peacock, when one of the many ghosts from my suddenly distant past fluttered up—Elizabeth and me in winter, in Mississippi, walking down a long country road following a rare snowstorm.

Ice-clad trees lined either side of the lonely farm-country lane, bowed and bent over; an ice tunnel, almost too cold to bear. The world glimmered as the morning sun rose and illuminated that ice with fire, and both of us realized, at the same time, with each shared breath, that we were in love. I thought I had been in the country of love before that moment, but I had not.

I had no map for it and did not know what I would find, but I believed in it, and went into it.

In the midst of the divorce, however, I lost my hunger not just for art but for most everything—lost my once-insatiable appetite for moonlit walks, for canoe rides on lazy winding creeks, hands trailing in the water. *Come look at the stars, wake up, come look at Venus.* In the territory of divorce—half the country, I suppose, knows this—it can be a kind of desert wandering. You're a little shell-shocked; your stomach shrinks. You no longer have either need or hunger. It's all memory. It's as if you, and not just she, have gone away.

But if it was no longer possible for me to be sustained all the way to the end of my life by the warmth and security and radiant foursquare pleasure of a happy home, something in me— something inextinguishable and still glowing faintly—told me to keep moving, despite being tired. In my fifty-fifth year, and those next few years beyond, I just wanted to rest and eat and sleep and read and walk and talk. And drive, and teach. I was trailing a stream of heart's blood wherever I went, but I had to keep moving. If I stopped, whatever was pursuing me would find me and finish me off.

I wondered why so deep into my life, I felt compelled to pursue this project, a seeming indulgence at a critical point. Over time, the answer became plain. It wasn't just my students

I was trying to nurture. I was trying to get one more shot at nurturing myself; was trying to crack open the marrow of who my heroes were, and suck out enough sustenance to get back, one more time, the same center-stream velocity with which they had once sustained me. The fuel, the energy, of purity, of newness, wonder, and hunger. I wanted to go back to where I'd come from. I wanted to regain that brightness of spirit. I wanted to learn, relearn, how to go after seconds, and then dessert, too: not just to survive, but to feast. And after a long time of not eating, I did begin to eat again.

Hunger. Wherever possible in this journey, we used seasonal, local, and organic ingredients for our meals. My freezer was full of wild game to choose from: turkey, spruce grouse, pheasant, elk, antelope, mule deer, white-tailed deer, wild boar, ruffed grouse, Hungarian partridge, wild duck, woodcock. Cristina's past stints as restaurateur came in handy, and we often raided her recipe book for inspiration. We made rich desserts—rhubarb pies, peach galettes with blueberry-caramel sauce, feta-and-goat-cheese cheesecakes with homemade gingersnap crusts, and lemon-lavender sugar cookies—and comfort foods: smoked-salmon-and-sweet-potato hash; black bean huevos rancheros with jalapeño pico de gallo and cold Mexican beer with lime; grilled Allégro cheese on sourdough bread with cucumbers. We grilled an antelope shoulder on mesquite coals with a dry rub of Tepin chili pepper, cayenne, cinnamon, paprika, brown sugar, cloves, and thyme; steamed halibut with ginger, orange, and lime; cooked elk burgers with ginger and blue cheese and arugula. And more, and more. I was rekindling my hunger.

Why go to the trouble? Because to hear the poet speak in his or her voice is different from hearing or watching a recording from the deep vault of the past. You can't measure it: the gestures with which he sprinkles salt onto the palm of his hand before applying it to his meal; the sudden stillness in her body when, in conversation, she overhears some line of dialogue or some small detail that is the truth of the matter emerging from the fertile soil of the soul.

The context of the moment—the quality of light and the weather, the time of day, the kitchen scent of the house, the characteristics of the family dog or cat and the way the writer softens in its presence—all of this matters to the student who must find his or her own way and who will benefit from seeing an elder who has been through all the challenges and has succeeded in traveling some distance ahead.

From Cormac McCarthy's *No Country for Old Men*:

I had two dreams about him after he died. I don't remember the first one all that well.... But the second one it was like we was both back in olden times and I was on horseback goin through the mountains of a night. Goin through this pass in the mountains. It was cold and there was snow on the ground and he rode past me and kept on goin. Never said nothing. He just rode on past and he had this blanket wrapped around him and he had his head down and when he rode past I seen he was carryin fire in a horn the way people used to do and I could see the horn from the light inside of it. About the color of the moon. And in the dream I knew that he was goin on ahead and that he was fixin to make a fire somewhere out there in all that dark and all that cold and I knew that whenever I got there he would be there.

This is what Erin, Cristina, and I—and those who joined us—did all along our journey: communed with the great ones who have carried the fire out ahead, into all that darkness and cold, and lit the way for us. All my life they have fed me, and continue to. The least I could do was to feed them in return, even if but one good meal.

ONE

Peter Matthiessen, RIP

On the phone, one of my greatest literary heroes, Peter Matthiessen, had sounded weak, fatigued, rocked. He said he was still working every day, still writing, but that he got tired. The chemo treatments were hard—a new and intense regimen, twice a week—and he'd also been getting a fair number of visitors, tiring in itself. I promised we wouldn't stay long, if he would indulge my request, which was that I and a mentee—a beginning writer, as I once was—would bring him a meal, serve it, visit, then leave.

It was an indulgence, I told him, partly about wanting to honor him, but also partly about feeding my own need. He laughed, said something like "I know that," and told us to come on. He said he wanted soup—and maybe a salad, he added, warming to the idea, and then, before our conversation ended, asked for bread. Not a bad appetite for an eighty-six-year-old man who'd been diagnosed with acute myelogenous leukemia back in the fall, and was undergoing rigorous chemotherapy.

So I brought a food processor in my checked baggage to New York. I was traveling with Erin Halcomb, a student of mine, a wonderful nonfiction writer who will be one of the voices of the future. She is a sawyer and a weasel live-trapper for the U.S. Forest Service. I met her several years ago, at a workshop taught by Terry Tempest Williams in Montana's Centennial Mountains. I believe in her, as folks once dared to believe in me, and I want her to meet as many of my mentors as possible.

We fix the meal the night before—a soup of fresh-dug parsnips (tarragon, butter, garlic, vermouth) with a rich morel cream, as well as a little avocado salad with a balsamic vinaigrette dressing. On the drive out from a friend's house in Brooklyn I stand in a field somewhere on Long Island speaking to workers digging holes in the ground, and hold my bright white sheets of paper fluttering with the directions Peter gave me, and read the words to the workers as though the pages hold verse, or the text of some document of near-biblical importance, and the men send us on our way with some general arm-waving. At last we reach Sagaponack. Peter told me the house was at the end of the road and we'd recognize it from the whale skull on the porch, and sure enough it's there, looking like a damned dinosaur fossil: tilted upright, house-tall, gray and pitted rather than desert-white, ossified and somber.

Carrying our wares now in one large cardboard box, we approach his house as if preparing to enter an enchanted cottage. The tiled porch is still in shadow on this first day of spring, the small hedge-bound yard sunlit, and the cold wind stirs the dry oak leaves of last year. Birds—sparrows, mostly—blow past like the leaves themselves, veering as if tumbling, wingflashes and pale bellies glinting. What's it like to have two younger people, acolytes, show up, not unlike the birds that flock, year after year, to the feeder?

We knock lightly on the French double doors, and wait. It's been almost ten years since I've seen Peter, back at the revel, or wake, for George Plimpton, with whom Peter cofounded the *Paris Review*, a magazine George published for fifty years, until his death. While it's not true to say that Peter hasn't aged, he's aged less than I have. He moves down his hallway on the other side of the glass carefully—more considered than casual—but with focus, presence, intent. A good day, then, maybe a great day.

He opens the door with an elegant, friendly manner. He seems surprised we showed up, and it occurs to me that perhaps in his long life, and his many adventures, he has nonetheless never had anyone materialize at his door wanting to cook him a meal.

"Come in," he says, giving me a handshake and then an embrace, and a courtly handshake to Erin. "I'm hungry, I was waiting on you, I was just about to eat something."

He says this without judgment or criticism, only with a slight marveling, it seems, that we arrived in the nick of time, the just-right moment to stay his hand—the fork already lifted, perhaps—and, unless I am imagining this, pleased, and a little surprised, by his appetite after so arduous a treatment. He wastes no time in leading us toward the kitchen.

Was it really thirty-eight years ago now that he was tromping in the Himalaya, hale and strong and healthy, if anguished, in *The Snow Leopard*? No small number of us read this book as very young men and women—often living in the American white-bread suburbs—and, shall we be direct, had our shit blown away by its blend of naturalism, science, adventure, passion, and spiritualism, set in those higher mountains in the world, a region that, in the 1970s, was arguably still the world's greatest physical and metaphysical wilderness. Readers can enter his work from any direction and become lost, in the best way, changed forever.

Where to begin with the work of a writer this capacious? So wide-ranging are his interests, beyond any possible horizon, that on paper it would be difficult for the structure to hold a straight chronological telling. He went to Paris as a young man, fell in love with the city as well as with a woman, a woman who also loved Paris, and he got a job with the CIA that allowed him to live and work there, which he did, in the 1950s—echoing the powerful literary generation that had preceded him there.

"It took me about a year," he says of his work with the CIA, "to realize what I was being asked to do, and that I didn't like it"—being untruthful to the people upon whom he was gathering information. "It drove me to the left," he says. "I realized I had to quit."

From that act of integrity—forsaking the pleasures of Paris for a matter of principle—it seems that wherever he went, no matter the subject or issue, it was for him as if a shining path of rightness was visible to him, like a shining silver stream or river in the darkness, and at each opportunity, each choice, he took it. During the publication process of his first-ever accepted piece in *The New Yorker*, a story about the mayor of Orleans being murdered by his wife, Peter so disagreed with legendary editor William Shawn that he sent "a strongly worded letter" asking Shawn to kill the piece rather than publish it with the recommended edits. Such cheek! A compromise was achieved, the piece was published, the ship of his career was launched into the surf.

Is he secretly attracted to tussles?

"No," he protests, spreading his hands as if in defense, "I'm actually quite cuddly." He laughs. "I *can* be ferocious," he adds, as if the two words are the most natural pairing in the world.

You can recognize both that ferocious integrity and his genius if you read only one of his books, *In the Spirit of Crazy Horse*, his magnificent nonfiction account of the 1975 killing of two federal agents on the Pine Ridge Indian Reservation, in South Dakota. Peter says that Leonard Peltier, who was convicted of those killings, still stays in touch with him all these years later. While he has deep compassion for the federal agents slain at Pine Ridge, Peter is convinced that Peltier was framed. Although Peltier has been serving consecutive life terms since his conviction forty years ago, he continues to hope, based on Peter's work, for amnesty.

When Peltier heard of Peter's illness, he understandably became concerned about the consequences to his own life should Peter not recover. Laughing a little, Peter tells us that Leonard cried out, most plaintively, "Don't leave me, Peter!" Here, too, is one of the great stories of American publishing, another typical path of Matthiessen's literary and artistic integrity: first in investigating with such exhaustive detail (thanks in part, perhaps, to his training with the CIA), and then in defending not just the book's veracity but himself against a $37 million lawsuit that resulted in the book's publication being tied up in court for nine years.

What humming energy circulates in his great skull, and why? More than with any of my other heroes, he has demonstrated, modeled, a life of artistic as well as political integrity, writing whatever his heart desires, in whatever manner he wishes. There are so many moving parts to the magic that has always been his life. He has followed that shining path sometimes through Amazonian swamps (*The Cloud Forest*), sometimes across Africa (*Sand Rivers*), and at other times into New Guinea (*Under the Mountain Wall*). *Shadow Country*, his great American novel in trilogy, was written from its Everglades setting. He talks about his days as a commercial fisherman. He was raising a family, had a wife and children, and had to get down to business, he says, writing about the only thing he knew well back then, fishing, which resulted in the masterly *Far Tortuga*. The quality of his work is matched only by the extraordinary length of his career, and because of the breadth of his mind—his curiosities and passions leading him to wildly different subjects—he is claimed by diverse tribes of readers. There is a feeling that he belongs to everyone.

The light in the kitchen is lovely. Peter tells us that the house previously belonged to a photographer who studied with Richard Avedon—that he liked it for all its windows, and the light. The work finishing the meal is done. The color of the soup, a pale yet rich orange, matches the midafternoon winterlight that's reaching through all those windows. Birds swirl past in the cold light and wind. Peter's wife, Maria, has arrived, just in time, carrying bags, and we all sit down at our leisure.

The dollop of morel cream dropped into the middle of the soup perches beautifully, does not dilute or wander. We can see the little golden-brown morel nuggets inside each dollop, and slowly we stir the cream deeper into the soup, then taste it. It's perfect—one of the best winter soups I've ever tasted, if I may say so—and it occurs to me, here on the first day of spring, we are pretty much in the high-noon balance of things—very near the precise time scientists have pinpointed when the tilt and cant and turn of things is such that we can say exactly that winter is behind us and spring has arrived.

Erin is telling Peter about the ruddy ducks we saw in the inlet beneath the bridge near Peter's house. As soon as we began crossing the bridge and Erin spotted them bobbing along in the cold wind and bright sun, I knew she'd left this world and was connected to the ducks; that they would be all she could see or hear and there would be no room in her mind for anything else.

We stopped on the bridge and she looked down upon the ducks as if channeling from them the essence of life: the very life force that would allow her to go forward, into the world. I was envious and happy. It was a glimpse at one of the reasons I'm betting on her and giving myself over to this mentoring. If she wanted to sit on this bridge for an hour or more in her duck-trance, who was I, as her mentor, to disrupt that? Peter himself would surely concur, I thought. Writing may or may not be able to be taught. But *being* a writer—which is to say, growing the unguarded heart, and inhabiting the exhilarating layer of atmosphere just above us as well as the sometimes frightening subsurface barely a spade's stroke beneath us—this can be taught, or at least encouraged.

I was reminded of the story of the Buddhist master who left a novitiate alone in a monastery for several days. A blizzard pushed through, and there was nothing for warmth. In desperation, the student burned a sacred table or chair, I forget which, and upon discovering this, the master was very pleased; the lesson of impermanence had been learned, along with several others.

Erin gazed down on the ducks for only a few minutes before emerging from her reverie, and then we continued on down the road, toward Peter, our holy man, who would be pleased, I thought, to know the ducks were there.

Erin has a question for Peter. Isn't it true, she asks, that non-fiction requires merely or mainly the yeoman ability to work each day and be dogged, committed, like a farrier, whereas fiction is more about courage, and greatness of soul? It's a para-phrase, I notice, of something I once told her when she asked me a similar question, and internally I find myself freezing midstride, like a busted, bandy-striped cartoon burglar with a pillowcase of cash on his back, illuminated with a single beam of spotlight glare. What if the maestro says, "Hell no, that's the most preposterous thing I've ever heard"?

Peter's head tips slightly downward, and he appears to be examining the idea with the practiced elegance of a raccoon turning a freshwater mussel over and over in his paws.

"Yes," he says, and he looks right at Erin with laser eyes of the palest blue, holds her gaze. "You've got to be ferocious. With novels you've got to be willing to be completely obsessed and committed, and for a long time."

And though he does not say it, another part of it seems ob-vious to me—you have to not care what anybody thinks. Or perhaps, if you know what others will think, to move stub-bornly in the opposite direction, unencumbered by crowds. From *The Snow Leopard*:

> I go slowly down the mountain, falling well behind the rest, in
> no hurry to get back to that dark camp. Despite the hard day
> that has ended in defeat, despite the loss of three thousand feet

of altitude that will have to be so painfully regained, despite the gloomy canyon and uncertain weather and ill humor of my friend, and the very doubtful prospects for tomorrow, I feel at peace among these looming rocks, the cloud swirl and wind-whirled snow, as if the earth had opened up to take me in.

Suddenly my heart swells, feels like it's doubling in size, my arms and legs incandesce with a fizzing in my blood, a feeling like light entering my veins, there is connection through me between future and past, as if by electric circuitry, and I know that my vision for this project is not harebrained or indulgent. My passion is somehow almost perfectly transferable. A thing that I love from the way-back has passed through me and been handed to a traveler in the way-future. Despite such a significant bridge of time—more than half a century's distance between them—two people whom I believe in know each other now. It's working. We have crossed over the low pass, the saddle, and are looking down into untrammeled territory where we've never been.

But just as quickly, time surges. It runs away from us. As we talk and ask questions and tell stories, the small clock within me whirs, as if tiny flecks of metal are being shaved from the cogs and gears of that internal mechanism. How ironic that when I conceived of this project, these meals, I mistakenly and romantically envisioned standing long leisurely hours in the kitchens of my heroes, maybe sipping highballs while the afternoon sun lengthened gold toward the sweet and perfect summer dinner hour.

Around the corner from where we are eating in the kitchen is an entire wall framed with photographs, not of Peter being given awards, but pictures from Papua New Guinea, where he participated in a tribal civil war. The quality of the photographs is astonishing—high art of indigenous people in loincloths and bead necklaces running at each other with lances and bows and arrows, their bodies and faces war-painted.

"Go look at them," Peter urges us. Thinking back on his life, I think. All the many wars.

As if inhabiting a ghost mansion, we do. These were fantastically stylized, full-blown choreographed wars in which everyone fights, but in which once a warrior has been killed, all hostilities cease. The ultimate ceremony. An evolutionary adaptation for extremely small clans and communities.

At last, as we're cleaning up the dishes, Peter craters. He had indicated earlier that two hours would likely be his energy level. We went two hours and eleven minutes, then two hours and seventeen minutes. He's absolutely got to go lie down. "Just five minutes," he explains. His manners and bearing are neither apologetic nor hurried, but they possess an element of regret, and some mild frustration, though not despair. In the old-fashioned sense of the phrase, he takes his leave, and Erin and Maria and I work quickly, efficiently, putting away leftovers, the three of us rotating without getting in each other's way, in the pleasure of a kitchen area that is just the right size, while Peter is already around the corner now, headed for a brief lying-down period with the focus of an athlete making a kick for the finish line: working only to reach the end, give it your all, run hard through the tape.

A short while later, as Erin and I wait in the study, we can hear Maria in the next room running through the answering machine's many messages, a litany of conferences, festivals, and various environmental benefits requesting that Peter fly to wherever they are and give keynote talks to support their causes. How to say "No thank you" or "I can't" or "I have to rest"? Another question for my mentor, but time is running out, has run out.

Peter reappears, resurrected, ready, rested. Where did he go, in those ten or fifteen minutes, while the clock melted? To the other side of the world and back? He still looks elegant. Wherever he went, it helped. We've asked for a picture, and gentleman that he is, he settles into his chair, books on the shelf behind him, and dons his mask—the restrained smile, the steady look of portraiture—and for a moment I feel an awful sense of leave-taking. Look, the moment of the meal is slipping away, look, we are no longer dwelling intimately and at depth—*snap, snap*—look, I am ruining the thing I love.

I'm chastened, but Peter is forgiving. The clock on the wall is moving at its regular pace again. It's time to go, past time to go—there are now just a few traces of shadows out in the yard.

Timing is one of the key elements of graciousness, and where my clumsy impulse, having overstayed, is to dash—to minimize the error—Peter's more elegant way is to effect a leisurely farewell.

For some reason he turns the conversation not to goodbyes but instead to wolverines and fishers, asking if we have ever seen any, out west. Funny he should ask: Erin tells him about her seasonal work doing research on mustelids, and, revived by his little rest, Peter leans forward, the two of them trading stories of fisher cats. As earlier, during the meal, my heart-swelling sense of what is passing between these generations returns. It makes me think, strangely, of the Bering Strait, and the way in which, during brief windows of time, there has been a passageway from Asia to the Americas, or vice versa: as if, for but a single day, geologically speaking, a gate would swing open, and great and powerful things, new beings and new ways, could flow from one place to another while the earth kept ceaselessly spinning.

The talk of fishers leads to a discussion of the few animals in the world that Peter *hasn't* seen. "I've never seen a right whale," he says, but a biologist friend of his has offered to take him up in a plane next spring, says he knows where they can be found at that time of year, and Peter's looking forward to it, like a young boy just starting out in the world. He talks about things he wants to show us when we come back, things we can do when we have more time. Fishing, maybe. A beach walk.

We emerge onto the porch and stand next to the whale skull. I can't help wondering how many more stories would spill from Peter if we could stay longer. As if on cue, he embarks on the saga of the skull, not as if the events of it had happened but a blink ago, still within the shell of this one man's life, but as if they had occurred centuries, even millennia, ago—as if he were not the whale skull's discoverer, but merely its interpreter.

One night, long ago, the skull presented itself to him while he was walking along the shore. He saw it from a long distance away, and from that vantage it must have looked not like a whale at all, but instead a large dinghy, the wreckage of some immense rowboat from decades ago. The skull was upside down, a leaden garden of wet, dense sand packed into the cavities where once a magnificent brain had carried for thousands of miles untold manner of thoughts, observations, and, surely, the most powerful emotions, traveling almost always beneath the surface, where skippers and sanderlings wheeled and whirled.

Peter says he knew the same tide that had brought the great skull to shore—tumbling and sloshing slowly beneath the rough waves like a single die being rolled across the ocean floor—would, in the next tide, or the next, take it back, or, worse, bury it beneath tonnages of the next tide's sand. And so he hurried home and got a cable, pounded a stake into the dunes, and fastened one end of the cable to the stake and the other to the skull, to mark its location and hold it in place until he could return with the equipment required for its excavation and retrieval. Again the image that comes to me is of a young boy excited by and for and in the world.

That's pretty much how it turned out, he says. Sure enough, the tide buried it, but he was able to follow his cable down into the depths of the sand—as if he had hooked the skull while fishing or trawling—and then fasten the cable to a truck, which dragged it farther up onto shore, to safety. Then, with the assistance of others, he loaded its heft into the back of the truck and drove it home.

Some writers hang deer or elk skulls on the walls of their porches, or place the bleached skulls of caribou or buffalo in their gardens; Peter has a giant whale skull the size of a dinosaur, lurking, looming in the shadows, and seeming, somehow, if you look at it just right, to still be thinking its enormous thoughts.

What, I wonder, did the various parts of the whale weigh? How much the caudal fins, how much the great broad flukes of the tail, how much the tongue, how much the heart? What are all the parts that make up the ponderous sum, and what immensity of years and near-infinitude of miles once passed through this great mammal's lungs, back in the years of its living, before it became lithified and but a talisman, a monument to the deep?

Peter is rejuvenated from that briefest of rests. He seems to be in his forties again, not eighty-six and buffeted by cancer. He accompanies us farther out onto that sunny, breezy porch and, before we part, leads us past his and Maria's little garden, out to his Zendo.

He pushes open the old wooden door and in the little foyer we slip off our shoes and then peer inside at the mats, the long bare stark meditating space—the splendid nothingness of it. As might be imagined, it is a space filled with ghosts, fine ghosts, an air dense with sweetness and stillness. Peter smiles his little smile, watches us stand there drinking it in, not saying anything, just breathing the different air. Our three hearts slow to beat as one. The deep galvanic pulse comes from one place, owning us and sharing us.

I don't know how long we stand there like that, but then it is time to go.

TWO

Amy Hempel,
Good Witch of Manhattan

Two months later, even as the wash of my visit to Peter with Erin is still echoing, Cristina and I are embarking on our own first trip, a strike into the heart of fiction. We're going to make a meal in Central Park for Amy Hempel, the short-story master, and one of the greatest of rarities, a short-story writer who has kept full fidelity to that form, with the exception of a lone novella. And beforehand we're also going to see Amy's and my once-upon-a-time editor, the legendary, flamboyant, controversial Gordon Lish, aka Captain Fiction, who edited Raymond Carver and helped save him from wrack and ruin. Did either man imagine that Carver would go on to become one of the greatest short-story writers of his time—the twentieth century's Chekhov? I intend to ask Gordon when we see him.

Philadelphia, Cristina's hometown, is flooding, a steady June monsoon that makes it hard to hear anything over the din. My rental car shudders and sleds through roads turned to rivers, with all the potholes hidden. Dogwood blossoms paste the sidewalks. When I arrive at her apartment, it takes a couple of minutes for her to hear my knocking in the downpour.

I step in and remove my shoes and socks, then place them neatly next to Cristina's shoes. A little about Cristina: in our interview at the University of Southern Maine's Stonecoast program, where I was teaching, when she was choosing a mentor she was all business. "People say my writing is cute," she said, almost crackling with hostility. "The breath of ambition. I don't want to be cute. I want to be good."

"Death to cute, then," I said. "That'll be the theme of the semester." And I believe we might have shaken hands on it.

It's with this same no-nonsense spirit that she informs me, even as her roommate is heading out for the night, that she is turning in, aiming to be up at six to write. With that, she calls it a night, and I lay my things out on the couch for bed.

Her dad used to run a boxing gym before he bought a pizza shop, she tells me the next morning. He was always remodeling old cars from the '50s and she would work on the engines with him. She shows me the pizza shop, and the gym, and the coffee shop where she worked later—all within two blocks of where she was born. She points out the house she grew up in; the next block over, her godfather's house. Her aunt's house—now the world's best dive bar, she says—is half a block from her old house, which is itself just a block away from her apartment.

As for our visit to Amy, such is her generosity that she has agreed to meet with us despite this being moving day for her. After more than twenty years on the Upper East Side, she is heading to Brooklyn, like much of the rest of New York. (There's a moving-and-storage company in Manhattan called Hot Movers, where the men are also models. In the summer they work shirtless. On the phone, Amy lamented she'd been unable to secure them; they were booked a couple of years out.)

The plan is to have coffee with Gordon, then lunch in Central Park with Amy. But I'm a little concerned, because we've been waiting for Gordon's call for a couple of days. I confirmed with him by phone earlier in the week, and spoke to him several times about Cristina's stories, which she had sent to him, and which he liked. He's been in regular communication with her since then. My original goal, which had seemed so bold, was to persuade Gordon to come out of retirement to edit one of Cristina's stories, giving her the opportunity to participate in one of the most significant editor-writer relationships in literature. But more than a story, he has read all her work. So when I got on the plane to leave Montana, I felt we were golden. Since I arrived here, however, I haven't been able to reach him.

When we finally bust out of Philadelphia, there's traffic galore, six lanes wide, and the stop-and-start erratica of a dismaying number of tollbooths. I had not known about the tolls. Flying would have been cheaper, I think. But it's going to be fun to knife into New York from the underbelly rather than flying in, as I usually do.

I fool with the radio. Our music's much the same, but our hearing's not. We spend the next many miles adjusting and readjusting the volume, subconsciously at first, but then with a gradual awareness of the other.

The thoroughfare, a parkway through the countryside, doesn't feel anything like a road that could lead to New York City. Hawks drift on the contours of thermals rising from the asphalt below. The closer we get, the more I remember the feeling from the old days, my previous arrivals, each of which was always attended by the belief that a path toward literature is so noble and beautiful a route for one's life that it might as well be a religion. That it too can contain the elements of salvation, redemption, and fall from grace again. And then the rescue once more.

With the city starting to come into view, I look over at Cristina, her rising eagerness, her wonderful combination of curiosity, confidence, and nerves. In her presence, I remember my own experience more sharply. I was still living in Mississippi. I had quit my job as a geologist and was consulting, prospecting— taking leases on my own and trying to sell prospects. Wildcatting. Falling in love with Elizabeth, and falling in love with writing. Driving up to north Alabama to do courthouse work, logging wells back in the hills and clay fields—driving to Houston, to New Orleans, to Jackson, to try to find investors.

When I was not up in the Alabama hills logging wells, I'd be in town, and on the lunch breaks when I didn't go to the bookstore, I'd walk to the park, especially in the spring, and sit under a tree and write. In winter (too cold) and summer (too hot), I'd go to the state capitol, walk up into the rotunda, and sit on one of the curved giant window jambs, behind an impossibly tall red velvet curtain, where no one could see me inside the building. I'd look down on the city through the ancient warped glass—like the gargoyles on Notre-Dame—and write. It was adolescent work, a necessary part of the ten thousand hours it's said one must first write to discover what lies below and beneath in an artist. In a person, maybe.

I'd been frequenting Lemuria, the bookstore, on my lunch

breaks, a young man in a coat and tie driving over there in the company car, looking for all the world like a person deeply at risk of becoming a Republican. Each day I walked into the little courtyard, past the trickling fountain in the garden plaza, up the stairs pebbled with pea gravel, to their store, and passed through their beaded curtains and into the wonderland of books. Each day I was saved, and saved again. They led me to the work of the Southern writers—Flannery O'Connor, Faulkner, Welty, Barry Hannah—as well as the Russians, whom they adored. They directed me to books by authors under the imprint of the legendary publisher at E. P. Dutton and later Houghton Mifflin, Seymour "Sam" Lawrence: Thomas McGuane, Tim O'Brien, Jayne Anne Phillips, Susan Minot, Richard Yates. He also published Brautigan, Harrison, Katherine Anne Porter, and Vonnegut's *Slaughterhouse Five*.

This was all in the early '80s, during the short-story renaissance, as exciting a time as might have ever existed in American lit: a time when great work was being done in the traditional, elegant, time-tested short-story form, and then, spilling over from that, and sometimes simultaneously, deeper experimentation from the likes of Donald Barthelme, T. C. Boyle, Joy Williams. There were maybe a handful of MFA programs in creative writing in the whole country. It wasn't something you studied back then, or rather, you did, but on your own, or you went out and found a mentor.

Great short stories were popping up every week—another one by Raymond Carver one week; the next week, just as newly minted, a story from Ann Beattie. Success was begetting success, and because so many classics were being written so fast, to a young writer it seemed that was simply the way it was done.

There was expectation that each new week would bring another great story. "Communist" by Richard Ford. "A Wedge of Shade" by Louise Erdrich. "Lust" by Susan Minot. "Self-Help" by Lorrie Moore. One didn't think of them as classics back then, but instead just the fodder for one's days. Like breathing; like youth.

Gordon Lish is credited—and I do not see how it can be argued otherwise—with sculpting and launching Carver, who when Gordon met him was just another hard-drinking relatively unpublished and unknown poet and short-story writer. Gordon is controversial, but back when he was editing, slashing, compressing until a kind of electrical superconductivity was achieved—finding the heart of the current that ran through Carver's heart and soul—readers were not complaining, and Carver, rightfully, was compared to Chekhov. Critics called Carver's style—and Lish's—minimalist, and stressed how technical it was. But in so doing, they overlooked the necessity of those technical movements overlying great heart.

I always felt bad, twenty years later, when Gordon got roughed up with the predictable revisionist backlash—"Lish eviscerated Carver's work"—but I chose not to wade into the conversation, because Carver's widow, Tess Gallagher, is a friend, and I didn't want to take sides or stir pots. My own experience, with the dust settled, is that Gordon, for all his eccentricities, was great to me, and a great editor. How lucky I was, to have been a self-educated writer, an oil and gas geologist living in Mississippi, and to fall in with one of the premier fiction editors in New York during the incandescence of the short-story boom in the 1980s.

Did I say he was eccentric? Yes. Arrogant? That's a hard one.

The line can be razor-thin. I myself saw only enthusiasm and passion, never arrogance. Nor do I recall hearing him utter a disparaging word about any other editor. His focus was on the sentences, the stories, and the writers. He worked from dawn until midnight, completely obsessed. He read several thousand pages each week.

Whenever I accompanied him out of his office at Knopf at five o'clock, he would be carrying a briefcase full of manuscripts, bearing his distinctive and barely legible cuts and scratches on every page. Captain Fiction, the press called him, and if he took pleasure in that, where was the harm? Looking back, I remember only great support. I think my relationship with him was helped by the fact that he wasn't my only editor, and that I already had not one but two publishers, each committed to me for the long haul—Carol Houck Smith at W. W. Norton for fiction, and Seymour Lawrence, at Dutton and then Houghton Mifflin, for nonfiction. This kept things with Gordon simple and pure: it was always only about one story at a time, for his literary magazine, *The Quarterly.*

He was generous with his cuts, generous with his praise, excessive about everything. Already middle-aged, he reminded me to be young, to stay young. He was editing Barry Hannah at the time—*Captain Maximus.* Gordon's fervor was that of a frenzied midsummer pollinator, drunk on pollen, shaking the yellow dust from stamen, pistil, anther.

One of his dictums was to write the one story you are most afraid or ashamed of. (A variation on this assignment was to write the one story you'd write if you knew you could write only one more in your life.) In his class, Amy (who would later become, for a while, his wife, and remain always his friend) walked into the fire that he spoke of and wrote for Gordon what many feel is the story of her life, the much-anthologized "In the Cemetery Where Al Jolson Is Buried." Two young women, lifelong best friends: one supremely healthy, the other dying of leukemia, a confessional story of the healthy friend abandoning the sick in her hour of need. John Updike called it one of the best stories of the century, and I concur.

With all of these memories from the days when I was so young, it's exciting to think of helping open the gate for Cristina. And now with our not being able to reach Gordon, we've had to scrap the idea of coffee—and ginger brew—with him; it'll just be Amy. When we arrive at Amy's she has only hours left in her old apartment. We enter the gilded lobby on the Upper East Side, the mahogany paneling and gold everything else, as if entering the lair of Astors, DuPonts, or Rockefellers, and I think to myself, *Well, who knew?*

We ride up to the third floor and, when the elevator door opens into a hallway, Amy's waiting for us. It's sudden and wonderful. Her hair's more silvery white than I remembered—it was just starting to go that way back when I last saw her, when I was still out in society, before I moved to Montana and dived deep into the earth. I've seen her only once in the last twenty-five years. Now her hair is wild, going everywhere, a little like Einstein's, but I'd recognize her smile across a century. I forgot how tiny she is, too. It's always a delight to encounter a small person with a huge smile. The quality of innocence I remember about her has grown only stronger. She's like a child welcoming two others who have appeared from nowhere to ask if Amy can come out and play.

One might think that among the great writers of our era there was a dark and brooding fretfulness, a low- to mid-level chronic dissatisfaction, and to be sure, there is a river of darkness in all the great ones, yet it's twinned with a river of goodness. Of the survivors, those talented young writers who persist to middle age and then into old age, the vast majority of them, I will find out in the course of these conversations, carry joy with them. Or have learned how to cultivate it.

I'm thinking of Raymond Carver, who stopped drinking and wrote about his new life perhaps most memorably in the poem "Gravy." Of Barry Hannah, pre- and post-drinking. There was definitely a bad Barry and then a good Barry. And even at the end, in that hour of dusk when the streetlamps begin to come on, Matthiessen was filled with a lightness.

It's such a paradox. To be a great writer you have to possess the psyche of an ox or mule, yet it can benefit you to be joyful, weightless. Amy, certainly, has got the joyful part down. She is a welcoming host even as her apartment is gutted; almost everything she owns is either in a box or on its way to a box. Only a couple days' worth of clothes hang in her closet. The apartment has to it a bomb-blast quality.

"All my dishes are packed," she apologizes. "I can't even offer you tea."

She shoves aside empty boxes, heaves against others that are book-laden. (There are still hundreds of books remaining on the shelves. They will be the last thing to go.) Joy Williams, Mark Richard, Mary Robison—other short-story masters of the 1980s and beyond. Random books, too, given to her by friends. A book Mark Richard mailed her, inexplicably, titled *A History of Spontaneous Combustion*. She clears a space for all three of us to sit: her overstuffed lounging chair, a straight-backed kitchen-table chair, and a tiny love seat, piled high with clothes, books, lamps.

"So tell me about yourself," Amy says to Cristina, with a graciousness so open it's almost laughable, like a *Saturday Night Live* skit about the absolute worst moments in one's life to receive visitors, with the hostess more accommodating and engaged as the circumstances grow dire.

Cristina tells her about growing up in the Quaker home school, about her writing program, Stonecoast, about Philadelphia, about her interest in food, and about our project, while Wanita, Amy's sweet old yellow Lab, sits at Amy's knee, regal as a lion, and receives an occasional petting.

I recognize what comes next in Amy as one of my own characteristics: a nonchalant, on-again, off-again relationship with time. "My goodness," Amy says, "we should go to the park, or we won't have time." We've had five or ten minutes of introductions, and now she's a New Yorker again; time has entered the doorway.

We gather our cloth tote bags, silverware rattling and glasses clinking. We leave her grand old apartment building, with the Upper East Side light coming through its high windows, and go down the hallway, and into the tiny, hissing, groaning cubicle of the elevator that has ferried her up and down so many countless times before, as if through the verticality of strata. Then it's back out through that gilded lobby, past the doorman who will tell her hello and goodbye just a handful more times now, and out into the brilliance of spring, and the rush of so many millions.

We've unwittingly picked the busiest-traffic day to visit— Puerto Rican Day. It's a street festival and parade, so certain chunks of the island will be closed, some officially and others unofficially. But it's the most gorgeous spring day. Blue sky, clean sunlight on buildings old and new, chrome and mirror, brownstone and brick—and there are flowers in all the planter boxes. We reach the breath of the park, green grass, ducks on the pond, people walking dogs, and the arch of trees: sugar maple, dogwood, hackberry, magnolia. Sycamore, sweetgum, tulip. The swell of hills, little ridges and knobs: the landscape revealed, like the true heart of the best stories, which hangs out for a while just beneath the surface before announcing itself.

We wander, casting and searching until we find the just-right bench. There are people on other benches within sight of us, but a little umbrella of soundscape offers a feeling of some privacy. The three of us take that bench and settle in, watching all the other park-goers in their comings and goings as we talk. There are some young mothers, young couples, pushing strollers, but also older people: the healthy as well as the infirm, summoned by this sweet day for sun and birdcall and fresh air.

They move like sleepwalkers. Now and again a power walker clad in his sweat suit, navy blue or fire-engine red, and striped running shoes, as colorful as a tropical fish, hurries past; but mostly it is a march of the old.

I remain impressed at Amy's amazing talent of being able to turn time on and off, all or nothing; fitting herself wholly into whatever reservoir of time exists. She said she was up for a picnic today, so, by damn, we're going to have a picnic, leisurely and sunlit, notwithstanding the impending move. She leans her back against the bench, lifts her face, her throat, closes her eyes, smiles. From time to time people with their dogs stop to say hello to her. She knows the names of all of their dogs and stops to ask after them. Bruiser and Falcon. Miss Maggie.

My hunger is making me impatient and awkward, but I force myself not to blurt "Are you ready to eat?" and instead adjust my pace to hers: Amy the sun-drinker. She's from Southern California, I remember, though that was a lifetime ago. And my restraint is rewarded in the next moment by what Amy begins to tell us.

For a long time, she volunteered at New York Animal Care and Control. "It's got the highest kill rate in the country," she says. The June sunlight is still filtering down, but a chill has entered Amy's voice, as well as a tenderness unmistakable as love. She's not speaking with the zeal of a warrior, but is nevertheless sharing with us the history of a war that began so many years ago perhaps she cannot remember a time when there wasn't war. "They just fired me," she says.

While she was there, she didn't merely insist on cleaner living conditions—the absence of which is the bane of every shelter animal. What she did, in addition to lobbying to extend the length of time animals could stay before being terminated, was some of the most compassionate activism I've heard of. She began coordinating the other volunteers to set up a system of hospice, where, on the night before a dog was to be executed, it would get special treatment at the shelter with one of the volunteers and experience "quality time," as she puts it— its last night on earth, before going to sleep for good.

"We'd give each dog a nice warm bath," she says—her voice quiet, registering the exhaustion of unconditional love, as well as the amazing journey of it. "A nice meal, and afterward a nice long walk." And then the next day, the volunteer would take the dog—clean-smelling, well fed, and changed within, one must imagine—to be euthanized. The shell of the body, the battered husk, would still be the same when the dogs were returned for their termination: but something else would be different, there at the end. Something that kept the volunteers doing it, again and again.

"They said it was becoming bad for morale," Amy explains.

She'd been fired once before, but had found a way to get back into the organization—I don't ask about the details; she has about her a natural elegance of manners that discourages any inquiry into unsavory matters—and, back in the old days, inside the Death Star, she had used another approach. She wrote press releases for each condemned dog, and sent out fax blasts. This was in the last days before the internet.

"I'd be up all night," she says, "writing these last-minute appeals. It was so intense. I was doing some of the best writing of my life." Pouring herself into prose with a shelf life of hours. Sometimes the dog was adopted, and sometimes it wasn't.

But the board didn't like that, either. "They said it was bringing bad publicity." And so once more the dog lover was terminated. Shitcanned.

"Will you try a third time?" I ask. "In Brooklyn?" An indelicate probing, but I can't help it.

"I don't know," she says. "They're definitely on to me."

We talk about Gordon for a while. She still sees him regularly, is curious to know what our perceptions are of his spirits. He's been feeling a little under the weather, she says.

The tenderness of the ex-spouse who still loves the ex: am I seeing this now only because I want to? The relationship might be unsalvageable, but the affection, love, and admiration still so strongly held as to be unerodable. It's a curious and lovely idea. One can hope.

I keep glancing at our sacks of food, hoping Amy will mention them, but she seems content to sit and watch people and their dogs, so finally I ask if anyone would like to eat.

Amy looks at our big bags with what I fear could be mild disinterest, or as if hoping they might contain books. But soon enough we are spreading the picnic, plates arranged in our laps and on the bench between us. I'm slicing the pear thin, the sunlight giving its transparency a stained-glass effect, and Cristina is cutting the Oregon blue cheese, its aged veins thick as the tangled inked contours of mountains and rivers. It's the cheese I have been thinking about, off and on, all morning. Cristina has selected the best grain crackers, and with pear and cheese situated on them, she now spoons little tendrils of honey onto the slices—the twirling honey glowing in the sun—and Amy begins to look a little more interested.

We pour the tall glasses of cold homemade ginger brew—sparkling orange—and Amy toasts Cristina and her work, and me for having traveled so far, and we sip the ambrosia, with its mule-kick bite.

I am struck by a feeling of fitness, of wellness, a deep if momentary inhabitation of health, which, as with other underpinnings of our happiness, we often take for granted.

This feeling of well-being seems to pause above us, in the way it seems to me spinning shapes of time drift over us all, carrying each of us forward in surges, at slightly different rates.

We sit in the sun and feel it. We eat our crackers and the sun sinks into our bones, and the food dissolves into our bloodstreams, spreading up into the domed pleasure palace of the brain. If what we were doing on this park bench was a drug, it would be illegal. I close my eyes, and Cristina keeps spreading cheese and passing crackers, until, too soon, we're sated.

I try to express my gratitude for Amy's story "In the Cemetery Where Al Jolson Is Buried." Leukemia was the disease my mother died from almost twenty-five years ago. I would sometimes try to read the story to students but could never keep from crying at the end, which disconcerted them and me.

Amy says thank you back, then asks what I've been teaching Cristina, and I mention I've been counseling her to work ahead without knowing how a thing's going to end.

"What about you?" I ask Amy.

"Oh, I always know the ending to every story I've ever written," she says. "I don't ever even start a story until I know how it's going to end."

Cristina's expression is inscrutable.

I ask Amy how she likes teaching.

"I love it," she says. Another small surprise, for it is almost de rigueur for serious writers to lament the time and energy taken away from their own work. "Wanita comes to class with me," she says, "and every day, my students say, 'Good morning, Professor,' and then they say hello to me."

But as if sensing that the conversation might be veering toward her, Amy turns it back to Cristina and her work. Cristina, likewise, shifts, to avoid crumpling beneath praise and generosity.

We continue to watch the park, with all the people coming and going, and I am struck by an old truth: no matter how much clarity there is in the moment, no one can see even five minutes ahead. This may be one reason we write: to attempt to go behind the curtain. Indeed, it might be why I love the Yaak, with its dense, foggy forests. Although it can be tempting at times to stay in the world of the mind, it would be a crime to let this world of flesh and stone pass by unlived, unobserved. So you reach for both.

We sit quietly—will it be another twenty years before I see Amy again?—and then time begins to awaken. On her busiest of days Amy has graciously given herself up to us and allowed us to take our communion-wafer bite out of her. But now she needs to get back and check on Wanita and finish packing. She won't hear of letting us help her.

We gather our bags and walk with her through the park back in the direction we came from. The shade is deeper and fuller, cooler, where we part ways, having crossed a footbridge over a rushing little creek. We thank Amy again, and she thanks us, and her last words are "Give Gordon my love."

THREE

Gordon Lish,
Captain Fiction

Cristina and I wander over to another section of the park and lie down on a grassy slope in the shade and watch the dazzle of young people playing Frisbee and chasing their children. Watching them, I feel about a hundred years old. Gordon is only twenty-one years away from being a hundred. He's up there in his apartment, behind us, barely more than a loud call away. I imagine that were he to open his window, he might be able to hear us hailing him—could hear the same shouts of the children we are hearing—and that he could look down and see the specks of us lying here beneath this tree, unidentifiable, just two more tiny figures among so many hundreds of others.

It's not fatigue that I'm feeling, I decide, but impatience; I still have work to do. And watching these young parents with their young children stirs a homesickness and nostalgia in me, which is quite an emotional cocktail indeed: the realization that my children are suddenly grown up. For the longest time, parenting was my identity. Now, although one never stops being a dad, the intensity of it has begun to wind down. Sometimes I can actually take a rest and reflect on all that sweet silliness adding up to—what? *Love.*

Cristina and I sit, waiting on Gordon's call, until we decide that a cold beer would be nice. We want to stay close so that when he calls we can hurry over to meet him before he changes his mind or says it's gotten too late. Cristina takes out her phone and speaks into it—"Where is the nearest dive bar?"— and, rising and brushing winter-dead grass fragments from our clothes, we begin following the directions, holding the phone in front of us like dowsers.

The inside of the bar is far too bleak, this sunny afternoon, so we go onto the back patio, which is reserved for the smokers, though there are none. We order our beers there in the courtyard with its rusty barbecue grill—if I'd known about this place, I would have borrowed it in advance of our picnic, would have grilled Amy a deer hindquarter.

It's getting on toward that point in the day where, if we're going to see Gordon with time to settle in over a glass of ginger brew, we're going to have to do so soon. The tilt of light is doing that thing it does in late spring when it crosses some lower azimuth and each increment of sixty seconds seems to grow faster than the other minutes that have been melting all day long. But you pretend not to notice the quickening. After all, where is the skill in being one of the first to realize the party is coming to an end?

Cristina and I finish our first beer, order another, and then—now it truly is getting late—walk back to the park. I call

Gordon and leave another message, saying we'll be here just a while longer, but would still love to catch up.

With the light now bronze as it spills down the city's corridors and canyons, we gather our bags and make our way to his apartment building, the site to which I've mailed so many postcards and letters over the decades. We greet the doorman and tell him we're friends, and ask if we can leave something for Gordon—that we know he's been feeling a little under the weather.

"Certainly," the doorman says.

We hand him the big glass jar of the murky orange-gold fluid, beautiful in the coppery light, with fragments of lemon pulp and ginger thread spinning.

He looks at it both suspiciously and admiringly, clearly thinking, *Hooch.* "I'll be certain to give it to Mr. Lish," he says.

We walk back to the park and wait until dusk. How the city changes and enlivens when the first lights glimmer and warmth begins to leave the concrete. You can feel people's hopes and dreams returning, seeping out as if through the cracks in their window jambs.

By now perhaps Amy's apartment is empty. By now surely Gordon is readying for bed. We have to leave.

I don't know if I'll see him again. I'd like to, but it's not what's most important. What's important is that he knows he is appreciated, admired. *Thank you.*

FOUR

Denis Johnson, a Long Time Clean

I had not expected one of the most reclusive of my influences to be the most welcoming. But perhaps because we have been such close neighbors for decades without bumping into each other, with just one long mountain range separating his valley from mine, Denis Johnson agreed to a visit later that fall. With neither Cristina nor Erin available, I would go to cook for Denis and his wife, Cindy, with the fiction writer Molly Antopol, a mutual fan of Denis's work whom I'd met at Stanford, where she was teaching, and who was mere months away from the publication of her debut, a remarkable collection of stories called *The UnAmericans* that would go on to be long-listed for the National Book Award.

"We'll put the big pots on," Denis wrote back to my proposition. "We'll cook with the big spoons." And the closer we got to the visit, the more excited Denis became about the meal. He called one day to say he'd already thought of what my first sentence should be: "When I arrived," he dictated, "the Johnsons were naked."

A high mountain wall, sharp and thin as a machete, separates the green forested bowl of Denis's valley from mine. Bears cross back and forth over this mountain, as do moose, even the enigmatic and exceptionally rare woodland caribou, looking like a reindeer in a children's Christmas story. No direct roads conjoin the two kingdoms. It is a sign of strength, I believe, that in these isolated valleys nature is free to go about its changes in the manner and at the pace it sees fit. Fires, blizzards, floods, and the four seasons, again and again. There just aren't a lot of people to muck things up.

With both of my daughters off at college now, with Elizabeth gone too, the empty nest is even emptier. The house is spacious without them, echoing with their ghosts. It feels like a long time since there's been anyone else in it, though really it's been only a little over a month since I dropped Lowry off in Wisconsin for the semester. I wake up each morning in the empty house and sweep the bare wooden floors in the autumn light, watch the alder leaves browning and detaching from their branches one by one: silver-coated with frost, like the marsh itself at daylight, glistening and steaming in the new sun, with the air so still that, when sitting on the porch with my bird dog, Callie, a German short-haired pointer, I can hear each slow-spinning leaf crash-land, quietly, onto the others already beneath it.

What is my life to become? I ask myself this at some point in almost every day now. To live without the security, or perceived security, of love can be like trying to sleep in the cold without a blanket. You can fall asleep, but at some point you're going to wake up and realize you are cold.

Molly has come up from California to make the trip over to Denis's with me. Given the usual emptiness and quiet of the big house, it's strange, but not unpleasant, to hear her voice today, speaking to Callie with great animation and delight. In the morning I drive her around to some of the valley's high-lights—old logging roads to hike, waterfalls, an overview from the high country. When we return to the house we cook elk burgers on the grill, and pass the time in conversation. Molly and her husband want to start a family someday—she's in her early thirties—and even though to her it seems still hypothet-ical, I can see that she has already stepped on a boat that has separated itself from the shore.

Slowly, we begin preparing. It's great not to be in a rush, and to be working in one's own kitchen. To be familiar with the location of everything, and with the space between things. To fit that space. Eventually, after preparing what we can ahead of time, we begin packing the car: baking sheets wrapped in foil to aid in kitchen clean-up; the potatoes and jalapeños sliced for the gratin; the ice chest loaded with tuna, cream, white wine, butter, and packed with ice. The pistachios cracked and chopped; and garlic, which a chef should never leave home without. Yaak Valley morels soaked and hydrated, then blotted dry, ready to be sautéed for appetizers. The cast-iron skillet.

It's so leisurely, spending the day getting ready, sitting on the porch with Callie. Time for a cocktail. Three-thirty, four o'clock, and finally, time to wander on, though we have a free hour, since northern Idaho—despite being only thirty miles away—is on Pacific rather than Mountain time. It's a two-hour drive, down out of my valley, along the Kootenai River, then north again, back up into Denis's valley, following an intricate system of logging roads more washboarded and torturous than my own. The glass casserole dishes and metal pots and pans jangle and clatter rhythmically, and the dust of autumn plumes. Our teeth rattle, the windows are down, music's playing.

When we arrive, the Johnsons, alas, are clothed. But friendly, as delighted to see us as if we were lost family, or travelers whose passage has covered arduous terrain, and whose arrival they have long been awaiting.

What do I notice about Denis immediately? His bigness of spirit, his joy, his unmedicated ebullience. His happiness.

The medicated violence, exuberance, wisdom, compassion, and turmoil of his classic works, such as his debut novel, *Angels*, and the story collection *Jesus' Son*, are legendary. Those masterpieces emerged after his days of hard living, hard partying. But those days of plummeting are gone, decades in the past. Denis is sober and clean. And the older he gets, the better he gets. Witness the National Book Award winner, *Tree of Smoke*, in 2007, and the novella *Train Dreams*, a finalist for the Pulitzer in 2011. His prose is often lean, sizzling like a wire stripped of its protective coating. His eye, his attention to the perfect and peripheral detail, strikes me as that of an extremely wise old animal, one that might have been wounded in the past, but survived the wounding, and has gone on to prosper, yet carries the wisdom of how that wound came to pass, and sees its shadow at the edges, knowing to keep its distance, and—if others care— to pass on a warning.

Something I want to ask him, but which I don't dare: he's been divorced twice. Did he give up hope? What was it like when he met Cindy? What does one do with scar tissue? I wish I had asked him. Instead, I just observe his deep, long happiness with Cindy. It is too intimate, and my nerve fails me, which I now regret.

They've been here in these woods for fifteen-plus years. "I want you to write," Cindy tells Denis, later that evening. "I want to help support you to do what you do best, write."

When a soul that has spent so long in conflict with itself, hostage to the mental war of chemical disarray, rights itself and finds centerstream, the peace, while not cloying, is unmistakable. Yet Denis also still possesses, thirty years later, the aura of the shipwrecked, the long-marooned, who has been rescued — who has rescued himself, and who sees now the world in its full and sharp beauty, while the rest of us, jaded, wander through its columns of gold with our heads cast down.

There's still a bit of daylight left. It's the last hour of sun, the sky still blue, the leaves of the aspen and cottonwood trees at their richest, most buttery yellow. Denis is eager to get out into that last and best light, and to show us their forest, and their meadows, eager for us to walk through the yellow sun of that late autumn light, cleaving it as one would cleave a lake while swimming. He embraces us, ushers us in, helping with the pans and dishes.

The view from their cabin is mythic. Looking south, down into the narrow, deeply forested valley, is like peering at an illustration in an old Bible — one of my ideas of heaven, with that light starting to lie flat across the land and the shadows lengthening gigantically and the spines of the mountains snow-dusted.

With a great and boyish pride, Denis shows us his generator and battery and solar panel setup, an intricate system so like my own. So many of my heroes are hermits, to the point where they remove themselves so far from society and civilization that not even the curls and tendrils of electricity can reach them. Denis takes us on a walk then, down the hill below their house and through a small dark forest, where he points out an old clubhouse he built for his nieces and nephews.

"I had this gold coin from the Yukon," he says, "and I offered it to any of them who could stay out in the woods all night. I'd send them out there with just a sleeping bag and flashlight and a walkie-talkie to call the house if they got scared."

No one ever won the gold coin, he tells us, because he'd always go out there and stomp around and make monster noises. Finally, however, his thirteen-year-old niece, Caitlin, made it all the way through. Denis stomped and roared, but she hung in there. What Caitlin had done, it turned out, was to throw the flashlight and walkie-talkie far enough away that she couldn't reach them. Then she burrowed down into her mummy bag and went to sleep.

Denis built the clubhouse on the spot where she prevailed, named it Caitlin's Cabin. He said it was an important rite of passage, her down there "dreaming some virgin dreams."

There's something so familiar here, where I can smell almost everything, just as I can in my own forest. Crimson-berried kinnikinnick, summer-dried lupine, sun-brittle pine. It's as if I can smell each individual needle on the forest floor, can smell the soft soil compressing beneath our footfalls and then releasing tiny currents of updraft as we walk through this forest separated from mine by only the one high mountain wall.

I like how Denis calls me "Brother." I like how he has taken what he needs from the world and then retreated to the place where he—and, therefore, not surprisingly, his work—is most powerful. He seems perfectly balanced. I am hiding my own freefall from him, and I watch him carefully, breathe the air he is exhaling. I walk alongside him like a peer but I do not feel like a peer, I feel like a wounded comrade who is hiding his wounds and is not calling out for help. Who is pretending all is well.

We emerge into a meadow then, and it is not the shimmering flutters of the gold-leafed aspen at meadow's edge that get our attention, or even the meadow itself, but instead, the immense abstract sculptures scattered throughout it like the remnants of a previous civilization.

Hippies, I think.

The sculptures have the appearance of giant rocket ships, brightly painted concrete husks twenty or thirty feet high. Some are still fully upright, like missiles growing from the soil, while others are tipped on their sides, or as if they have all crashed into this one meadow. A repository for the weird.

"They were here when we bought it," Denis explains. "The guy before me was an artist."

We wind our way through the meadow, viewing the funky tilted monstrosities, marveling at the strangeness of the human brain. Out here so far from any town, or even any other humans, they seem somehow like a cry for help. Though who would ever be wandering this way? With the sun down behind the high wall of the mountains and the light turning sepia, we walk in the new chill of the evening back up the old logging road to their house on the hill, and that view: the seemingly unending blue waves of the mountains, their folds soft against the approaching darkness.

Along the lane, we talk about writing a little bit, with Molly asking specific questions. Denis, while allowing he doesn't much care to think about such things, answers with intelligence and gentle nods of assent, or wry silences if he feels otherwise. Does a story need to be moral? A look, almost perplexed, off into the woods, but with a small sweet smile; *almost* a shake of the head, which I interpret to mean, "I don't think about any of that kind of stuff." Can writing make someone a better person? Pause. He starts to speak, then smiles again and points out a late-season bloom of bellflower. Such gentle tact: beauty, or wreckage? Please, he seems to be saying, consider the former; there is such lesser talent in identifying the latter!

No small number of my heroes have wiped out and hit rock bottom in long-ago days, or at least damaged themselves on the shoals. Denis, it would seem, Barry Hannah, certainly. Tom McGuane, Jim Harrison, the painter Russell Chatham. Is this the same percentage of wipeouts as exist in the general population? I don't know. More germane to my journey, and that of my writers, is that there are plenty who did not; who were not as tortured, who somehow moved ahead without the vertiginous amplitudes of bipolarity, addiction, self-medication, despair.

We talk a little more about writing, but do so before the last light fades, which feels healthy. For me, if one is to get into the earnestness and dread that can come from too considered an analysis of why literature works, it is best done in the light of day. The life of the mind is, after all, for better or worse, a morass of the abstract. Why further envelop it in the unseeingness of nighttime?

Watching my mentors, coupled with my own experience, has led me to suspect that when it comes to writing, one of the key areas for improvement over the long run of a life is not so much about bearing down harder on the nouns and verbs as it is about learning how to take care of one's mind. How to let the brain properly cool down, after asking so much of it. The smithy of the soul. I'm referring here to "James Joyce's Refrigerator," the great *New Yorker* cartoon by David Jacobson, which showed the great bearded poet perusing a scrap of paper attached to his refrigerator, a shopping list, which read:

1. Call Bank
2. Dry Cleaner
3. Forge in the smithy of my soul the uncreated conscience of my race.
4. Call mom

I remember hearing a story about how when Denis was teaching in Austin, his front pants pockets were always filled with dollar bills. Denis explained to a new friend that they were going to have to drink a lot of coffee in Austin, because he had about three hundred one-dollar bills that he needed to get rid of, stuffed in his pants pockets. When he had lived in San Francisco, he had always carried around a similar stash, so that whenever a homeless person asked for money for coffee, he could help them out. But in Austin, it turned out, he never came across someone asking for help. Still, he told his friend, he wanted to be ready.

"I didn't want to risk being ungracious," he said. "So you and I may need to drink about 150 cups of coffee."

Denis is talking about contemporary editors—how he's noticed a tendency in the crop of twentysomethings to try to take out whatever the one most weird thing is in any of his stories.

Molly and I are surprised, because in addition to that component often being one of the strengths and surprises in Denis's stories, it would seem that a youthful editor would embrace this weirdness.

"But if I pull out the most weird," Denis says of some of the young editors, "the next-craziest thing steps up to become the most weird, and then they're going to want to take that out. And so on."

Even heroes have heroes, of course, and our talk turns to Raymond Carver, and the business of how much a writer allows him- or herself to be edited: when to agree, when to disagree. Carver, of course, was famously and thoroughly edited by Gordon Lish. Although Denis's work is popular in Europe in its own right, he tells us about being at a literary festival in Croatia where all anyone wanted to talk to him about was his friendship with Raymond Carver. Denis says he finally had to go into the bathroom to try to get away from them asking him about Carver, Carver, Carver, but that even there, they kept coming after him.

Two things a reader might not know about Denis: he can remember names, even people he met once fifty years ago. When I tell him my younger daughter's name is Lowry, he snaps his fingers and says, "I won't forget that. I met a fellow, Bill Lowry, in the 1960s, down in Arizona."

And this: he's violently allergic to shellfish. "Anything with an exoskeleton," he says. "One *kernel*, and I blow up."

Molly and I do a mental scan of the menu, but he says it doesn't matter, and that he didn't tell us on purpose—that he never does. "I'm into the ceremony," he says. "Whatever people want to fix for me is good enough."

*   *   *

When we return from our walkabout to their cabin, we visit like the neighbors we are, while Molly and I go through our paces, relaxed, prepared, confident, happy: heating butter, coating the salmon with the pistachio. Blending the triple-chocolate Texas sheet-cake batter, greasing the pan. Placing the gratin casserole dish in the preheated oven and relaxing as the fragrance of jalapeño begins to fill the cabin. *Autumn.*

When we are done, and begin serving, the food is knockout perfect. The slab of salmon gleams with its green-crisped pistachio crust, looking so over-the-top that when it comes out of the oven there are gasps. My old favorite, the comfort food of a gratin, is extraordinarily beautiful, perfectly browned, and more fragrant than usual. The twice-baked sheet cake finishes off the meal in style as well as substance. And though I have never before met Denis—my woods neighbor!—I am suffused with the sense that he is my friend. It feels comfortable being over here on the other side of the mountain, like I'm already home.

The talk moves to the difference between "hero" and "mentor." You might admire a hero, we decide, for the path they took or blazed, and for the work they did, whereas a mentor is someone who teaches you, and from whom you learn directly.

"I guess Chekhov was my mentor," Denis says. As he was to Carver as well, and to so many others.

When at last we are leaving, Denis—the hermit, the recluse—insists we should do this again.

It is bittersweet to me to see his great contentment: with the meal, with his house, with where he lives, with his partner, with the person he has become and the person he left behind, and with the work behind him, and the work—tomorrow morning's—ahead of him. He came through mayhem and survived it, with his core values intact. He began taking care of himself, and then, on a roll, taking care of others, with his great generosity of spirit.

If there was anything I could have done in my marriage, I would have. Anything. But doesn't that sound trite? Sometimes, at dusk, it's a thing almost like panic. I have wrecked my life. Did I mistake happiness for love? Am I capable of it? And is writing itself a form of running? Of manipulating a thing from the way it is into the way one wants it to be? And if so, what are the consequences of investing in such an alternate reality day after day, as if building up a fortress against the real world, stone by stone?

Terrible thoughts. I gaze upon Denis and Cindy's happiness with the hunger of a jungle explorer witnessing something he has heard of, and read about, but does not fully understand.

Molly and I load all our pots and pans into the Subaru and go rattling down the hill, lids and jars jangling louder than ever, the lone beam of my one working headlamp lighting the lane before us, down and out of the woods in which, behind the dense wall of trees, strange rocket ships rest, waiting.

I am surprised. Because I knew Denis to be a genius with his sentences and perceptions, I imagined he might not be wise that way with the rest of his life, and with the allocations of his heart. But as with the best of meals, we were fed what we needed, and strengthened.

Two years later, he will be gone: whisked, lost to a fast-moving liver cancer. Now, leaning forward into the wind, we must carry his smile and the books he handed off before he went, like the fire in the horn.

I remember the time he challenged all poetry students in the Northwest to a slam at the Home Bar in Troy, Montana. There'd been a movie being filmed near there, Denis had been hanging out with the stuntmen, and one of them had given him an asbestos glove. For his reading, Denis donned the glove, lit his book aflame, held it up and began reading from it, his arm and hand a burning torch.

For a man with a yard full of rocket ships, how, really, could it have been any other way?

FIVE

Doug Peacock,
Hayduke Still Lives

I've heard it said you can be too close to a mentor, and while certainly there's a danger, I'd like to think the rewards of a greater intimacy outweigh the risks of a weaker writer, or weaker mind, becoming only imitative of his mentor. And what mentor of integrity would choose someone who would settle for the status quo rather than trying to extend whatever greatness was offered? In the most productive mentor relationships, the simple act of conversation inflames parts of the mentee's brain that need stimulating, as wind stimulates a fire, as fire regenerates a forest, as a forest shelters its rivers, as the whole cycle keeps rolling along forever.

The best thing about being a writer is the isolation; the hardest thing about being a writer is the isolation. And so the best mentor doesn't edit or give publishing counsel or anything so practical, but simply supports you in your tribulations and tells stories from the old days, as the elders have done since the time we lived in caves and ice huts.

I met Doug Peacock, my most cherished mentor, in the spring of 1989, after hitchhiking to Edward Abbey's desert memorial, outside Moab, Utah. My rental car had run out of gas because I'd never before seen a car with one of those locking outer gas cap lids that require the flip of a lever under the seat. I sputtered to a stop a few miles from the gathering.

I'd run out of more than gas—had used up all my savings in Montana and taken a semester teaching job down in Austin, and was already terribly homesick for the West. When the first car to pass stopped and picked me up, it was with an intense sense of homecoming that I squeezed into the back seat next to these happy sage-scented ragamuffins, each radiating joy at being on the road in the red-rock country on a fine blue-sky morning in March, even if we were on the way to celebrate the life of a fallen hero.

Terry Tempest Williams, whom I'd never met and wouldn't have recognized, scooted over to the middle to make space for me. Her hair wasn't silver! She was a *baby*. We introduced ourselves quietly while other folks continued their joking and chattering and bullshitting. I'd just published a collection of short stories, *The Watch*, that had gotten a lot of reviews, and Terry knew my name from that. She gave me a look—some flash moving behind her eyes—and she reached forward and gripped the shoulder of the driver and said, "Have any of you read that story collection, *The Watch*, by that new writer Rick Bass?"

I saw it all in an instant—her delight in the quickness of her own mind. A trifecta, where with a single sentence she brought herself great pleasure, her victim excruciating embarrassment, and her unwitting foils great—what?—*punkedness*. She knew I'd sit there quietly and take it, hoping somehow to ease through the awkwardness.

"Yeah, I read it," said the driver, with some interest yet also ambivalence, and his passenger in the front seat nodded with—was I being hypersensitive?—reservation.

Terry looked over at me, delighted. She leaned forward again. "And what did you think?"

"Well," the driver said, and I cringed further, knowing it was going to be a drawn-out explication, "there were some good things, and some things I didn't care for."

Hope surged. A fair-minded critique. I was going to escape.

But then Terry's hand was on the driver's shoulder again. "Tell me what you didn't like," she said.

"I thought some of it was a little over-the-top," he said.

What a plum dessert for Terry, what a luscious moment of life. "Well, he happens to be here with us. This is him, sitting in the back seat," she said.

We proceeded down the red dusty road in a cloud of deeply uncomfortable politeness.

At the memorial, hundreds, maybe thousands, of river runners and mountain scramblers were perched throughout the red hills. Speakers came and went. A raven circled one speaker, cawing. Stories were told—great stories of mischief, passion, and resistance. I was so young, I drank it in. At one point, a freaky gust of wind snatched up the spindly pole of the American flag, whirled it up, then tossed it down.

The first time I saw him, Doug didn't look as if he possessed a thread of greatness. He was drinking and maybe drunk, erratic yet powerful, with a wildness so palpable as to be galvanic, as if a current of moray-eel electricity attended wherever he went. Dressed in camo, stubble-bearded, sweating, hair askew, he was moving through the crowd hunched over and glancing around like a man being hunted, which he was; the feds were intent upon breaking up Earth First! and were looking for him. They'd already arrested Doug's close friend and EF! cofounder Dave Foreman, busting down his door in Tucson in the middle of the night and hauling him off to jail, after which Doug fled. He'd been on the lam for the last two hundred days and nights—had tended to Edward Abbey, his own mentor and dear friend, in his dying, and had, according to Abbey's wishes, buried him out in his beloved black-rock desert. The feds were after Doug for that, too, claiming you couldn't just go around burying people wherever you wanted, and especially not on federal land.

Anyone could see he was a man falling apart, a humpbacked wolverine, feral, done for. His marriage was delaminating, he was unemployed and unemployable—was still psychically stoved up from all the bullshit in Vietnam. He was still physically powerful, but the shrapnel he carried had begun to irritate him. His crowd-wandering continued to veer unpredictably. He was careening, certain this was where the feds would get him. Certain that any fed worth his salt would know that, like Robin Hood, Doug would return home.

A flash of pistol in Doug's coat, a cold beer at 10:00 a.m. That royal-blue sky, spring returning to the land. Doug said his words for Abbey, then whirled off, preparing to go back on the lam—orphaned, in a way. Terry made a quick introduction, we shook hands. He trusted Terry, but I was short-haired and respectable-looking from my days as a geologist and from teaching a semester in Austin, that skinny year. Clearly he thought I was a fed, a plant, they were everywhere, and he bolted, vanished for another year off into the blue, off into misery.

A year later, nonetheless, we had become pals, and in the fall of 1990 Doug and I went into the wilderness of southern Colorado on an extensive search for proof of the last grizzly bears in Colorado. I'd been in college in Utah, in 1979, when the reputed last one was killed, by a bowhunter. Grizzlies can live to be thirty, almost forty years old, and thus there were still rumors of their existence in the San Juan Mountains eleven years later. Doug and I backpacked for weeks, gathering scat and hair samples for DNA analysis. We climbed mountains, descended into deep ravines, and scoured the autumn wilderness, sniffing the air, observing bent or chewed grasses. We combed damp places for tracks, listened for elk bugling, watched the stars at night, gloried in lightning storms and early-season snows. Every autumn for three years we did this, and in the ancient tradition of the true apprentice, I followed in Doug's every footstep, observing whatever he drew my attention to and learning, eventually, to notice even that which he did not point out: the faint disturbance of bark, where an animal had rubbed against a tree; the subtle breath of warmth, midslope on a mountain, where the chanterelles could be found; the sweet scent of a tiny spring, far back in the shade on a north slope, which elk—and bears—would seek out on a hot day.

Every step, those three years, I followed. Later I would return to my home valley in the Yaak, so different, and apply what Doug had taught me to that landscape, where I finally began to learn on my own how to be in the woods, with maximum intensity and observation, and how to be alone with my work, as each writer must learn to inhabit every piece of writing before bringing it back to the reader like a village hunter returning to camp at the end of a day, saying, "I have found something special, here is something of worth."

After a long mentorship, including many years of conservation work, Doug became a friend, and his friendship now informs me even more deeply than did his mentorship. As with so many of these heroes, even more than his writing style it's his life that inspires me. He will defend with every last cell of his being that which he loves. "He is the complete American renegade hero," says Carl Hiaasen. "Outraged, badass, and deeply, unshakably moral."

Doug's skills in diplomacy are less than zero, but his feist quotient exceeds any known scale of measurement. An iconic eco-warrior and spiritual godfather of monkey-wrenching, he's the author of five books, including *Grizzly Years*, one of those texts, like Terry Tempest Williams's *Refuge* or Edward Abbey's *Desert Solitaire*, that nearly every environmentalist winds up reading. More than any one person, Doug has helped change the way we think about grizzly bears and the big wild country they need to survive.

The Abbey connection is no fluke. Doug also served as the inspiration for one of the author's most memorable characters: George Washington Hayduke, the hard-drinking Vietnam vet and eco-saboteur in Abbey's 1975 novel, *The Monkey Wrench Gang*. "Hayduke Lives" T-shirts and bumper stickers remain common sights in mountain towns everywhere. Indeed, it would not be a stretch to say that the environmental movement can be demarcated into pre-Doug and post-Doug. "Peacock's life makes nearly all of the environmental movement look like an upper-class bridge tournament," Jim Harrison, a longtime friend of Doug's, once said. He had a point: How many tree huggers, really, have been shot at? And, more pertinent, how many have shot back?

But Doug had always had an anti-authoritarian streak. While attending the University of Michigan as a philosophy and geology student in the mid-1960s, he brought Martin Luther King Jr. to campus, over the protests of the engineering school dean. "He took me into his office and started showing me all this FBI shit about King's sexual activity," Doug says. "I stood up to him. But I knew right from the start that King had powerful enemies."

In 1964, he made his way to Berkeley, California. When his draft notice arrived a few months later, he enlisted in the Army. He was no fan of the war in Vietnam, but says he wanted to bear witness. He became a Green Beret and served two consecutive tours as a combat medic stationed in Vietnam's rugged highlands among the indigenous montagnard people, who served as his command's mountain troops. "I always identified with them," he says. "They were treated so badly by their own country, like our blacks or Indians. And they knew the land. I was immediately comfortable with them."

Doug was shot at and splattered with shrapnel. He suffered multiple concussions. He spent much of his two tours sewing together blown-up children. During the Tet Offensive, in 1968, the U.S. refused to let wounded montagnards from Khe Sanh into hospitals in Da Nang, arguing that they could be Viet Cong operating undercover. Furious at the decision,

Doug went AWOL. He stole an Army two-and-a-half-ton truck, cruised the country picking up wounded montagnards, and drove them to his own Special Forces hospital.

What finally got him out of Vietnam was a firefight in which 180 men, women, and children were killed or wounded, and he was the only medic. He couldn't figure out which arms and legs were supposed to go back on which bodies, especially the smaller ones. He found himself holding a dead baby up to the sky in a monsoon and cursing God. "I was given my 'death eyes' that day," he says. "I was ordered out of the field. Arrangements were made for me to leave." He was flown out by helicopter. Soaring down the coast, he passed over another battle, saw soldiers returning. Someone fired up at his helicopter. He assumed it was enemy fire but later found out he'd flown right over the My Lai massacre and it was likely his own deranged troops firing at him. "March 16," he says. "My Day of the Dead."

Doug returned to his parents' home in Michigan, aimless and lost. He'd been back barely two weeks when King was gunned down. "It didn't surprise me at all," he says. "It was what I expected of the world." Eventually he made his way to Wyoming's Wind River Range—he'd spent long nights in his tent in Vietnam studying these very precincts by flashlight, and says it was the dreams of that wild country that got him through the war—and from there he went north, up into Yellowstone country. He had it in mind to find a hot spring to soak in, to lick his wounds in solitude. And so he crawled into the lair of bears.

From the start, there was something about the grizzlies that intrigued him. He started tracking them, following at a cautious, respectful distance. "I began to have relationships with certain bears," he says. Bitter Creek Grizz, Black Grizz. The animals tolerated him and never attacked. And Doug began to feel better.

When the weather got cold and the bears went into hibernation, Doug made his way down to southern Arizona, where he met Abbey. He had read Abbey's memoir, *Desert Solitaire*, and admired his pro-wilderness, anti-authoritarian philosophy. In retrospect, Doug realizes, he was "looking for another war, a noble war, one worth fighting." He showed up at Abbey's ranger hut at Organ Pipe Cactus National Monument with a six-pack of beer and a bottle of whiskey. ("Good manners," he says. "That was how you did things back then.") The two men hit it off immediately and began going for long rambles deep into the desert Southwest. It was during these excursions, Doug says, that he found his true calling: "The preservation of wilderness."

After that Doug split his time between the Montana Rockies and the Arizona borderlands near Tucson. In Montana he house-sat the ranches and homes of agents, movie stars, famous authors—Bob Dattila, Jeff Bridges, Jim Harrison—and in Arizona he kicked around with Abbey. He got married, had two children, bought a little home in the desert and settled down. He took a job as a fire lookout in Glacier National Park. While he was there, an oil company's helicopter was mysteriously firebombed the day after it buzzed his lookout. "Me?" he said, when friends asked him about it. "I was in the lookout."

He wrote a memoir, *Grizzly Years*, which *National Geographic* named one of the hundred best adventure books of all time. All the while he remained dedicated to wilderness preservation and to the activism he learned from Abbey, who once wrote that "sentiment without action is the ruination of the soul." Doug puts it more concretely: "One action is worth a thousand books."

On this particular trip to see Doug, Erin will accompany me. She too subscribes to his credo assiduously, and I have been pushing her hard to write a book that takes in her time as a fire lookout in Oregon.

It is winter now, and I pick Erin up in Salt Lake City, where she's finishing her master's thesis, in a rental car, having left Montana earlier in the day. (My old Subaru, with its lone working headlight, is gut-busted with head-gasket issues again.) I have two dogs, Callie and Linus, in the back seat, and Kiowa, a mixed-breed heeler, Erin's dog, makes three. Fur's flying everywhere, which will result in a huge cleaning fee later. (You think, at first, *Oh, I can brush that out*, and then, *Oh, I can vacuum that*, and then, later, *Ah, fuck it*, and you write the check and hope the car isn't ruined.) I've also got an entire antelope shoulder and front leg thawing slowly in the trunk and, whenever I stop to camp, have been stabbing it down into a snowbank to keep it cool. Migration: the march of the antelope, working its way from the Canadian border down to the Mexican border, where Doug and his wife, Andrea, winter and where this antelope will find itself atop mesquite coals.

On the long drive, Erin and I are nervous for different reasons. Abbey, like Doug, is a huge influence on her, as he is on so many nonfiction writers, particularly Westerners, and even more so on environmentalists, who, up until the time of Abbey, resided too often in a culture of victimization and high-minded passivity that was hard to stomach as bulldozers broke open the desert and chain saws and skidders erased the deep forests, turning them to dust bowls. Abbey fought back, in word and deed, and he mentored Doug. All of this makes Erin nervous, which I think is great and is as it should be.

My own reason for nervousness is that Doug, a great cook himself, can be prickly. He's definitely going to be peering over my shoulder. And he knows me from our early camping days when I'd bring a can of Vienna sausages or beans, stick them in the fire, and call it good. Doug's culinary world is inhabited by Bandol wines and blue cheese and freshly foraged chanterelles cooked in butter and a white-wine sauce. He makes his own chimichurri. The man has high standards, is what I'm saying, and he doesn't mince words about the way a thing tastes.

Darkness falls and the night scrolls past. We're into the desert now, the winter stars are brilliant, and I listen to Erin's eclectic playlist with bemusement and pleasure. The Beastie Boys, Outkast, and yet also Lucinda Williams and the Avett Brothers. My old CD mixes are so much less edgy by comparison. Neil Young's "Heart of Gold" and Gillian Welch's "One Little Song." All of Martha Scanlan. All of Sera Cahoone's *Deer Creek Canyon.* John Prine's haunting song about Lake Elizabeth. Will I hurt forever? I feel certain I will, and must simply learn to accommodate it. Will running help? I aim to find out.

Somewhere north of Las Vegas we stop to nap in a sand wash, cold as hell, our breath pluming like smoke, the glow of Sin City to the south. Then, after some sleep, a pink dawn, coffee on the Jetboil, and more desert driving, drawing ever closer to Mexico. We pause often to stretch and run the dogs, and to collect six-packs and whiskey for Doug. Dazzling blue skies, and mild warmth, finally. Erin, meanwhile, is asking me to stop at seemingly every other yucca, saguaro, or paloverde so that she can raise her binoculars at the various desert dazzlers they house: olive warblers and flame-colored tanagers. She is made rapturous by the sight. I myself am red-green color-blind, and envious. Suddenly another day has nearly gone past. How fast they go by when one is not seated at the desk all day, "blackening pages," in the words of Tom McGuane.

Neither Erin nor I have a smartphone. As we approach Ajo, Arizona, we're navigating by a folded, hand-drawn map. Across the second sand wash, past the tennis courts, turn right at the old abandoned army tank.

When we arrive there are hugs all around from Doug and Andrea. These full circles: Montana to Arizona; Doug's and Abbey's past; the tradition of preserving and defending the West passing from Doug to me to Erin. It seems vital to me that these two warriors, young and old, meet each other.

Doug is delighted to see us, in the great singular merriment perhaps known only to any old-time mountain man who finds himself safely ensconced in warm Arizona sunlight while the blizzards go about their own business to the north. He can't believe we drove nonstop from Montana. Nor, when we show him the now-thawed antelope shoulder, shank attached, and describe for him the dry rub we've prepared, can he believe we've brought it all this way. I tell him it was a young one and should be tender.

"Well, whatever you do," he says, "don't burn it." And his

voice drops a register into a gravelly, no-nonsense gruffness devoid of humor. "Mesquite cooks *hot*. You look away for an instant, it'll dry out," he says, and jabs a finger at it.

I just laugh, pretend like I don't know and that he's instructing me.

It's strange and wonderful to be cooking in the ground, in Doug and Andrea's backyard—particularly for the wildest, grizzliest of my mentors. As dusk falls and doves swoop into the yard to bathe in the birdbath and spray seed from the feeder, I prepare the fire, laying the chunks of mesquite just right: building the fire up (a little too large, I can tell Doug is thinking as he squints at the showers of sparks rising to the twilight) so that the big chunks will burn down to the just-right pumpkin-glow scatter, which they do, magnificently.

Doug goes into the house and reappears with a bottle of red in each hand. There are old folding chairs around the fire ring, and he and Andrea settle in. Doug wants badly to cover the meat with foil, so I allow him to, and we spend the next half hour, as darkness spreads across the land, lifting the foil up and pushing it back down.

In the end, it's the best I can remember ever tasting. Doug, gracious (as well as deeply relieved), doesn't hesitate to say so.

The night is black, the stars brightening. A pack of javelinas goes trotting down the alley, just on the other side of the chain-link fence—an adolescent gang, Doug says, looking for trouble, and he grabs a broom and runs out after them, shooing them on down the alley. A man who's been bluff-charged by six-hundred-pound grizzlies isn't one to be made shy by a pack of young pigs.

*   *   *

In the morning we go for a walk, birding, which with Erin means a crawl. I'm a rambler, a horizon seeker, while she is stunned, mesmerized as if to paralysis, by any little flutter back in the bushes. I imagine her vision like that of the fractured spectrum of a dragonfly, able to see 360 degrees, with puzzle-piece imagery of leaf patterns coming into her mind at warp speed as she searches the mosaic of the tiny spaces between the sun-struck leaves. A speck of iridescent green or cobalt, a flash of scarlet feather.

Doug gives us a map to the petroglyphs, also urges us to carry Abbey's old .357 Magnum for protection against drug smugglers who frequent the area. Neither of us wants to take it but he insists, and I can see that it's ceremony. Doug waits for us up on the rim while Erin and I slow-walk to the petroglyphs. Somewhere beyond them lies Abbey's mummified carcass, beneath an unmarked black-rock mound where vultures soar.

We examine the antiquities. I don't know how any of us, our species, makes it this far: scratching our names, our dreams, onto the sides of rocks, then passing on into dust, heat, wind, light. A flash of memory winking, then—what? (*Books*, maybe, if we're lucky. Stories kept aloft, however briefly.)

We turn and hike back up to the rim, where Doug is waiting for us with a bottle of Bordeaux and some cheese and crackers, a little red-checked tablecloth draped on the back of his tail-gate. It's actually Abbey's old truck, a posthumous gift to Doug. He gives us the wine, cracks a cold beer, toasts old Ed, welcoming Erin to the clan. He points to the horizon and describes hikes we'll take next time we're down.

We watch the sun sink lower, then get in the truck three abreast to drive back to Ajo. From out of nowhere Doug mentions his dear friend Peter Matthiessen. "Peter's not going to make it," he says, his voice thick. Something blue flies across the sand road in front of us, and Doug stops so that Erin can lift her binoculars.

Meanwhile he grieves the impending loss of yet another cherished elder. Erin, somber, continues watching the little bird jumping around in the juniper, while I, with similar scrutiny, take discreet note of Doug's hollowing pain: the unspeakability of not being able, for once, to save a thing beloved.

SIX

David Sedaris,
Trash Collector Extraordinaire

The funniest man in the world, David Sedaris, is the youngest of my heroes by a long shot, only a year older than I am. And afterward, I'll visit my oldest remaining mentor, John Berger, high in the French Alps, where he's lived quietly, almost anonymously, for the last four decades.

Why Sedaris? Beneath the craftsmanship and the glittering tears of laughter in his work, entire cultures and civilizations move. He abhors injustice, ignorance, prejudice. He can be savage or caustic, but he can also be sweet. Both strands are within him. His work quivers with the voltage of his intelligence.

Erin and I have brought gifts: dried morel mushrooms from Erin's home in Oregon and elk meat from mine in the Yaak Valley. If, as an agricultural product, they pose a problem for the customs officer at Heathrow, in a pinch I will ask Erin to wear the morels like a necklace, or a lei. As for the elk, frozen brick-hard as the day began, wild meat doesn't spoil easily—in fact is best eaten cold and raw—but I am concerned about TSA agents confiscating it. Yet I encountered no trouble in Spokane, the origin of the journey, nor in Seattle, where airport matters are taken more seriously. I passed through these checkpoints safely, with the frozen meat in my carry-on bag. Now I have made it even through JFK, which I assumed would be the most problematic, and am here with Erin aboard the red-eye to London, a whole row to ourselves.

Heathrow customs will be the biggest dragnet, but I have a plan. I'll bury half the meat in a checked bag and store the other half in my carry-on pack, doubling my chances of being caught but also increasing my odds of at least one piece getting through. Earlier I also asked Erin to try to carry another piece.

"You shouldn't have told me," she said. "Now when they ask if anyone unknown to me has given me any item to carry, I have to say yes."

"But I'm not unknown to you."

She made some kind of expression I couldn't read—exasperation?—tabling the issue for future discussion.

There are a couple of pounds of ground meat for elk burgers, and a length of backstrap, thick as a man's arm, which I have marked "tuna," since you can bring fish into the European Union. I'm hoping that at Heathrow they will not really know what elk looks like and, since the meat is bright red, will believe it is indeed tuna.

Erin and I settle into our seats with that fizz known specifically to travelers starting out on an adventure to the faraway.

My daughter Lowry will be meeting us in London, coming from college, having just finished her first year. Sedaris is her hero as much as mine, and she's psyched not just to meet him but to do so at his home in West Sussex. Meanwhile, Erin and I cram as if for a test, reading our favorite passages of Berger and Sedaris to each other, and catch up on gossip, keenly aware that we have no idea what's in store.

Upon disembarking in London, I feel moisture trickling down my spine and think at first that it's the perspiration of the guilty. "The wicked flee when no man pursueth." But something about it feels a little different, and I realize, with a spasm of panic, that the meat is thawing, and doing so rapidly. Both packages have become bags of blood, and the Ziploc seals are failing.

Ahead of me, the same phenomenon is happening to Erin, but I can tell she doesn't know it yet. A broad bloodstain begins to Rorschach itself down her back, and now I see we're both leaving a splattering, dripping trail behind us. I take Erin by her arm, whisper to her, and just before we reach the customs line, we detour to the restrooms (surely video cameras are witnessing our suspicious behavior), where we can repackage the elk meat and wash up.

There at the sink, I avoid the alarmed looks from fellow travelers—so much blood—and can feel the fumes of fury emanating from Erin in her own washroom: the scrubbing and rinsing, the sink full of blood as we pour off the excess from the Ziplocs, then seal them back up. Tuna, my ass.

Yet we clear customs without a bit of trouble. No one asks us anything, we declare nothing, we don't even encounter anyone. Did we somehow go around the checkpoint, pass through the wrong door while other passengers stood in line? Whatever the reason, our entry to the United Kingdom goes pretty much undetected.

We wait downstairs in Heathrow's cavernousness for Lowry to arrive from Boston, and it's a great thing, a feeling all middle-aged fathers know, to see her come walking out, all grown up, wearing her sweatshirt and pulling her roller bag. To be in a crowd of what seems like millions, in an unfamiliar place, and then to see one of the ones closest to me in the world lifts my spirits indescribably.

We navigate some midmorning subways to a train station—David has sent detailed directions on how to do this—and, jet-lagged, take our train seats, craving sleep yet unable to find any, for the entire train car is filled with small screaming boys. They run up and down the aisles like a troop of monkeys, throwing things and shrieking, whacking each other with sticks while their parents lie comatose in the slumber of the deeply medicated.

The din is so great that we cover our ears with our hands. At one point I speak to the pack of boys as they howl past, and they lower their shrieks a few decibels, but only temporarily. Meanwhile the meat in our bags is still leaking, and the high-speed train is pitching and swerving, swaying and clacking, and it is as if the boys are driving broadswords deep into the travel-inflamed meninges of our brains. Two more hours to West Sussex.

Not a moment too soon, the three of us spill from the train, into the meadow-scented green wonder of West Sussex. Across the valley, soft yellow light bathes the Downs—a long ridge separating the valley from the English Channel—and the fields and woods glow. David and his partner, the painter Hugh Hamrick, drive up in their old Volvo, step out, and welcome us, smiling the greetings of hosts, but curiosity is etched on their faces as well.

The world unfolds as if in a dream. We drive straight away to the butcher, David and Hugh up front, Erin and Lowry and I in the back seat. Hugh, I will soon discover, is all about food— a great chef, and great shopper—and I begin to feel I am here under false pretenses. I'm certain that whatever meal Erin and I make will fall short of what Hugh himself could create.

Technically, David is not a mentor. I was already learning to write—had already published my first book of stories—by the time he made his breakthrough with "The Santaland Diaries," an NPR essay about being a department-store elf. He's possibly Lowry's mentor more than mine. *Woodsy* is not a word you would associate with him. He has spent his adulthood in New York, Paris, London, and now the English countryside. In truth I hadn't expected him to say yes to the project. I was surprised he did.

I've been particularly daunted by Hugh from the beginning, a feeling that will only amplify throughout the day. In our first correspondence, David informed me that Hugh had directed him to let me know that the stove is "a Rayburn, sort of like an Aga." I had no idea what this message meant and still don't— I didn't look it up. In our second correspondence, David mentioned that Hugh had just made a delicious spanakopita, using wild nettles from the yard.

I have my mind set on using the elk backstrap we brought as an appetizer, with Cornish game hens as the main course.

At one point in our emails, when I mentioned I might attempt to express-mail some frozen meat ahead of our arrival, David nixed the idea, saying that it sometimes took days, even weeks, for FedEx to reach him. He suggested an alternative might be for me to hunt and gather some of the local pheasants. Sometimes he couldn't so much as go out of the house without stepping on one, he said. Lowry, who had just secured her hunting license, was intrigued by this idea, and began suggesting various box traps and deadfalls we might set up in the English countryside. I in turn feigned Montana bloodthirstiness to David, saying it sounded like a great idea. I began to imagine he might have expected to greet three Westerners dressed in coonskin caps and fringed leather boots.

There are two butcher shops in the village, and as we drive, David and Hugh engage in conversation about which one is open on a Friday, and which one is better. Will their favorite butcher be cross if they go to the other shop, seeking a hard-to-find item? In the end they decide to throw caution to the wind and visit the farther, less frequented butcher.

Inside, it's meat happiness. Pale naked fowl hang from hooks and chains. Thick chops of pinkish-red meat—lamb, surely—line the racks, and fat little sausage links bulge in silver trays. Everything's behind a glass counter—ducks, squab, quail, chickens, pheasants, geese—but there are no Cornish game hens, and when I ask at the counter if they might have some in the back, the butcher has never even heard of that type of bird. Strange to think that *Cornish* may be a misnomer.

Whenever Erin gets stressed, she eats, and now she has set her gaze on a curious monstrosity, huge as the eye of a Cyclops, a nut- and bread-crumb-crusted orb the size of a grapefruit. It's a Scotch egg, David tells us, and it seems roughly a third of the shop is devoted to these, as if no one has bought one in decades but they keep bringing them in nevertheless. They look both disgusting and delicious: the British equivalent of a corn dog.

Two other guests, Frank and Scott, friends of David and Hugh's who are renting their flat in London, will be joining us later in the evening, and so I'm shopping for seven. I'm tempted by the pheasant, but with a gourmet's intuition Hugh says quietly they had some pheasants from this shop the other day and he found them a little tough. Directness coupled with tact is a rare talent, and much appreciated.

I'm unaccustomed to thinking of birds and meat in this manner. Mine always begin in either feathers or fur; I trim and pluck and butcher them myself. They each have a character, are woven of the muscle required to stay alive. The birds still possess the prickles and goose bumps from where their pinfeathers were. But all the meat here—so fat and pimply—looks ghostly. I feel trapped by the customers stacking up behind me, and by the frivolity of the butchers in this sunlit room, wearing their cheery white aprons and their little red paper hats, like one would wear at a child's birthday party. This, coupled with their big smiles of expectation, has the effect of making them look like clowns, but with cleavers. Every fiber of my being is telling me to get out.

Erin's no help; she's still ogling those eggs. And Lowry is keying in on the sausages. Am I being hypersensitive, or are David and Hugh starting to wonder what they've gotten themselves into, as the minutes stack up and the store fills with a steady stream of other customers, so that where only a short while ago we were inhabiting a dreamy patch of time, there is now an accruing tension? The scent of bleach is coming from somewhere—the back butchering room, I guess—and I'm fading. I just want to go back out in the sun and lie down in the grass and have someone else take over. I want a nap, a good meal. Everyone is looking at me.

"Quail," I say, "we'll have a dozen quail."

Why I've said this I don't know. I can't imagine a more challenging form than quail—the haiku of poultry—how tiny they are, how difficult to cook well. The birds' bodies, ill fitted to a grill, are thick at one end and tapered at the other, so that you've got to cook the two ends of the bird at radically different temperatures, rotating them every several seconds. Is it my imagination, or are Hugh and the butchers giving one another a WTF look, and is David—always cunning, all-seeing David—amused, delighted, by this display of sprawling human foible and terror?

Like a bandit in a bank heist, I take receipt of a bag of frozen quail, a bundle of minted lamb-sausage links, and a Scotch egg, and we escape. Not until we're back outside do I realize I've been holding my breath.

From the butcher shop we drive into the heart of the village, park, and walk down cobblestone streets past quaint businesses with storefronts harking back to the nineteenth century. Well, almost. I realize I'm short of cash and stop at an ATM. When it transpires that it's out of order, David reaches into his wallet and hands me £100 in fresh bills.

"Don't worry about it," he says.

Lowry, knowing my forgetfulness, gives me a don't-mess-this-up look.

We walk on, and at a fresh-vegetable market with beautiful potatoes and luscious greens I remember the winter parsnips we found for Peter Matthiessen, who died a few weeks before this trip. I'm so grateful to have gotten the chance to cook for him.

When the list is finally executed, there's barely room for our overbrimming boxes and bulging sacks in the back of the Volvo, which groans already beneath all our luggage. We leave the village and drive through the woods with the sun filtering through the trees in gilded, dappled columns. A fox hunt is in progress. We pass the emerald fields of hobbit land. Brilliant rooster pheasants scuttle across them.

A group of old people is walking along the road and David calls out, "Look, *ramblers!*" There's a rambling club in the area, he explains, and bevies of older hikers go on nature walks, all suited up in wool knickers and cardigans and berets, wearing high socks and toting wooden staffs.

This winding road flanked by stone walls, Hugh tells us, has been a road since the dawn of the Roman Empire: only a wagon track, back in the day.

At last we stop outside a cottage surrounded by bursting wildflowers, a fairy-tale scene, with more stone walls and a picket fence and gate leading to an updated old farmhouse from the sixteenth century. *Home.* There are also two guest cottages on the property, one of them converted to David's writing office and the other to a studio for Hugh, who is a painter. The sun glints on the freshly scrubbed windows.

In the kitchen of the farmhouse Hugh shows us what's what, as a resident physician might explain the setup in the OR to a visiting surgeon. I'm carrying the bag of elk, eager to refrigerate it, and no sooner have I crossed the threshold than it drips a spot of blood onto the immaculate tile floor. Without a word, before I can even move, Hugh wipes it up in little more than a nanosecond.

"You'll probably want this," he says, and shows me the spice rack.

"I forgot the curry," I exclaim. "I forgot the cashews, for the salad."

"Not to worry," Hugh says. He has cashews and can whip up some curry. From his cabinets he pulls the various ingredients—coriander, cumin, turmeric—and calmly grinds them in the mortar while we sip the tea David has prepared and try to convince ourselves we're not exhausted.

Then David and Hugh take us to our rooms. Erin will be upstairs in the main guest room, a lovely loft with lace curtains and a view of the Downs. Lowry and I are given the cottage containing David's office, long and open, with a kitchenette at one end, a big sunny space in the middle, and at the other end a bedroom and bathroom with a claw-foot tub.

The ceilings are high, the bookshelves filled with fiction, particularly with short-story collections. There's a broad simple wooden table in the center of the room, presumably for writing. Very few knickknacks adorn the shelves. A stuffed gray squirrel crouches above the sink, looking intent and engaged, and a bottle of Fairy dish soap rests on the sink itself. Other than that, there's little if any of the whimsy one might associate with David. It's an elegant chamber of calm, a room in which it is almost impossible to imagine writer's block.

David glances at the clock and smiles, watching us settle in. He inquires about Lowry's and Erin's lives, how they came to be part of the project, and then announces that he thinks there's time for a walk, and that we can prepare to leave at 4:15.

He is smiling, but he does not say *around* 4:15, and I notice the electrical currents that sing silently between him and Hugh, as between all longtime couples, indeed as they once sang between Elizabeth and me. Though I am not in the crackling cross fire of it, what I *think* I feel coursing back from Hugh is a kind of reminder: *These folks aren't used to being punctual, don't get your hopes up.* And what I think I feel roll back from David is something along the lines of *I know, I know, but if we don't leave at 4:15, there's not time to do everything precisely and perfectly.*

It seems like all the time in the world—it's barely four o'clock—but before Lowry and I can change into our rambling gear, David takes us out onto the grounds through an elaborately landscaped rock-and-flower garden. Above the garden, out on the sprawling verdant lawn, there is an item so improbable it appears almost to fit. A lone covered wagon sits as if stalled; as if its team of six white horses has merely wandered off for a while. It's not a Conestoga, but instead the much smaller design, used by sheepherders since time immemorial. Inside, the cabinets are tiny, as are the twin bunk beds, the bookshelves, the woodstove, and the window, like the portal in a ship's berth. The only gesture toward contemporary culture is a transistor radio, from analog days, by the bedside.

"Sometimes Hugh comes out here and listens to the radio," David says simply. Tenderly.

At exactly 4:15 we walk out of the cottage and proceed, five abreast, toward tea. Along the way David stops to pick up any scrap of trash he spies and puts it in a sack he carries for that purpose. Whenever adolescent boys see him doing this, he says, they taunt him, thinking he is simple and this is his job. He's got a keen eye and misses not even the tiniest glint of gum wrapper or single Styrofoam peanut, earth-colored with age. Lowry, delighted, joins in. Together the two of them scour the road.

The next village is about a fifteen-minute walk. Once there we enter a garden—there's outside seating—but David and Hugh want to sit inside, it's still a tad chilly, so we go inside and sit beside a light-bathed window. Our tea steams. Before us are slices of rosemary-lavender and ginger-and-walnut and carrot cake. We begin sharing it around and after all the trading is done, or has paused, I realize there's a little unfinished business: I have not yet tasted Hugh's cake. But because there are a couple of shimmering conversations going on, for me to *ask* for a taste of the unsampled cake would be an interruption. Instead, in the interest of what I think is good manners, I reach my fork toward Hugh's plate and break off just a *flake*, and consume it with silent satisfaction.

Lowry's eyes scold me—*I can't believe you did that! He doesn't want your nasty old fork stuck into his cake!*—and once again I have dismayed my younger daughter. In the absence of Elizabeth's civilizing influence, I do worry that I will go to seed, or even further to seed, as I have seen happen to so many heart-broken men of divorce, as well as widowers. Perhaps I can put it down to the sleep deprivation. Indeed, I'm looking forward to a spot of sleep, but first there's another walk, to the Downs, and a meal to cook. We're only starting.

At some point, mentally revisiting the dishes for the meal, I become aware that I did not buy enough butter, certainly not taking into account the other two guests coming. Hugh volunteers to hurry back to their house, get on his bike, and return to the market. He thinks he can get there just before the store closes and then drop the butter off at the house before taking the car to the train station to pick up Frank and Scott, as if in some West Sussex version of the most genteel triathlon ever.

When the proprietor brings David the check I offer to take care of it, but David says no, that he would like to, and so without that boring fanfare of back-and-forth on such matters, I just say, "Thank you." Again, Lowry gives me the look—strike two—and we step out into the glorious springtime and head south, for the Downs.

Before I know it, we're out of the village and on a gravel road that leads to a busy two-lane highway, a winding autobahn. We cross it and start up a steep grade of what seems, enchantingly, a dirt road to nowhere, with ancient oaks above us on either side of the banks carved by the road. The scene reminds me of Mississippi: red gravel, with sun piercing the deep shade, and everywhere the color green. As in Mississippi, cattle stand amid that green, chewing, grinding the grass, and watching with dull stupefaction as we pass. The bracing tonic of the pastoral. We gain the ridge trail to the Downs and strike north, all pastureland now, and a hundred miles of trail. To the south, the English Channel glints metal-colored. There's nobody else out on the trail today, just the cattle.

David and Lowry are collecting trash once more, when David's Fitbit beeps. He likes a day in which he takes ten thousand steps. He says he hit that number yesterday, but not until eleven o'clock at night.

As we walk I find myself slipping unaccountably into a football metaphor, telling David that I know we don't have anything in common, but I love how he uses humor to drive-block the story, to clear a gap and impose his will upon the opposition like a pulling guard, so he can then run a misdirection, or a trap, or really whatever play he wants: a bubble screen, a quick out to the slot, a post, a curl, a sluggo, anything. (Lowry is out of earshot, and so I avoid another vexed look.) I tell him I admire the turn at the end of his stories, where, after all the laughing is done, the story announces, then concludes itself.

David smiles, does not agree or disagree, just smiles and walks on, pleased with the day and the elevated view and, I think, the eager curiosity of this pilgrimage.

I ask him if he thinks about getting older; if he has an image of himself as an old writer. "So many of my old heroes are choosing to stay in the saddle," I say. "I'm not sure that's the model for me. I mean, what's the difference between, say, fifty books, or fifty-one?" And I ask him how he imagines being when he is our mentors' age.

"I find that I'm getting meaner," he says.

"I have to kind of work at it now sometimes," I say. "Not being mean."

"I don't mind it," he says, and allows that he'll probably just keep rocking on, traveling, and giving talks; that it's his life and he likes it. Then he says something that renders me speechless. "I know there will come a day when my publisher doesn't want me," he confides. "It happens to everyone, eventually. I know it. It's just a business."

Part of me is thinking, That's *my* line. My last novel, my thirtieth book, sold fewer than five thousand copies—less than a hundredth of what David's books sell.

Erin's got an on-and-off day job, a working spouse, and no family responsibilities beyond that. She doesn't yet have to make a living from her writing, and so these words, which are caught by the wind and whisked off the green ridge and out toward the channel, aren't crucial for her to hear. But we're back in earshot of Lowry now, and I hope she's hearing them. She seems to be lost in contemplation: wondering, I can't help thinking, *Why has my dad chosen such a tenuous calling?*

David is so *taken* with Lowry. He keeps looking at her sideways, with a small smile on his face, looking right at her in a way young people tend not to get looked at—*Who are you, what's your story?* They're hitting it off splendidly. She's comfortable enough with herself to go into her own brand of humor in his presence without showboating, and I sense that they're using humor to map each other's character. It pleases me more than I can say to see my daughter's literary fantasy metamorphosing into reality.

"You could survive here, couldn't you?" David says to her.

Lowry looks around at the radiant green countryside—dandelion salads and wild violets at this time of year—and out at the channel, an obvious no-brainer with the bounty of the twice-daily tides: fish, shellfish, and who knows what else delivered to shore. She mentions the two calves we just passed. "I guess I could get a strand of that fallen-down barbed wire," she says, "and take care of them with that."

It takes David a second to realize that by "take care of them," Lowry does not mean build a new corral.

We descend into a small patch of woods—*shelter*—in which

Lowry notes the runways of rabbits and pheasants, good places to set the snare of a deadfall.

"Yes," she says simply, so beautiful, so young and strong, so self-assured.

It is at moments like these—here to witness something in our daughter without her—that I miss Elizabeth most intensely, recalling times so good, so powerful, that the roots of them seem to reach all the way down through the soil of the past into the underlying bedrock, the stone, that was here before any of us. Other times I feel relief at a thing as simple as the freedom of emotional and physical space. Just to be. To disappoint no one, to be free of seeking the adulation or even the small kindness of a spouse.

The two lenses, the two sets of memories. Is one real, and the other not? Or are they both real at once? And is it better this way, or that? Did I mess up? Could I have done better? There's no way to know. Time has gone on past.

We descend from the Downs. David, invigorated by the walk, emerges from the woods with the vitality of a deer and practically bounds down the side of the two-lane highway. Benzes and Audis, as well as delivery vans and buses, rip up and down the winding bumpy road with its yellow middle line painted as if by a drunkard. David strides along the unshouldered edge, inches from the howling traffic. Road weeds wave in wild semaphore. The cars pass with the sound of tearing cloth, shearing the air right next to us.

I'm right behind Lowry, and, as if she's six or seven again, I find myself watching closely, making sure that there is always as much space as possible between her elbow and the side mirrors of the procession on this autobahn. In a strange and irrational way I'm admiring David's carefree enthusiasm. He does this every day? Puts his life on the line for the cleansing benefits of something as basic as a walk in the country?

When we finally reach the crossing-over place, he looks left, right, then dashes across. Erin and Lowry and I follow like ducklings, gliding to safety, and with the roar behind us, we are again on the gentle country road that leads back to David and Hugh's cottage in the woods.

We're walking with leisure now, our hearts slowing beneath the high canopy. David and I stroll side by side for a while, and now comes the part that I was hungriest for without realizing it: the building of community, the starting anew. Meeting someone who was around at my beginning and who has aged. Being reassured and inspired by the sight, the proof, that in the greats this fire is never extinguished.

We talk of Chekhov, Alice Munro, and Welty. Faulkner, Barry Hannah, and Richard Ford—we're Southerners, after all (David grew up in North Carolina). It turns out David and I share a love for the stories of my dear friend the late Larry Brown, who died of a heart attack when he was younger than I am now—a brilliant writer, and one of the sweetest hearts imaginable. Raymond Carver, Ann Beattie, Joy Williams, Susan Minot, Amy Hempel, Lorrie Moore: the breath of the eighties, this magnificent tide that rolled across the country, west to east and south to north. David and I came of age in the intoxicating draft of it, being pulled along and following behind it.

There was nothing but space in front of us, nothing but momentum, and walking down that country lane, talking quietly, with the day so beautiful, I feel like I did before.

When we return, Hugh's out in the little covered wagon, listening to his radio. He's secured the missing butter and now departs in a rush to get to the train station in advance of Frank and Scott. Shadows are coming on fast, and there's a strange moment in which David gives us a look that seems to say, *Okay, that was a lovely afternoon and now I'm passing it off to you, I trust you to do what you said you could do. I wish you well, I wish you luck, thank you, and goodbye now.*

His dark eyes fix the three of us and he smiles and backs away like a lion tamer who has opened the cage door.

Later, having returned from collecting Frank and Scott at the train station, Hugh is pouring an absolutely first-rate gin-and-tonic for each of us, except for David, who retreats to the front of the room with a cup of tea.

Erin, who *must* rest, says she is going out into the garden to smoke a cigarette, and for a moment I am struck by the idea that I might never see her again. Without even having napped on the flight over, we've now gone a day and a half without sleep.

From the kitchen, Lowry and I can hear David and the other guests laughing loudly in the other room. Hugh has lit a fire in both fireplaces, one in the front room and one here in the kitchen, and the cast of firelight across his face illuminates planes and angles of concern as he busies himself around us, cleaning up our minor irregularities before we have really even begun. A spilled quarter-teaspoon of kosher salt here, a drop of elk blood there. One last cleaning, before the onslaught of the barbarians. One of us, made nervous by his concern, knocks over and shatters a wineglass, which Hugh sweeps up almost before we can register it.

Hugh attempts to show us how to work the stove, the rhythm of which excites him—the way you can move the skillet around on top of it, inch by inch. There are no burners. Instead, it's like something a sorcerer would use, placing the food on the one magic spot where it will cook perfectly. Except that the perfect place changes, over time, as the wood burns, so that it's like playing a piano with a migrating keyboard. There can be no more gin-and-tonics during this process.

Erin returns from her walkabout and helps us spread the food out along the narrow dining table, and on all the counters, without a word. The fancy, complicated stove sits there like some great ticking *being*, some kind of Buddhist presence, with its inscrutability and its mysterious dials. *One* means 150 degrees Celsius, Hugh tells us, speaking rapid-fire, as if agitated. *Two* means 200, which is who knows what in America, *Three* is 250, *Four* is 300, and so on. Meanwhile the measuring cups are in alien denominations like deciliters.

The three of us work quietly, moving around one another gracefully and efficiently, but our physical fluidity belies the inner tensions of the exhausted. There's no conversation, only a kind of grim focus, the focus of not wanting to mess up—tunnel vision more than focus. Sometimes you can look right at a thing and not see it. Where's the pepper, where's the cumin, where's the spatula, where's my joy?

The yellow sunlight has flattened; it flows across our hands, across the food, across the table, bathing the kitchen with its last touch before darkness.

We spread the quail, gleaming with oil and glinting with salt, on a foil-covered baking sheet—a dozen of them, each a potential disaster. Even without heads or feathers or feet, they still somehow look evasive, as if poised for flight, and my dread builds. Ideally, I'd grill them instead, but I don't have the nerve to rig up skewers and hunker by the fireplace, cooking them like marshmallows. This is a first-draft world, a ragged militaristic campaign—*make the landing, establish the beachhead, control the perimeter*—and I do not give the fireplace a second glance, knowing the chances are not insignificant I could burn the house down.

Lowry will make the balsamic-and-fig glaze, as well as her famous gingersnaps with molasses. To this we'll add great mounds of leafy greens, so fresh and local they might have been growing this very day in the deep black soil, and our old go-to, potato chili gratin. Erin and Lowry are pros at this by now, and they slice the potatoes to perfect thinness, arrange the peppers just so. A team effort.

But almost immediately there's too much smoke. The quail are sputtering their sweet grease everywhere inside the oven. Hugh appears ready to cry. Smoke and the smell of wild meat permeate the house—no doubt soaking into the furniture. Hugh opens a window and the blue smoke dissipates. From the other room come the sounds of jocularity. Notwithstanding the smoke, the quail is finishing just right. Meat is the one thing, maybe the only thing, I can do well, in any kitchen, knowing when it's done sometimes just by the weight of it in the skillet. Meanwhile, Hugh glides behind and beneath us, scrubbing and burnishing as if the kitchen is an EPA brownfield site, cleaning up the slightest spill before it can linger. He seems almost to be able to reach out a sponge to catch a drop of olive oil or a sift of flour before any of it can touch the floor.

With her part done, Lowry leaves to join the party in the front room. Erin and I try to do some damage control on the accruing mountain of dirty cookware. At some point, Hugh relaxes—gives himself up, I think, to the project, and to the evening. He does not cede the kitchen entirely, but appears to determine to enjoy the festivities in the other room. Soon all five of them, Lowry and David and Hugh and Frank and Scott, are laughing steadily, sometimes uproariously, and I am happy for my daughter.

A pine-nut tart—the dessert—is baking in the strange high-tech oven, the salad is tossed, the fat little quail are dressed and wrapped in bacon. The gratin meanwhile is browning and bubbling, filling the cottage with its lovely scent. Outside, night has fallen. It was not so many generations ago that we gathered thus around fires in caves, and in forests, and in huts and cabins. The blood remembers things the mind never knew. The body leans toward these old invisible things.

Now that I have a moment to rest, Hugh has fixed me another fantastic and stout gin-and-tonic. Great gusts of laughter continue to rollick in the front room. The only thing left to do now is to throw the backstrap of elk meat into the iron skillet, with salt and pepper and the hydrated morel mushrooms. Everything else is under control. A quick glimpse at the tart, which I have been bragging about, having succeeded with it once before, shows it to be gleaming a bit brighter than I remember. There's quite a sheen of oil, but it's actually prettier that way, and I close the oven door, take another sip of that incredible drink, and focus my attention upon the skillet, and the elk, forsaking in my mind everything else.

The backstrap is the best cut of meat, the most tender and

delicious, taken from an animal I hunted for five weeks, traveling up and down steep mountains, through dark forests and across windy snowfields. Each day that I went out I awakened long before dawn and hiked all day, not returning until late at night, only to do it all over again the next day, and the next.

I lift the perfect elk out of the skillet, medium-rare, and slice it into medallions, then hurry to the front room; the temperature must not fall below a certain threshold. I urge everyone to eat it immediately, and they do, lifting it to their mouths as finger food and wiping the juices from the meat on paper towels I've distributed, licking their fingers and eating every last scrap, until all that remains on the plate is a little juice. I nearly sprint back to the stove and throw another length of backstrap into the skillet and we repeat the process.

David, the most enthusiastic consumer of the elk, comes into the kitchen to watch the wonder of its preparation—salt, pepper, butter, iron skillet—and when he returns he can't find his napkin, and has to get a new one. "Odd," he says, "I left it in my chair."

Has my nineteen-year-old fan-daughter snatched it in his absence as a souvenir for her friend back home, a napkin with the bloody handprints of their literary hero? I suspect so, but I don't rat her out.

Dinner at last. We take our seats, light the candles, and begin to serve the extravaganza of dishes. The quail, alas, are mostly tasteless. The best thing about them is the bacon draped across them, and even that could have been improved with pepper or maple syrup. But the company is good, the setting elegant, and—I hope—we're still riding the wave of the magnificent elk. We're out of gin but the wine, a Bordeaux, is delicious, and I pour it often.

One of the highlights of the evening is a word game that David and Lowry, who are sitting next to each other, engage in.

"Which Hollywood actors or historical figures have tree names?" David asks Lowry, innocently. "Like, you know, JenniFIR Garner, and Annie OAKley?"

Lowry pauses, fascinated. Her hero is addressing her directly, *knighting* her, it seems, by asking her to join him on an expedition into the legendary territories of his mind. *I believe in you*, he might as well be saying, and as he knew she would, she delivers, thinking for only a few seconds before answering, "ASHton Kutcher."

David nods, thrilled, as though it's easily the best thing that's happened to him this whole trip. Better even than the elk. He casts about for only a moment, then says, "Charles BARKley."

They're in another universe, he and she. The rest of us strain and search, but we can find nothing, even as David and Lowry go off like flashbulbs.

"John TREEvolta," David says, slyly, and as if with a tennis volley, Lowry answers, "Robert PLANT," and David could not be happier. "SPRUCE Jenner," he says.

How many, really, can there be?

For the rest of the evening, our dining is punctuated by these random utterances, like public service announcements.

The meal might yet prove salvageable, I'm thinking, as we move through the entrées with polite murmurings, but I have not reckoned on that pine tart, which has been baking at whatever indecipherable and arbitrary temperature pulses within the implacable Rayburn, the considerable heat of which we can feel all the way from the kitchen. The tart is meant to be the centerpiece of the evening and our salvation from what was otherwise (with the exception of the elk) an attractive but underwhelming meal. As people are finishing the quail, I rise to check on the tart, and what I find inside the maw of the stove is a health hazard.

It would be easy for me to blame the oven, or the butter here, or the pine nuts bought in bulk, or Hugh's Pyrex dish. It's tempting, as I stand there staring at a lake of melted butter and oil, to blame all of England. I'll never know the culprit. A super-oily batch of nuts? Too much heat for too long? A too-small dish? There seem to be *a lot* of pine nuts—did I accidentally double the recipe? Or was it faulty estimation in my conversion from English metric with the great block of butter that I hewed and hacked into the dough while knocking back those gin-and-tonics? As for the dough, it resides far beneath the depths of clarified butter and the iridescent ribbons of rich oil from all the nuts streaking the yellow lake.

Maybe if I blot up the excess butter, I think, it will be as if it never happened. And this is what I attempt, with a fistful of paper towels that grow quickly saturated, so that it's as if I'm holding the dripping wick for a Molotov cocktail.

"Careful with that!" says Lowry, who has come into the kitchen to see about the holdup, meaning, *Mind your heat sources!*

Stubbornly, I bring the bloated disaster to the dining table and plate it, as if there is special merit in soldiering on despite evidence that one should retreat. With all the hubbub, Hugh's hard-gotten relaxation is taking a hit. David appears curious and disappointed at the same time, while Erin looks at the tart and says only "Ewwww," an unambiguous statement that she had nothing to do with this.

Everyone makes a pass at the tart with their forks, but it's foul—somehow greasy and chalky at the same time. An annihilation. For those adventurous enough to lift it to their mouths, it takes every bit of civility not to gag.

"Lowry," David asks sweetly, "how about some of those lovely gingersnaps?"

At last we say our goodnights—so many hours without sleep, but our job done. Erin goes upstairs, and Lowry and I to the cottage that serves as David's office, where we will sleep in the work space of a great and important writer, a man who summons one of the rarest things, again and again: laughter.

All that laughter—millions of people laughing, sometimes until they're crying—coming from this one quiet office, with no one in it now but me and my younger daughter, who might one day be a writer. Alone, we look around as if at a piazza fountain, or the wellspring for some magnificent and timeless river, and then we go to bed, finally, and sleep the deep and dreamless sleep of healing.

In the morning, the green-gold light of spring slides across the pasture and into the cottage. Outside the mullioned windows of the south-facing French doors, a fox digs in the grass at the base of Hugh's wagon, hunting for crickets, I suppose, or the rest of last night's pine tart.

No one is stirring in the windows of the farmhouse. Lowry

has asked to be awakened one hour before it's time to leave, and Erin has made no request. Knowing they are both sleeping soundly, I sit and write for a while. Maybe I should do some yoga, after the brutality of the plane and the train, or go for a walk, but I feel like writing on this beautiful morning. I fix a strong pot of Italian roast and, perhaps to my discredit, sit at David's desk and scratch out a couple of paragraphs in that wonderful stillness.

I cannot stop. I have scant years left, and in whatever supply, that mysterious number, always smaller than it used to be, is one that would motivate any self-respecting geologist to sit up straight in cold terror.

After a bit I walk over to the farmhouse and find David and Hugh up now. We toast some peasant bread from town and spread butter and blackberry jam on it. The morning light, so golden, turns the house into a movie set, and we sit around in quiet satisfaction, in a strange mix of rest and fatigue from the late night before.

David looks out at the light. The door to the kitchen is a stable door, allowing the upper half to swing open while the lower half remains shut. David walks over and opens the upper part, and the soft light pours into the kitchen. He smiles a deep and distant smile. "I had that door specially made to do that," he says. "I was thinking of mornings like this."

It touches me deeply, his pleasure, the absence of humor, only the quiet marveling at great beauty and the associated peace of home. I think he's glad we came. I know I am—pleased, more than anything, by the inspiration Lowry has gotten from meeting her favorite writer. The difference in their ages, it occurs to me, is greater than was the difference between mine and Matthiessen's, and for a moment I feel dizzy: the force and ceaselessness of the old river of time.

Frank and Scott drift in, pour cups of coffee. We all slouch like the haggard survivors of an all-night card game, one in which everyone won. There's not a lot of time left before the cab arrives to take us to Gatwick Airport, from which we'll fly to Geneva, where we'll rent a car and drive to Mont Blanc, in France, to see John Berger.

I return to the cottage and wake Lowry, who's a little grumpy—how a teenager craves and needs deep sleep—but when she realizes that time is telescoping, she jumps right up. Back in the farmhouse, Erin comes downstairs. A good night for her is twelve hours. Her sentences crackle with the intensity of glass being broken, slinging their refracted light from the sharpest shards of words with the prismatic wonder of a kaleidoscope. But they do not get written early in the morning. She does not say good morning, does not say anything, just sits down with a cup of coffee. Only the call of a bird, or a cigarette, could rouse her from her stupor.

The cab arrives ten minutes early, and while I can't speak for the natives, the North American contingency is as dismayed as if we were prisoners for whom the executioner has arrived. Perhaps we could live in the covered wagon.

The cab driver tells us not to worry, no rush, and we walk out into the garden and sit on the rock wall amid the boisterous flowers. We visit lazily, as if we have all the time in the world.

But I sense a faint whir beginning in David, not antsiness or impatience, but a coiling, a readying for the day. It's an energy that's almost athletic in character, as if for him each morning is game day. He has not yet crossed over that threshold, though. He is still present, still peaceful, there in the garden, and with a sweet generosity he turns and bestows the last of our time upon Lowry.

"Lowry," he says, "you're a princess. Come back anytime." He steps in a little closer to her. He's staring down at her feet, the toenails painted a glorious plum color. "I want you to do something for me," he says to her. "It's very important to me."

We are all listening carefully, aware that this is a farewell moment, and that there's a great possibility that he might be about to dispense some life advice. Lowry can't even speak. She nods.

"I want you to treasure this moment," he says. "I want you to stop and be fully aware of how beautiful your feet are. They're so beautiful and perfect. I want you to remember this moment, and how perfect they are."

We're all staring down at Lowry's bare feet now. *Is this a dream?* she must be wondering.

"Mine," he continues, breaking the sweet spell in order to release us to our cab, "are gnarled, like little *hobbit* feet. Like hooves."

Lowry laughs. "You should channel your inner hobbit," she says. "Gambol in that field barefooted." And David smiles, as if imagining it.

Then the clock owns us once more. We shake hands, hug. Mercifully, I remember the leftover elk meat still in the freezer—needed for a recipe at Berger's—and duck back in to grab that bloody frozen bag, which I see I inadvertently tossed into the ice-cube maker, so that some of the cubes are tinged red. A new recipe for Hugh's gin-and-tonics.

In the cab, the driver wants to chat, but none of us can think of anything to say. Eventually he comes to understand this, and we ride in silence through the English countryside. Lowry's feet, I imagine, must still be tingling as if in a fairy tale, imbued with magic dust.

SEVEN

John Berger,
Old Man of the Mountains

At the baggage claim in Geneva, my suitcase—a new red roller bag—is among the last to emerge onto the carousel. I pick it up and have ferried it only a short distance when I realize it feels lighter. *Shit*, I think, *did customs search it and extract the meat?* I wheel it to a bench and unzip the suitcase.

What I see is not for the squeamish. At first it appears to be a woman's dismembered leg. But there's no blood, only a shapely calf, bare, attached to a feminine foot. It takes me several seconds to realize it's a prosthesis.

Also in the suitcase are two large packages of adult diapers and eight cartons of shortbread cookies. Nothing else. *Where is the heroin?* I wonder.

Feeling like a criminal, and yet also that I've been set up, I dash to the nearest security guard. This would be an opportune moment to speak French. Instead, we find ourselves

being escorted to a sterile detention center. The red suitcase containing the woman's leg is taken from us and we
are told to wait in the holding room. I fill out some papers.
The security guard tells us they've discovered who owns the
leg, presumably the same person who has my bag: an elderly
gentleman whose wife is in a wheelchair. The two of them
live far away in the mountains, near Lake Lucerne, the guard
says, and we must remain here until the couple realizes their
mistake and comes back. It could be hours or days. It's a very
large inconvenience, he says.

The man leaves and Lowry makes a pallet of sweaters on the
floor and goes to sleep. Erin curls up catlike in one tiny chair,
her legs jackknifed over the armrest, feet on the end table. I
pace like a tiger in the zoo. There's nothing in the room but a
clock. I feel my troops' will is sagging to a new low, one from
which no pep talk will rally them. *Hang in there*, I think, *fatigue
makes cowards of us all. We're going to see John Berger, by God—
keep the faith! When you're trafficking in beauty, searching for the
mother lode of excellence, of course the way should be lined with hard-
ship!*

When the bag finally comes, it is anticlimactic. I had envisioned the old woman stumping along with her peg leg, the
man trolling my bag, perhaps an exchange in the center of the
abandoned baggage area wherein we would get to see her put
her leg on and become whole again. But when the bag arrives,
it is being rolled instead by a man in a uniform—a general, it
seems. Before I can claim it the general asks me to describe my
bag's contents, open it to verify, then sign some papers that, for
all I know, warrant I shall never come to Geneva again. But the
elk meat is still there! I shudder to think what the old woman

thought when she saw that. Her first intake of breath as sharp and sudden as my own.

We trudge out of detention and through the empty airport—night has fallen—but our trial is not over yet. Due to some technicality—has a hold been placed on my passport?—we spend a terrible amount of time at the rental-car counter until, just at the edge of weeping, we regain our freedom. Quickly, before anyone can change their mind, we pile our bags into the car and make our way up into the French Alps, toward a village called Quincy, on the road to Mont Blanc and its perfect, snowy mass: a beauty so vast it can absorb almost all ugliness and imperfection.

After some stress navigating the cobblestone streets of Geneva in the dark, and a fruitless stop at the sole open grocery store on our route, we cross into France and begin to pass one merry little stone tavern after another. None of us has eaten anything since our morning toast at David's, but the consensus is *Drive on.*

All day I've been trading phone calls with kind and patient Yves, John's dreamy, fiercely intelligent son, who has given me meticulous directions to the place we'll be staying, a pension run by friends of his. But when we finally roll into Quincy, in such darkness and beset with bone-deep exhaustion, we drive around the small town a couple of times and make multiple passes around a roundabout without locating the place. Given that I've already called Yves four or five times during the day—updating him about the luggage fiasco and the delays, getting directions, then clarifications on the directions—I'm determined not to destroy his peace one more time with yet another clang of the phone in the stillness of his country home. The trouble is I can't read my own writing on the napkin scrap where I wrote it all down: Mansion something something; something about a hallway; something about a hill, and a security code.

We reach the cemetery at the edge of town and turn back. Then I spy a larger building on the hill, beneath a big church adorned with a cross, and I hope it's our lodging and not simply someone's nice home. Up the hill we go, through a series of gravel switchbacks, with tall grasses swishing the sides of the car. I park and we stumble out, desperate travelers. Three countries—England, Switzerland, and France—in this one day alone.

We approach with caution. All is dark inside the building, and when I pull on the door, it is locked tight—not so much as a wiggle. But beneath the handle there's a little keypad, such as you'd find on a cell phone. Now I recall the four-digit number Yves gave me, which I thought was some kind of street address or telephone extension, but after I go back to the car for the napkin scrap, decipher the numbers, and key them in, the door clicks. Euphoria! We open it and step inside. At the top of a set of narrow stairs we find two empty rooms, one on the left and one on the right. The beds are neatly made and we pile in, hoping they are ours. *Goldilocks.*

I've met John before, after a literary festival in Lyon, when a mutual friend, Marc Trivier, a Belgian photographer and stonemason, introduced us. Elizabeth was with me then. In John's backyard, where apple trees were blossoming, we sat in the sunlight drinking cassis made from the blackberries in his garden while he smoked cigarettes, and I remember the smoke blue in that light, with Mont Blanc above us so close we could feel the icy draft of its glaciers. We visited about our respective valleys, his in France and mine in Montana, and how nice it was to live among people who worked with their hands, and how important it was for a writer to work in some physical way. Then John had to leave. His wife of fifty years, Beverly, had just been diagnosed with cancer, and was on her way to another doctor that evening.

It got me thinking how fine it would be, as John had Yves and his family, to have my children, and eventually my grandchildren, living in the same village, only a nice walk away. Taking Sunday meals together, holidays. For a long time this is the way things used to be for us as a species. And it's how it was for me, until my daughters went off to college. I did my best to carve out such a life, and here in Quincy, John was still living it, as was Yves, with the sweetness I once had. Unbeknownst to John and Beverly on the day we met, in less than two months all of that would be gone from them. Beverly was dying, though they did not yet know how bad it was. We enjoyed the meal and the company, and went to bed that night sated and content.

Up until a couple of years ago I envisioned easing into a dignified geezerhood of exactly the sort John was living, good-natured bantering with a longtime spouse, with the increased congeniality of having passed through even more years, and challenges, together. A lengthy campaign, perhaps, but with peace finally inhabiting the land. With parenting duties mostly behind us, I imagined, Elizabeth and I would do some traveling and take a breather before preparing for Act Two, grandparenthood. I was ready. Now, however, those images had disappeared—there was nothing to sustain them—and I could think of nothing to take their place.

What I love most about John is how, though an intellectual, to some degree he turned his back on what many would call civilization and moved far up into the mountains, into a beautiful little valley, and immersed himself into his art as if diving deep into a lake.

John writes best of all about peasants, in a trilogy of books called *Into Their Labors*, but he is probably better known for his novel *G.*, which won the 1972 Man Booker Prize (the profits of which he is famous for having split with the Black Panthers). His book of art criticism, published the same year, called *Ways of Seeing*, which grew out of his TV series for the BBC, has sold more than a million copies, and has never been out of print. He has published scores of essays of art criticism. I love the clean, elegant, and direct way he explains what is going on within the brushstrokes of a painting, and beyond the edges of the canvas.

You can read all you want about how to write. But to stand in the presence of living greatness has inexplicable and inexhaustible value. I never did sit on Miss Welty's back porch and sip lemonade with her, never did stroll her backyard with her and shoot the shit about metaphor—but I remember tiny things, tiny gestures, from my mentors: Harrison's labored breathing, and the rasp of his voice in telling a story. The terrible, wonderful mischief in Sedaris's eyes during my fiasco at the butcher shop. It's not that I think John, or any other hero, is going to lean forward and say to Lowry, or Erin, or Cristina, "Begin each morning by writing at least four sentences in iambic pentameter," or dispense any other advice. I just want my mentees to know what greatness looks like—to see it in person, and not just in the space between the lines.

We're due at John's farmhouse by noon on this lazy Sunday, and in the late morning we load the rental car with our gear and food and begin to wind our way through the green countryside, and along a river flanked on both sides by forested mountains. We pass lakes seemingly too small and shallow to hold any significant fish, and yet people stand fishing alongside them. Farther on, brightly clad men and women have gathered with ropes, but no helmets, to climb the cliff faces, some of them already attached to the rock, like spiders. All the while the road curves up through green fields and snowy mountains rising all around us like a dream.

We enter the smallest of villages—just a tight cluster of stone farmhouses—and then John's home is before us. There's a motorcycle parked beneath the porch, beside a neatly stacked woodpile, and Yves's van is also there, filled in the back with the most gigantic rhubarb ever—absurdly so, as all we aim to make of it is one pie.

John is not yet present, but Yves is, and the three of us step forward, shake hands, embrace him. Yves is still youthful, and his daughter, Melina, is seven. Together they help us carry our boxes of food inside to the kitchen, which could be a tableau from 1930, or 1880 for that matter: pie safes, worn tables, church pews for benches.

Melina is delighted by the activity. She exudes the confidence that inhabits seven-year-old girls—I remember this elixir as the wellspring of my own girls' early years. They've grown into wonderful adults, but what a magical time that window was between the ages of five and nine. Melina glides from her father's elbow out into the space around each of us, curious as to what each is doing. She drifts from one to the other, asking what she can do to help. A dreamer and a doer. Peel the potatoes, deleaf the rhubarb, slice, dice, wash, mix, stir; she fits right in, a good hand. I feel a tug at my soul. This is the life I wanted for myself, my family, my children. I wanted my mother to know my daughters, to know lazy sunlit Sunday afternoons such as this one, filled with the quiet pleasures of family and food, but the closest we came to it was my mother getting to feel Mary Katherine, our first, kick in Elizabeth's stomach when she was pregnant. It was not enough. It is not enough.

John writes beautifully about his own mother, and in his 2005 novel, *Here Is Where We Meet*, the veil disappears between the living and the dead—who, if they have burned brightly enough in life, never fully go away. The narrator, an old man himself, motorcycling through years of memories, and the great cities of the world, confesses to his mother of having been scared by one thing after another. "I still am," he says. "Naturally," she reassures him. "How could it be otherwise? You can either be fearless, or you can be free, you can't be both."

At last John himself enters. He has been in the front part of the house, whether napping or reading—or, more likely, writing—I do not know. He comes striding into the room with great animation for a man of any age, much less one nearing ninety. My first impression? How *fit* he is. He's dressed in navy pants and a white long-sleeved shirt, over which he's wearing a powder-blue fleece vest. He looks like a mountaineer, a guide.

His hair is whiter than it was just two years ago—less silvery, more snowy—and his shoulders a little more stooped, but he remains sprightly, robust, coming around the long table like a relay runner rounding the final turn. The only sign of Beverly's passing since I last saw him are his eyes, broken by grief.

But what a hug! He's almost speechless, except that his brilliant smile says everything. "Welcome, my friends," he says, grasping for all of our hands at once. "You have come so very far, I cannot believe it. This is *incredible* what you are doing. My heart is"—he pauses—"my heart is too full, it is overflowing." He stands there, smiling at us, his eyes glistening, and grips our hands with his powerful stonemason's grip.

Holy shit, is all I can think. *We did it. We're here.*

John is glowing. "This is so wonderful, what you all are doing," he says again. "This is just magnificent." He moves among us in the kitchen much as his granddaughter did, touching us on the elbows, on the back. Studying us, and the meal that is unfolding in his space. The brown curls of potato peels, the flesh of the potatoes, opening white as bone, brilliant in the spring light through the window. The ivory pool of flour spread on the chopping-block table in the center of the kitchen. The bowl of raw elk meat, which we've kept moderately chilled with ice cubes; the green-gold chunks of ginger being minced. Rhubarb everywhere.

John's eyes shine again and he addresses each of us one by one, speaking in French. He speaks for quite a while, and we're smiling, but as he goes on, our faces, though polite, must reveal our confusion.

"Oh!" he cries, switching back to English, "how foolish of me! Forgive me, I did not realize..."

And for the thousandth time it occurs to me that I really should try harder to learn something besides *s'il vous plaît* and *merci*.

"The mere fact of your presence feeds me in a way that no meal ever could," John says in his rich, deep, gentle voice. And there are no words in English or French that could have made us feel more at ease.

He takes a bottle of wine from his cabinet, opens it, pours, hands a glass to each of us. "*Santé.*" He's not having any—"I'll wait for the meal," he says—but for the rest of the afternoon he does not allow our glasses to get empty.

As Erin washes lettuce leaves for the salad, Melina chops the rhubarb, and Lowry peels and slices the potatoes, I work the dough for the pie and John continues to shower praise upon us.

You can pretty much tell, even in the rolling, how a crust is going to turn out, and this one is so-so. It doesn't have that magical mix of sticky and light, that perfect density and stretch. But that kind of crust is rare. All you can really do is be careful with the ingredients, pay attention, and take care of the little things: chill the butter, the water, and the shortening; make the measurements level; be attentive to moisture; refrigerate the dough before rolling it out. Most of all, though, don't handle it too much, because the heat from your hands can destroy the potential for flakiness; as if there lies buried within you some curse that will ruin anything you try to hold on to for too long.

Marc, the friend who introduced me to John two years earlier, arrives with his friend Daniel, also a photographer. They were in Switzerland for the weekend, and when I told him I'd be going to see John, he said he'd try to stop in. The guests pass easily between English and French. John makes sure all of our wineglasses are filled again, then retires to his chambers for a spell while we continue to assemble the food.

I go outside to make a fire in the grill for the elk burgers. The side porch there is stacked neatly with firewood, and an old maul and wheelbarrow lean against the farmhouse. Crepe myrtle hangs and droops like an old woman's jewelry.

The burgers are prepared just the way I like them, with the diced ginger and kosher salt and coarse black pepper mixed in, along with soy sauce this time instead of Worcestershire. But the wood smokes too much, and smells like creosote, as if I'm cooking over a fire made of old railroad ties. And how am I going to melt the stubborn blue cheese atop the burgers with no way to trap the heat? The burgers will cook faster than the cheese, and the longer I try to melt the cheese, the drier the burgers will become.

The only saving grace in this regard is that I have already been informed by all parties European that they desire their meat to be as well done as possible. (Perhaps this has something to do with the sight of a large Ziploc of thawed and bloody meat.) "Dry," Marc clarified when I asked if they were really sure they wanted it well done. "The drier the better." And he shrugged. "That's how it is here," he said. "Burn it."

I wish I had more confidence to cook it the way I want it. I wish I had poorer manners, more brashness. *Here, eat this, I'm going to tell y'all how things should be. You're mistaken in your tastes and values.* Because the glory of these burgers is when they're big and round and juicy, cooked just until the juices begin to run clean out of them, trickling like snowmelt from the side of the mountain in June. A flavor explosion of medium rare.

But as I squat by the smoldering black char wishing I had brought my mesquite, a feeling of great calm descends on me. Cows are grazing on the hill above me, pushing through the belly-high green grass, their bells tinkling and clanking. Apple blossoms float like snow just as they have in these mountains every spring, or for as long as agrarians and pastoralists have lived here. *The Old Country.* Even the limestone cliffs above the village have been polished smooth by the creep of time. Meanwhile I'm confident in my chefs back in the farmhouse. We've made these dishes before. Besides, there's no need to impress John—he's going to savor whatever we've got, even if I serve him a little black briquette.

As luck would have it, all the pieces come together at once, and on the long table, with all of us gathering, it looks magnificent. Melina has picked immense bouquets of wildflowers— sunflowers, daisies, roses, lilies—that the salad leaves complement perfectly. The gratin glistens in the late-afternoon light and the rhubarb pie rests by a window, fragrant with sugar and butter and browned crust. Once again, John is walking around the table pouring wine for everyone. There's bread and cheese. We've got everything we need.

We eat wantonly, indiscriminately. Whatever looks good and is on a nearby serving platter, we reach for. Let the lettuce merge with the coins of gratin, let the garlic-infused cream and jalapeños adorn the lumpy little meat cakes. Sometimes there's small talk, but everyone is hungry and for the most part it's just eating. From time to time I look around at Lowry and Erin and try to gauge what they might be thinking. They're pretty quiet, and a little glassy-eyed, and I feel certain the three of us are under the same spell.

*   *   *

Pie time. Ideally we wouldn't have eaten quite so much before serving dessert, but so be it. In anticipation, John, our faithful sommelier, rises and navigates the long table once more, refilling glasses, the wine like rich paint in our sunlit crystal goblets. He places his hand on each of our shoulders as he pours, trembling not with age, it seems, but joy. He sits back down at the head of the table, just to my left—Yves is at the other end—and I can't resist letting loose the question I've been carrying around and trying to ask each of my mentors, timing be damned.

"I'm here to share you, my hero, with these two young writers I believe in deeply," I tell John. "But I'm also here for myself. What do I need?" I ask him. "What will life look like, from here on out?"

If he was unprepared for such an earnest question, or considers it a gauche imposition, he does not show it. And although the timbre of my voice is casual and the words are not arranged with any particular gravity or elegance, he recognizes the intensity behind the calm. He locks my eyes with his own: those icy, unclouded blue eyes, translucent in their depthlessness, unsettling if they weren't so beautiful.

"Courage," he says. His answer has such emotion in it: firmness, understanding, and gentleness, with more sorrow in his voice than I would have expected. "Courage," he repeats, not as incantation but as echo, a shadow of the first utterance. As if the word, the thing, is so substantial that it has that shadow at all times.

Something's passing between us, and I can't help but wonder if he's remembering standing where I am, at a point in time where he still—despite some significant years having passed by—had the opportunity to make a change, maybe a dramatic one, with his life. Is that what brought him to this farmhouse in the mountains, with a few peasant farmers for neighbors, and the freedom of anonymity?

"You come to a spot," he says, leaning forward—his eyes still have not lost their lock on mine, so that I feel like a horse being gentled—"and you make the hard decisions and go on." His eyes bore deeper now, telling me that he's been where I am. "It's hard," he says. "Not many do. That's all I'm going to say." He straightens up in his chair, holds my gaze long enough to imprint these things, and then we speak of it no more.

After that, the conversation shifts in tone, takes on even more depth. At the other end of the table, Yves is talking about the differences between store-bought meat and animals acquired by oneself, whether hunted or raised, and specifically about a pig he raised a full year for slaughter, and the ceremony of the day they killed it.

He speaks of the gratitude they felt for it, and how every step of the process—the cleaning and butchering, then the curing—was done with the attentiveness of art. He uses the word *sacred*. Before eating, they passed around the knife that had been used to kill the pig. The same knife they then used to carve the meat. "It was very special," he says in his quiet way. "Very moving."

I tell the story of the elk we have just consumed, how it stood at the top of the mountain, in the sunlight, while I was hiking up out of the valley's autumnal fog—how the elk was poised at the leading edge of that fog, as if it were a lake to which he'd come to water. I could see him on the other side, as the fog tendrils began to burn away in the light of the day, though he could not make out what I was. I raised the rifle and took him, and was grateful. I spent days afterward cleaning, butchering, and packing him out, while in subsequent days ravens and eagles circled what remained, coming in to feed on the bones, and after I was gone and had taken everything, bears and wolves came and carried away the bones. I froze the meat, and now, a year later, have carried it to John.

John excuses himself from the table, disappears into the back room, and returns with a large envelope. It's the loose galley pages of a book Yves and John have written together: *Flying Skirts*, which was Beverly's nickname. John hands the package to Yves, and Yves, with even greater care than his father, pulls out the pages, the loose pieces that will be sewn and bound into the book, not bringing Beverly back to life, but fanning her spirit back into their lives.

Yves delivers the book to me with both hands. I take it in my open arms like a tablet, and, making sure that my hands are spotless, begin turning the pages. It's as if everyone's heart slows and there is nothing beyond these mountains, this meal, no world beyond this one.

I read some of the vignettes: concise, elegant, raw but without lamentation. In one of them John writes about how she informed the pages of his work, and hence his life.

Courage.

Each piece is more beautiful and intense than the last. It's too intense. I fold the pages, hand them back to Yves with an apology. "It's too much for me at once," I tell them both. "It's so beautiful. I'd like to read it while I'm alone, if I might."

They understand, and the envelope is carried away.

But like a tide, and as graceful, John begins to churn the heart's country below. He goes to his room once more and returns with a poem, "Carrying the Songs," by Moya Cannon, an Irish poet with whom he's been corresponding. He reads it beautifully, his rich voice deepening to a gentle but powerful baritone. It's an actor's voice, Shakespearean—and though there is no brogue, somehow it feels, sounds, Irish.

We all sit quietly. He has cast a trance upon our hearts.

I'm still thinking about the answer I got from him, my treasure. Does he know of the drift in my life, the severance? Has Marc told him? I'm not sure, but it wouldn't surprise me at all if he knew things without their ever being spoken.

"You have such a beautiful reading voice," Erin says, and I love how John is neither self-deprecating nor its close cousin, vain. He just smiles, pleased by her happiness.

He sits back down at the head of the table, clears his throat, dons his reading glasses, adjusts them as might a hunter examining the optics of his scope, thumbs through the pages of one of his books, and then seems to relax, finding what he was searching for. As he reads a passage from *Bento's Sketchbook*, about a character named Bento (a diminutive of the philosopher Spinoza's first name) in a municipal swimming pool, we sit mesmerized and sheltered beneath his voice. I listen to his breath and imagine how it must have been when he joined these words and sentences together, the slow-rolling sound waves that bring the story into us. He finishes and sits back, happy again with our silence, and only now, for the first time, does he look even the least bit fatigued.

He pours more wine for us and then goes back to his room. After we finish it, the rest of us walk outside and climb the wooden ladder to Yves's painting loft. The ladder goes straight up, vertical rung-and-rail nailed to the side of the barn. We pop into the loft, walk past the hay bales, which glow in the late-afternoon attic light, and across the wide planks to the studio.

When we open the door we are greeted by the smell of paint and a flood of white light, along with an extravagance of easels and canvases, cans of soaking brushes of all sizes and lengths. And the mountain. Always the mountain.

The most famous peak in Europe, the iconic Mont Blanc—the wild soul of Europe, or what's left of its wild soul. Of course these two men, father and son, would live at its flanks, milking that wildness from it each day and night. Of course their family has settled here as the outside world slips into the future. Mont Blanc fills the huge window. One cannot prepare for opening a door and stepping into a small room in which is housed an entire mountain, much less *that* mountain.

I worry that I can't properly describe Yves's paintings. I don't have John's facility for art criticism, after all. If I use the word *figures*—apparitions—coupled with the adjective *abstract*, the mind drifts away from rather than toward the subject. The paintings are thickly textured, in hues of smoke—blue, gray, purple, black, eggplant, mauve—and would seem to have nothing to do with Mont Blanc, which, I realize now, is the point. It is Yves's knowledge of the view when his back is turned to the mountain that lets him go wherever he wants in his painting. The mountain will always be there when he turns around.

His counter space, and every scrap of wall space, are filled with talismans: shells, nests, feathers, bones, stones, and myriad pictures, including photographs of his parents when they were young and brimming with verve. Looking at the pictures of John then—in a sedan outside a restaurant, smoking a cigarette, or on a motorcycle on a county lane in the fall—one understands why he is still as powerful as he is. Such a light can never go completely out.

I imagined that in these journeys I might discover some things even more valuable than the answers for which I had gone searching. What is the nature of greatness? The depth of commitment required to make even the faintest impression upon the implacable stone of history and culture? How ought we to teach, how to learn? How to grow old?

What I had not guessed was that I might come closer to understanding the nature of time itself. I know that my heroes, like everyone else, are mortal. And yet when I am in their presence, time slows. It folds in on itself. They cannot inhabit this stillness forever, of course. Eventually time resumes its plummet. But these elders manage to move through it in a way different from the rest of us.

Marc and Daniel are waiting for us at the bottom of the ladder outside the barn, trying with their European manners to be casual, but letting us know also that the light is going away and now is the time for a group photograph. We step inside to check in with John, who is seated alone at the long table in the dimming light, on the telephone, speaking to someone in that same rich voice with which he spoke to us.

"I am dying," he says.

It's chilling to hear the words, but he says them with such pleasantness, almost cheerfulness, that he seems to mean dying in the general sense, in the way we are all dying every day, in the way the light is leaving, or will be soon.

"This is nothing," he says.

He looks over at us then, standing at the head of the long table, waiting for him, our leader, our host. What little light is left in the room finds its way into his eyes. He concludes his conversation, hangs up, smiles, rises, takes me and Erin by the arm, and together we walk outside to sit on the long bench beside his woodpile for a picture, just one, in the last moment of light.

EIGHT

Gary Snyder and the Road to Kitkitdizze

We travel together the best we can, Erin and I, but she begins to wobble a little under sleep deprivation of the sort we had on the trips to see Peacock and Sedaris. I've driven twelve hours west from the Yaak to pick her up at her home in Ashland, Oregon, and we're traveling on south, to the Sierra Nevada, to see the Zen poet Gary Snyder. We've ridden a long way in silence now. I wish she'd say what's eating her, but she keeps quiet, and I do not pry.

How did it work, I wonder, in *On the Road*? What I love about that book is the birdsong joy of the journey, the jazz-burst thrall of youth. But there can be no mistaking that it's a boys' book, and, more dated yet, a boys' book in the 1950s. The women in it aren't really given the same depth of characterization as Sal Paradise and the rest of the guys.

Home and the road are antithetical pleasures for me. What

I love most, back in Montana, is to go out to the solitude of my cabin by the edge of the marsh and to tuck in at my writing desk and work, looking out at the sheets of rain or snow; or, if the weather allows, to take up residence at the picnic table outside, nestled in the bower of alder and red-stemmed ceanothus, through which bright warblers dive.

But apart from the tension today, I've been enjoying traveling with Erin and Cristina. I'm not ready to return to utter solitude yet. Thinking of Kerouac, a young man in his twenties during the adventures he wrote about, makes me want to start again.

The summer-yellow fields slide past. I've been traveling hard this past month since the trip to England and France, grading papers and giving readings, and have not made time to plot the journey. Now Erin opens the old-school road atlas that's been floating around in the back. She gives me a few recommendations for the route to Nevada City, the nearest map coordinate, and then we ride in further silence. I want to say it was half a century ago that Kerouac longed for California, but look, now it's sixty years. Blink and it will be seventy. Kerouac yearned for crazy all-night talks on literature, art, photography, music, but what I love about my time with Erin is the intensity of her focus on writing. We talk about the woods, but she's also a sponge for my ferocious views on commas, on the perfectly shaped short story, on the toxicity of adverbs—and again, this teaching feels almost as creative as the writing. Some days, more so.

She asks if we can stop for a minute for her to smoke a cigarette and see what kind of birds are back in the oaks we're passing. I park in the shade beneath the big trees—a blaze of yellow foothills beyond—and stay in the car while she watches the birds. The light dazzles. I roll the window down. In her dark glasses, Erin glares at the sky as if daring it. She lights a cigarette and puffs it not with leisure but in short bursts, as if she's trying to extinguish it and smoke it at the same time. I know she has doubts about her writing, and no amount of coaching can keep hope or faith or confidence aloft forever.

My hope is that these visits to some of her heroes will help when she reflects on them. Along with Matthiessen and Peacock, Gary Snyder is a writer who fits right in Erin's wheelhouse: he, too, was a fire lookout in the Cascades, a chain-saw guy and a fire lover, but also a teacher, poet, logger, essayist, activist. However you turn the prism, there's always something else to see about him. In his late eighties now, he has become more complex with age rather than less. Gary is a science writer who believes in magic. He loves the forest, but also loves the ax, the chain saw, and, most of all, fire.

We're certainly not the first seekers to pass this way. Built in 1970 by volunteers Snyder had recruited the year before, Kitkitdizze is intensely local, constructed of Ponderosa pines gathered within a few hundred yards of the house site, river rocks from the Middle Fork of the Yuba River, and siding from local cedars. (Dana Goodyear's 2008 *New Yorker* article describing the construction of Kitkitdizze reports "they felled the trees with a two-man handsaw. Days were hot and nakedness prevailed.")

Since its beginning, Snyder's home has served as a waypoint for spiritual seekers. Legendary Beat poets such as Lawrence Ferlinghetti and Allen Ginsberg were regular visitors, as were Kenneth Rexroth and the artist R. Crumb. Snyder's first wife,

Masa Uehara, said they "probably hosted a dinner five of seven nights"—and whether for literary luminaries or anonymous drifting-through hippies, no matter. Into the 1980s, California governor Jerry Brown came to Kitkitdizze to meditate.

Back in the car, Erin twists in her seat to look up at the forest through which we're driving. Shuttered light slants through the summer-green needles. The road becomes more of a trail, and the way is padded with the soft matting of pine needles. Eventually, after a missed turn and some backtracking, we ascend a gravel drive, rolling slowly, windows down. Glinting birds back in the forest deflect the sun off the shield of their wings. I can smell the crush of dried pine needles, can feel the crunching of the pine straw as our tires roll across it. We park, get out and stretch, look around. Erin's eyes are wide, the way they often are when she's stressed out, muscling through something. We wander toward the house, approaching the porch with caution, and the light continues to fall heavily on us.

Kitkitdizze. The word is on a wooden sign. This is Synder's place, named after a plant in the area.

Nearby there's a little pond. An empty firefighter's water-tank backpack, the twin cylinders resembling a scuba apparatus, leans against newly split firewood. When we peer into the house, sunlight falls down through the high ceilings, illuminating the rich blond-red wooden floors and furniture.

Everything comes at me at once. A carved wooden mask on one of the nearest end posts. The writing table right by the door, the books stacked nearby on the small ramparts. The bookshelves throughout the house; so many sunlit books. A small gas oven, and a wood-burning stove. So much light in the house. Some framed photographs of people on the bookshelf on the far back side. A stereo system. A large dining table in the center of the room. The quiet is overwhelming, and I wonder if Gary is taking a nap, or meditating. I cannot raise my hand to tap on the door and break the stillness.

We wander off the porch, past the firefighter's gear and the neat pile of kindling. Each of us, I think, leans toward one of the four elements more than the others. He's a hero of mine for so many reasons. His instinct seems always to have been that of an outsider, even when amid outsiders. He hung out with the Beat poets but was never, he says, "a Beat in a literary sense. I'm a historical part of that circle of friends, and I was part of the early sociological and cultural effect of it. My work did not fit with the critics' and the media's idea of Beat writing, ever. We were all so different from each other, all these unique cases. That makes it really kind of untidy."

This fluctuation, I think, is the essence of fire: the great un-making force, yet the great creative force. Gary, despite his easy, mellow demeanor, has a fondness for fire, for the swirling ability to remake, to consume one's own self as the fire eats the very for-est that feeds it. Besides a firefighter, he's been a Navy officer, Beat poet, Buddhist, scholar, and environmental ethicist.

Erin and I pass an outdoor patio—a barbecue grill that will be perfect for our tried-and-true elk burgers—and through dappled shade make our way down a narrow path flanked by tall drying grass to the small muddy pond, which glints in the sun. The heat is buzzing, and before long we return to Kit-kitdizze, where we find Gary standing inside that column of sunlight, smiling. It's the same smile of his twenties, though in a face lined by time. He's fit, and moves without the imbalance of the old.

A dog is at his heel, a tall well-groomed poodle, champagne-colored, as poised as Gary. "Emi," he says by way of introduction. The dog is eerily human, like some canine of the underworld, but benign, seeming wise and magical.

It's strange, standing there next to Kerouac's buddy, immortalized in *The Dharma Bums* as the poet Japhy Ryder and credited not only with introducing Kerouac to Buddhism and mountaineering but also with inspiring him to become a fire lookout. I don't think of him that way, though. Gary moved on—became a man who, like Erin, made a living from watching fire, and produced some of his most evocative work from those long summer days in the high country. His writer's brain was wired from such dreamy days of watching and writing. Now he is as steadfastly local as Kerouac and his other pals were peripatetic. Home defines him.

After showing us around the house—the tatami mats, the sleeping porch, the workings of the hot water and the electricity in this solar-powered place—he inquires about our project: he wants to know the *why* of it. We sit down at his table and take up a Socratic discussion about art and the artist. I want to nurture my best students, I tell him, and make a bridge to the masters who have mentored me, as well as to feel again that sense of community and support myself.

Gary's expression is stern. "But it's never really been that way, has it?" he says, and shakes his head. "The spirit that makes great art has always gone its own way."

His reaction surprises me. I know he insists on going it alone—it's one of the things I admire about him—but I get a little defensive. My mind whirs with the contradictions, in my life and in his. "I know what you mean," I say. "The best work is done alone at the table. But I think the knowledge that you have friends and a community out there—even if just one or two—is helpful." I know it's that way for me, with Doug and Terry. "The project is also about saying thank you," I add.

Gary smiles, nods, as in, *point taken.* But although he's happy to have us, he also intimates that we should be spending our time right now at our desks, rather than driving around the country. Nevertheless he's prepared a portfolio of papers he thinks we'll find interesting: a commencement speech he's just delivered and, just out this week, a book composed of letters written between him and Wendell Berry. Yet we've not been in his home fifteen minutes before he also pretty much tells us not to expect him to be the hermit of myth. He received a letter from a fan, he says, who expressed her disappointment that he owned a car. Gary says he wrote her back and informed her that he owns not only a car but also a truck, and that he drives it back and forth to the dump, and sometimes it is filled with firewood he has cut.

We fix him ginger tea and rummage through his small kitchen to find the skillets and pots we'll need, and the kitchen fills with the steamy hiss and fragrance of the tea, so that just the act of breathing feels healthful. A homey calm descends.

Gary leaves for a moment to go fuss with the generator, which is on the fritz. As I look through the sunny window at him walking across the carpet of pine needles down to the little outbuilding, I have a flashback to rinsing some dishes in Peter Matthiessen's kitchen and imagining all the times Peter would have looked through that same window, and here too I find myself experiencing a view Gary must have witnessed thousands of times.

Not long after he returns he excuses himself to his office—a neat, tiny book-lined room toward the back of the house—and continues to allow us the run of the kitchen. We chop some more ginger to mince and mix into the elk patties. This task is the old standby, the thing you can do almost with your eyes closed. After the sound and fury of the preparation for Sedaris's dinner, it feels good to enjoy this simplicity, with the summer light coming in through the windows and falling upon all the colors of Erin's salad—the deep red of the beets, the greens, the marbled blue cheese, some golden raisins, and, a flourish I'm proud of, some violets gathered from behind my house the day I left and kept in a Ziploc on ice. And for dessert, rhubarb again, not a pie this time, but a cobbler, with whipped cream.

An hour melts, then two. I take in my surroundings. A bucketful of kindling for the woodstove. Old *Encyclopedia Britannica*s. A rifle hanging on the wall; snowshoes.

When at last we eat at the picnic table in the pavilion, it seems our leisurely time of preparation has imparted itself into the splendidness of the food. Gary eats with purpose and satisfaction until his plate is empty.

And then, as if it's a natural extension of the meal, he tells us he has a tattoo of a raven and asks if we want to see it. We do. "It's big," he says, pulling his T-shirt up over his head and shoulders like a boy at a lake in the summer. It covers all of his chest. I admire the boldness. There's no part of him that's not raven, so much tattoo that Gary disappears within it. Above it there's just his face, smiling—do we like it?—and I'm so surprised I don't even think to ask when, where, how, who, how much, why. All I can do is state the obvious: "Wow, that's really big." Gary puts his shirt back on and we proceed to sip our wine.

I ask a few questions about Kerouac—what was he like, what were those times like?—but I sense a wariness from Gary: am I here to celebrate and converse with him, or to mine the much-mined rubble of sixty years ago?

"We were different" is all Gary allows. "He was very, very social." And Gary stares out at the pond, perhaps thinking, *I had work to do.*

And though I wanted to know what it was like being Kerouac's roommate, I let it go.

With darkness comes a drawing in, a deepening feeling of clan. I ask Gary if, before the evening closes, we can hear him read aloud, and if Erin can read one of her essays to him. Erin is usually imperturbable, and when she blanches at the suggestion it's the first time I can recall seeing that reaction in her.

Gary does nothing to indicate the request is unusual. "Of course," he says. "I've got something I've been working on recently, I'd love to try it out."

There is an absence of ego in him. I suspect that all of the greats are able to banish ego during the white-heat, childish purity of the creative process. *Make something up.* I'm reminded of Jim Harrison commenting that his mother, late in her life, said to him, "Well, Jimmy, you've made a pretty good living with your little windies."

I want this to be memorable for Erin. It's good training. Reading out loud brings an awareness to every word, forcing the writer to assume full responsibility for every pulse, cadence, rhythm, and sound; for all the clumsy, stilted passages.

And while Gary goes to find his poem-in-progress, Erin says she doesn't know what to read. Her signature essay in the collection she's working on, about her time as a fire lookout, while compelling, is a tad long for the lateness of the hour; I suggest instead the essay about her mother.

The lights are off in the rest of the house. Gary comes back with a couple of lit candles. With little preface he settles in with a poem about wildfire, set in the West. A poem about the unstoppability of things and the what-will-be, with some geology thrown in. These elements are well-traveled territory for him, and this circling back to old material interests me keenly. Is it something many great writers feel compelled to do on the farther side of their journey?

During her turn, Erin's voice is tight and high owing to her nerves, but the essay's so good it doesn't matter. I feel a mix of pride and fascination as she adjusts her voice to the text, following the landscape of the sentences, remembering her mother and forgetting, sometimes for long stretches, that she's reading a bedtime story to Gary Snyder.

Gary listens intently, eyes closed, head tipped down as if in church. How much attention can he be giving, really, at this hour? And yet when the essay is finished he nods with somber satisfaction, and there's a new light in his eyes. "That was fierce," he says.

And with that, it's time for bed. I will sleep on one of the tatami mats. Erin, as is her wont, goes outside to sleep, beyond the porch and out into the tall summer grass rustling in the wind. She reminds me of Doug in this manner. Hers is a quiet wildness, but the flash of fire is there regardless. What to do with that fire? It is a question everyone must answer each morning—how to end the day with no sticks left unburned, so that you're like a cooling mound of phosphorescent blue ash, ready to rise again, fully formed, the next morning.

We're up early. After a quick breakfast of toast and coffee, Gary shuffles a great stack of his books he has assembled to give us. One by one he ticks through them, asking if we've read them, and if not, he inscribes each one, loading us up with the bounty of his mind.

He's got little books that few people have heard of, books of all sizes and shapes, books written about whatever he pleased. *He Who Hunted Birds in His Father's Village: The Dimensions of a Haida Myth*, and *The Great Clod: Notes and Memoirs on Nature and History in East Asia*. He arranges the stacks like a card dealer. Two more for Erin, three more for me, another for Erin, and another. Feeling gluttonous, giddy, mortified, I ask him to sign one for Lowry, and he does that too; how I wish she was here.

Erin and I are feeling the pull of the road. Ahead of us awaits an overnight drop-in at the home of famed landscape painter Russell Chatham, in the remote, winding hills of Marin County, overlooking Tomales Bay. And following that a visit to the Oregon home of Barry Lopez and his wife, Debra Gwartney. But beyond the schedule, there's also the code of manners, which is nearly lithified in both Erin and me: *Don't overstay your welcome*.

Gary, however, has other designs. He's warming to this idea of apprenticeship. He keeps signing books, sliding them across the table to us as if loading us up with food for our journey. I want to believe that greatness can have an element of sloth, but

Gary is so neat, so precise, that he ledgers into a special notebook the date and other specifics of this gifting.

"I wish we had done this more," he says, speaking of the old days. "I wish we'd had more of these conversations."

This surprises me. My image of the '50s and '60s is of nothing but deep talk. In my mind, *On the Road* is a nonstop celebration of art and artists—but in the rereading, it does come across as more of a rolling drift, with an emphasis, then as now, on how to come up with money for gas and food; how to make ends meet and when the next meal will be.

Kerouac departed the world early, before he was fifty. What would he be doing today if he had avoided drinking himself to death? Could he have weathered as well as Gary? Can I imagine the two of them sitting in the shade on a hot California day, two old men playing cards and talking as the grasshoppers clack and spur past in the yellow sun? It's hard to picture. Gary feels like the last of the last, strong and powerful into old age, ablaze now as he was in the beginning.

We're at the car, making preliminary gestures toward leaving, when Gary asks us if we'd like to see his Zendo; as if he, too, wants to leave no stone unturned. *If you are to know me, you should know this.* Who could say no? We follow him down through the big pines. The needles, sun-scented with the rich smell of turpentine, are soft beneath our feet. When we reach the Zendo, the word *compound* comes to mind. Connected by boardwalks are three buildings there in the dappling of sun and shade, one low and long, another high-ceilinged like a church, and a third resembling a cabin. The wood on all of them is stained dark by time. An enormous bell is stationed between the long bunkhouse and the churchlike one.

The Zendo, which he calls Ring of Bone, was built by volunteers, Gary tells us, like Kitkitdizze itself, and you can still feel that vibe of yearning and community. It's modeled after a famous one in Japan, where Gary studied as a young man and met his third wife, Masa Uehara, who lived with him at Kitkitdizze for twenty years and is the mother of his two sons. The three of us pass from room to room as if through the chambers of a heart.

There's a kitchen, which surprises me. It's tucked away neatly in one wing. But of course: Buddhists need to eat, too. Surprising to me also is the lone photograph hanging on the wall, of a young man. Somehow, without ever having met or even seen him before, I know who it is. I know the young man's father, Tom Lyon, a friend of Gary's, who taught a short-story appreciation class I took my freshman year at Utah State University, one of only two literature classes I would ever take, back when I was studying geology.

Tom's son, Max, was one of those legendary young men who backcountry skied, white-water kayaked, ran marathons. Tom talked about him in class all the time: "Max and I are going to the Brooks Range, Max and I are going to the Wind Rivers." When Max died in a freak avalanche in the night, it broke both of his parents' gentle souls. Nearly forty years have gone by since college days, but I say to Gary, "That's Tom's son, isn't it?" And Gary looks at me with surprise—he didn't know I knew Tom, much less Max—and says, "Yes, it is," and then mentions what an amazing young man Max was. On we go, walking, looking, and the great bell outside that has not yet been rung seems nonetheless to have been sounded, and is echoing within me as though I am a hollow vessel.

For me the Zendo is a lonely place. Elegant, yes, a church for the ages, hand-hewn and classic—but it matches the human condition of emptiness, and I cannot get out of here fast enough. The open road beckons.

A thank-you, an embrace, a rearrangement of the crates and cartons of books, olive oil and avocados, guidebooks and dirty laundry and wine. Erin keeps the trunk of the rental car as neat as the shelves in a hardware store, while my belongings—loose notebook pages, an unstuffed sleeping bag, open laptop and various charging implements, socks and sandals—writhe in the back seat. But neatness will not address any inner emptiness, I tell myself. Soon enough we're gone, knowing only that although we came to give, once again we received.

NINE

Russell Chatham, the Painter, Recently Hospitalized, Emerges from Seven-Figure Debt and Alcoholism, Ready to Paint

The painter's house on the hill is ablaze with light, though tiny against the darkness. We've been driving for hours, down from Gary's place in the Sierra Nevada and out to the California coast, before heading north to cook for Barry Lopez at his home in Oregon. The painter is not easy to find. People see him around—in Inverness, California, where he has a studio, and in Marshall, where he lives—but he has an elusive quality, disappearing into his work for long stretches. He's the greatest living landscape painter in America, famous for his outlandish appetites for food, wine, travel, art, music, literature, and the sporting life.

No one I know is more of a financial wreck than Russell Chatham. For decades, his creditors have been hounding him. The IRS has been garnishing his wages while he tries to paint his way out of this last century and into the next. It makes no sense—even the smallest of his paintings sells for tens of thousands of dollars, while a large commission is an honest seven figures, yet his debts are huge. He spends *forever* on each painting, getting it just right. His deepest vice is fishing; other than painting, it's his greatest obsession, one that has been with him all his life. Any time he gets some money, he goes fishing somewhere. There aren't many places left in the world he hasn't been. His friend Tom McGuane, who was his neighbor when Russell was living in Montana, has called him "a man who has ruined his life with sport," who "skulks from his home at all hours with gun or rod."

Always I study Russell closely, with fascination, admiration, and the tingle of adrenaline that can precede either great accomplishment or a grand wipeout. At seventy-four, he's painting as well as he ever has, with some new tender subtleties coming in—a haze creeping into the cottonwood bottoms along the Yellowstone River, and rising into his paintings of the ridges above Tomales Bay.

Erin and I wind our way up the long gravel road that leads to Russell's ridgetop, past the grove of giant eucalyptus, solitary among all the tall grass of the rolling hills. He's always chosen the most beautiful places to live (back in Montana it was along Deep Creek, in the aptly named Paradise Valley), and when Erin and I finally pull in, the night is scented with blooming roses, and every window of the house burns yellow in the darkness. We can hear opera music—Wagner? Puccini? Is there a party going on?—but there aren't any other cars. The music's too loud for a knock to do any good, so I open the door, and the sound washes over us like floodwaters released by the bursting of a dam.

Elegance within: all the surfaces are clear, save for a pen and a notebook, a laptop, a bowl of fruit. His magazines (*Wooden Boat, Saltwater Fisherman, The New Yorker*) are arranged neatly on the coffee table. Erin was dubious about coming here—a painter as a writer's hero?—and this full-volume hilltop opera in what seems to be an abandoned house is doing nothing to convince her otherwise. But although Russell is also a writer, and a good one, it's his paintings that have informed me most as a writer and a Westerner. They are the reason I want Erin to meet him. Moreover, these words from his essay "Advice to a Young Painter" are at least as appropriate for young writers: "First and foremost, determine if wanting to be a painter is just a passing romantic or otherwise fanciful notion, or whether in fact it is a genuinely primal calling you must follow to be whole. Then, know what you're getting into. The number of people in America today who can understand and appreciate real painting is about the same as the number of wild condors in California."

I go over to the stereo and turn the volume down, and with the house seeming to tremble in the new silence, we walk around looking at the neatness of things, perhaps merely a tip-off to the volcano that shudders within. Erin has brought gifts—she always carries morels, the desiccated, mummified little treasures rattling in her rubber-sealed glass jars. There's not room in our schedule for a meal, and for this I'm relieved. What, really, would an amateur serve a famous chef and restaurateur? For these are among Russell's other talents. Our goal this time is simple: to say hello and then go straight to bed. We'll be up and on the road in the morning before Russell wakes. It'll almost be like we were never here.

Beyond the spacious living room, there's an all-glass porch, where he ties his flies and repairs his rods and reels. The sunlit space is filled with cubicles containing feathers of all sizes and colors and styles, boxes of hooks arranged and long worktables with chrome visors and surgeons' lights overhead, and magnifying glasses.

There are numerous bedrooms, all empty. It's the house of one person, and all the larger and lonelier for that—and again it is with a tingle of dread and familiarity that I stare at what could easily be a possibility for my own life, beyond middle age.

Russell comes out of one of the many rooms and greets us. "I've decided to stop drinking," he says. Another of the things I love most about Russell—beyond the paintings themselves and beyond his ethos—is his ebullience, which some might term manic, but which I prefer to think of as merely enthusiastic.

Of Russell, Jim Harrison has written: "Along with others I have spent a great deal of time worrying about Chatham. For a long time I thought he had too much humility to survive, and in some respects he nearly didn't." There's an integrity in every one of his brushstrokes, in every composition, and it's there in every day of his life. He's slow and careful on the canvas—painstaking—while intuitive, immediate, impulsive, explosive within. The disparity between these two beings creates a quivering tension that few others could withstand but which seems to allow Russell's work to flourish.

"I just got out of the hospital," Russell tells us. This time the doctors said he has to stop drinking or die. "I want to paint," he says. "My best work is ahead of me. There's so much to do.

I don't have time to drink." He rubs his hands together like a man preparing to sit down to a meal. "I'm ready to kick ass and take names. I've never felt stronger, I've never been painting better."

I wish he was still in Montana, but the call of home is strong—he was born here—and the estuary force of Tomales is so much of his blood that his brain knows when the water is coming and when it is leaving. He learned the bay's rhythms as a child, attuned to the excitement of the birds' feeding calls and then the reassuring quiet. Elegy is his birthright. He was five years old when the most influential man in his life, the Italian-American landscape painter Gottardo Piazzoni, his grandfather, had a heart attack at breakfast one morning, pitching forward suddenly but managing to say "Goodbye" before he died. Because of his grandfather, Russell carried a paint box and easel everywhere. He hunted quail and ducks and rabbits and fished like a fiend, and he painted. "By the time I was nineteen," he says, "I had painted a thousand paintings."

In that same essay counseling young painters, Russell is unequivocal about the education a painter needs:

> There are probably places you can still access serious formal training in drawing and painting, but I don't know where they are. To be on the safe side while you're looking, steer clear of the so-called art institutes, as well as the pointless, ineffectual art departments at colleges and universities. Instead, be proactive by drawing, painting, reading, and traveling. This will eventually result in a real education and a path of your own while at the same time being far less expensive than a fraudulent degree.

As Thoreau spent each day guarding his moods, so too does Russell. He's handsome, in a craggy, European way; tall, with a nose hooked like an eagle's. He dresses down, in baggy faded denim overalls and an equally faded paint-speckled T-shirt. His huge brown eyes look perpetually amazed. He's been married three times, is impossible to live with, but remains best friends with his second wife, whom he taught during a brief stint in his twenties at a school for young nuns-to-be.

There is a moral code in Chatham's paintings. Over the course of his life, he has shown us how to really see California—with its umbers and mustards, its taupes and soft hills—the solitary respite of shade, a lollipop shape of a single oak on one of those muscular hillsides. He has shown us how to look at the American West.

He left California for Montana, where he had to learn all over how to paint, he says. In Montana, the landscape was too vast. You could never get it all onto one canvas. "I had to learn to get down in a gully and look up," he explains. "I'd never been in a winter before. Color goes away in winter. Not completely. But almost. I had to learn to find some color in winter."

He's in some deep water right now with his taxes. He's digging in and trying to get up out of that gully. Rising eager for work, working long hours, taking care of himself, and going to bed each night dreaming of the next day's work.

Working from Paradise Valley, by the banks of the same river that Bierstadt painted, Chatham painted the gates of the mountains in their natural duality—glaciers on the icy peaks while the valley below was already verdant. He painted the agricultural lands along the Yellowstone: the homesteads, the solitary cabins with their tiny window square of light at dusk, and the darkness beyond the fields; the big cottonwoods along the wide river. The great artist changes how we see the world. His genius is to see things the way they are, and to make us see them that way too. How many times have I heard someone say, beholding a landscape, that it looks just like a Chatham painting?

The great artist can celebrate or lament. Edward Hopper, certainly, captured the brooding American menace—the guns and knives of the American heart, the culture of detective dramas and unsatisfied lives and, almost always, the chill breath of violence rarely far away. I'm reminded of the words of one of Hopper's contemporaries, D. H. Lawrence: "The essential American soul is hard, isolate, stoic, and a killer." But it seems to me an eye trained only for darkness makes for a lesser path, in art as in life. So many of Russell's paintings portray not just weather, but *seasons*—the duality in the transition from one to the next, and in the crepuscular periods where one thing, dawn or dusk, is dying, and the other thing is being born.

In the morning, Russell scrapes down and sands lightly a painting he's been waiting to finish. Sitting with it for days, the way a good writer will sit with an ending. Waiting to be sure—waiting for the delightful vapors, the satisfying fumes of completion, to wear off—and then waiting a little longer. The painting, maybe six inches by nine inches, has taken him a month.

"No one spends a month on a small painting like this anymore," he says. He'll take it to an exclusive auction in Great Falls later in the month, carrying it onto the plane like a newspaper under his arm. He's not complaining as much as slightly mystified. He blows on the painting, shakes it, puffs on it again, then sands it lightly, holds it at arm's length, and is satisfied. And it is beautiful, even better than before.

"The artist does not simply hold a mirror to society," he has written. "If the world now is greedy, the artist must be generous. If there is war and hate, he must be peaceful and loving. If the world is insane, he must offer sanity, and if the world is becoming a void, he must fill it with his soul."

Erin and I gather our things to leave. Russell needs to get back to work. He needs to return to his studio, solitary and great, stranded in the moment, but returning, in his paintings, as I think many of us long to do, to some deeper, older place.

TEN

Barry Lopez,
Carnivore for a Night

Leaving Russell's early, I make a bewildering number of
wrong turns in the fog. And though Erin's still roused by the
maelstrom she encountered in Russell, the mist appears to have
brought back some of her self-doubt. Few fires can burn as hot
as Russell's forever. I think it's for this reason that I am so hungry for my aging mentors. I know how they did it when they
were young. But how have they managed to keep burning later
into life? I want to peer at them closely, to take in the center of
the fuel they are feeding into that fire.

We're headed north to see Barry Lopez, whom I've known
since I started writing. Where do I begin, with Barry? I don't
want to start at the beginning—him being a theology student
at Notre Dame. I don't even want to start with his books—
River Notes and *Desert Notes*, which influenced an early work
of mine, *Oil Notes;* nor with his classic, *Arctic Dreams*, the Na-

tional Book Award winner, about time spent in the far north, nor another classic, *Of Wolves and Men*. I want instead to begin with the woman he's married to, his second wife, Debra, one of my best friends.

I met her at a writers' conference, the first I ever went to, Writers at Work, in Park City, Utah. Debra, like me, was a student. She was living in Arizona with her young family. She was Elizabeth's and my age, twenty-nine, but already had four daughters: Amanda, nine; Stephanie, seven; Mary, five; and Molly, three. She had brought them to the conference, these four cherubs, each of them with her bright blond hair.

It was 1987, Elizabeth's and my third year at the conference. We had just moved to Montana. We had grown up some, because we were no longer camping as we had when we drove out to the conference the first time, but instead had a hotel room there. This was before Park City became what it is now. When I think of Park City I instead always think of camping in the mountains, getting up early to make a campfire, cooking breakfast in that clear early cold with the sound of the creek nearby, bacon in the skillet, coffee steaming, Elizabeth wearing her big coat, and a whole life before us, none of it known.

One bright sun-filled day at the conference, Debra came up to introduce herself. She told us she felt compelled to share with us the most wonderful dream she'd had the night before, in which she and her daughters came up to visit us in Montana, and were riding horses bareback, there with us, in a green summer field.

Elizabeth and I had seen the girls racing pell-mell, four brilliant paragons of exultant childhood, splashing and shrieking in the hotel pool. These were the children who first began to make real our hopes for making a family of our own.

Well, we told Debra, you'll have to bring them up.

The next June, Debra and her husband, Bruce, and the girls showed up in Montana, books spilling out of the van, and we hiked and camped and swam in the lake, cooked the fish we caught and swung on tire swings, played in the garden and stayed up late reading stories and talking about books. We fed horses carrots and sat the girls up on those horses, just as they had been in Debra's dream.

How long did they stay? I have no idea. It felt like the whole summer. I watched intently the way Debra was with the girls, communicating her love to them, and the delight she took in each of them without fawning. I saw her working to strengthen them at each little opportunity. I saw her making sure they knew in every moment of their childhood they were loved, and that there was a right and a wrong. I saw her giving love and moral compass. She always put them first, and she was fed by that, fortified.

Such is the nature of the best love: inspiriting, not fatiguing. She was a wonderful mother, and we loved the girls and they loved us. Living in a fairy-tale manor, the old hunting lodge back in the dark forest, we were as exotic to them as they were to us. From that summer, I have one indelible image: a meadow, the grass already tall. There's an explosion of daisies in the field, and whatever previous pandemonium there had been has suddenly been distilled into quietude. The girls and Debra and Bruce and Elizabeth and I are sitting in the grass and the girls are picking daisies. I can hear the *rip rip rip* of each green stalk being pulled, there's no other sound, just the heavy breathing of their focused efforts and a mild breeze, and their hair brilliant, seeming in that sun almost as bright as the white of the daisies. Back in the forest, the croak or laugh of a raven.

As Debra, Elizabeth, and the girls and I began to travel the West together, I quickly became immersed in the girls' lives, learning and embracing the code and logic of girlhood. They each went out into the bright world of the day expectant; they were magical, confident, boisterous, loving, idealistic, fierce, at different hours every day, and I dared to hope for daughters of my own.

After Debra and Bruce divorced, she moved with her daughters up to Oregon, where she eventually met Barry and the two of them got together. When that happened, Barry sent me a note, saying how much he loved her, and the girls: this *family* he'd stepped into. With grace, consideration, and love, he fit himself into their lives. He had endured his own divorce after a long marriage, and now his solitude of one amplified to become six.

Erin doesn't have any idea what's ahead of her, meeting Barry. She knows a couple of the basics—that the girls would come and spend time with Elizabeth and me in Montana during their growing-up years—but of Debra's and Barry's generosity, she has no clue—and we push north, back toward home.

In a strange little Oregon town—a hybrid of European mountain village, backwoods methland, and once-upon-a-time 1950s "safe" white Americana—we sit down at a brewery to talk about the menu. Salmon, of course, with a dry rub of brown sugar, thyme, salt, and garlic. We *have* to serve Barry and Debra salmon. From their window they can see the McKenzie River riffling through the old cedars. Barry says there is one certain date each year in September when the spawning salmon push past their house, heading up farther into the forest, as they have always done. Several years ago he went down to the river and sat waiting as he had every year, and there were no salmon. His heartbreak was beyond despair. And he waited, and waited. Finally—three days late—a wild salmon returned; and for one more year, his world was right.

Debra has insisted that she help us with the meal, and I'm thrilled. It's been a long time since we've been in the kitchen together, and it will recall many great dinners, in all seasons: Thanksgiving feasts, Christmas celebrations, winter spicy stews in Tucson, venison chili and turkey enchiladas in the Yaak, grilled trout in summer. It'll bring back the old days, when we were young and just starting out and the girls' heads came only to our elbows as we worked in the kitchen.

There's a recipe for sweet-potato galettes with roasted pumpkin seeds that I couldn't resist adding into the mix. And I've brought another length of elk backstrap from the Yaak. Barry's not eating red meat, but he said he'll have one bite for ceremony—a significant acquiescence, since it's huge for him to bend any rule.

We pull up into sun dapple, a cabin on the slope of a hill tucked back in the trees. Barry and Debra are standing outside looking at a little generator that's been acting up, and it's déjà vu from Gary's.

Seeing Debra feels just like it did thirty years ago: her

brightness of spirit hasn't changed a bit. She's the world's most resilient person—a striver for happiness, even in the hardest of times. Barry, too, looks good. A little pale and maybe a little worried, but happy. It's good to see him, and while he doesn't look his best, he doesn't look like he's carrying inside him what he's carrying, either. His prostate cancer is spreading to his bones, and he's had to be conservative in expending his energies.

There's a nice new stack of Douglas fir logs, orange and sweet-scented, flanked by a hatchet and a few bright chips of fresh-cut kindling beside a large stump, and I want to ask Barry whether he's well enough to be cutting and splitting his own wood—as if that's one of the most fundamental arbiters of health there is. But I say nothing, and he and Debra take us over to her beautiful new writing studio. It looks like something from *Architectural Digest:* a wooden deck, glass doors and big west-facing windows, lovely blond fir floors, a desk and a little kitchen, a tiny bathroom with a tile floor, and a small bedroom. All a writer needs here is time.

In addition to teaching at a low-residency writing program in Seaside, Oregon, Debra is an award-winning journalist and author of the beautiful memoir *Live Through This.* And as she was and is one of the world's best mothers, so too is she one of the best grandmothers, to two young grandchildren, who are the same age, essentially, that Debra's daughters were when I first met them, a fact I cannot quite comprehend.

We unload the groceries and, spying the morels, Barry and Debra ask if we'd like to go up into the woods and look for some oyster mushrooms. Of course. A nature walk. We step through the emerald ferns behind Debra's writing cabin and into the old forest. It's like stepping through a curtain of green. The soil is blacker here than in the Yaak. Pulpy, rotting orange mulch blazes bright amid all the green and atop that black soil. We ease deeper into the woods. On our right, a silver creek rushes, small enough that a child could jump across it. Barry says forty years ago he used to sit in that creek sometimes while writing, and now the grandchildren play in it. This is the same creek in which silver salmon surge their way up with only one thought pounding in their ancient, illuminated minds: *Ascend.*

Debra finds the oyster mushrooms in their typical spot, growing from the side of a fallen tree. They come and go like fireflies—they're always around here somewhere, she says. She cuts them carefully and we carry them home in cupped hands.

"I wanted to name this Debra Creek," Barry says, "but when I petitioned the county, they said it already had a name, that it's called No-Name Creek." He laughs, and this is another of the things I remember about him—his easy sense of humor. As if his mind needs uncomplicated humor after laboring long hours amid the fumes of despair. I forget how boyish and enthusiastic he can be, too. I'm sometimes guilty of thinking of him only as who he is on the page—an esteemed and moral voice in matters of mankind and nature. But he also gets as excited about fun as he does about big ideas and the burning world. Not many people know that part of him. They see the passion in his thinking and his prose, or they attend a profound lecture of his and think, *Holy shit, that dude is… intense.*

We've barely gotten back from our walk when Barry asks if I'd like to see his work space. Feeling a bit like Tom Sawyer handing off the paintbrush, I make sure it's all right with Erin and Debra, then vacate the kitchen. The small building, like

Debra's, is elegant. I think of my own rough little cabin in the woods, a trapper's cabin from 1903 homesteaders, which I dismantled, hauled farther into the forest, and then reconstructed, log by log, at the marsh's edge. Barry's, however, is the office of a board retreat. A little stove. Bright orange-red flooring and walls. There's a special map drawer. Barry opens it and shows me maps of expeditions he's been on. There are a lot of them, and they are all neat, none folded cattywampus, as mine are, none with crude or illegible notes. Everything in its place. There is an order in his mind that is so unlike mine that I wonder if he and I are the same species. His is a life devoted to order. How strange to know someone for so long, and yet upon deeper inquiry to discover something new about him. I knew of his rigorous internal attention to order and rightness, but having never been in his office, I had not fully realized this carryover of precision into his physical world.

I feel like I shouldn't even be in this space. As if the whirl of my asynchrony might begin to tilt the lightbulbs in their elegant overhead tracks. I believe I could ask Barry what birds he sighted on a particular river in Alaska on a particular day forty years gone by and he would need to take but two steps to a certain filing cabinet, slide open the drawer, lift a sheet of paper from a folder, and tell me.

We wander back to the house, and when we step inside we are greeted with the Thanksgiving aroma of sweet potatoes baking. We stop in the mudroom first, where Barry slides open another drawer and shows me his letter-writing kit—folders and binders with various stamps of all different denominations. The artifacts of a craftsman who composes thoughtful physical letters, typed or sometimes handwritten in elegant script, to anyone who might write him. His attention to detail carries over even into the envelope in which he posts his return missive: choosing stamps appropriate to the message.

Amanda, Debra's oldest daughter, arrives, driving in from Ash Valley—juggling work and school and the children. I haven't seen her in a couple of years. She's glowing, and she leans into the kitchen chores with a grace identical to her mother's. They work on their dishes but also look over Erin's and my shoulders at the recipes spread everywhere, knowing what we'll need before we can ask for it. How many meals has Debra prepared in this kitchen? She glides through the narrow space, never in a rush, but with confidence and authority. And while part of this is her disposition, I recognize that part of it is the hardwiring of deep experience from being such a great mother to so many for so long.

Barry comes back in with the day's mail, which includes a letter from a friend whose prostate cancer, having been in remission, has returned. He asks again about Gary Snyder's health. Debra, who's helping Erin tear the leaves in the enormous salad, is quiet for a moment, and then says only, "Mortality has entered our home."

In one corner, at the far end, by a window and the screen porch—as out of the way as possible, characteristically reserved and observant—Erin is now working with the morels, and then a decadent old-school ginger chocolate cake made with buttermilk, applesauce, vanilla, Dagoba chocolate, cinnamon, and a lot of ginger. The length of elk backstrap, muscular as an anaconda, sits on a plate, glinting with the light olive-oil sheen, coarse salt, and newly crushed black peppercorns that adhere to it. It will go into the cast-iron skillet last, along with some of Erin's morels, and plenty of butter—and all around us, the unassembled pieces become something recognizable as a meal.

There's also a spectacularly beautiful cilantro salad, which Amanda is working on: two full cups of cilantro, parsley, spinach, a full cup of tarragon, a pile of basil and arugula, and a cup of pomegranate seeds, glistening. And for my old mentor, the comfort-food standby, the jalapeño potato gratin, with sweet potatoes and cream, garlic and sage. Next to the salad, the centerpiece—sweet-potato galettes, the baked sweet potatoes perched on top of an egg white–glazed puff-pastry square, with sour cream, goat cheese, red-hot chili pepper, garlic, parsley, and toasted pumpkin seeds. Last, king salmon two ways: two giant silver-scaled slabs, one with the traditional grilling recipe, the dry rub, the second baked with a hazelnut crust, and a salsa of red bell peppers, chives, garlic, lemon, apple-cider vinegar, cucumber, a spot of Dijon, papaya, mango, red onion, red chili peppers, a splash of Thai fish sauce, sugar, and some more ginger.

The kitchen is filled with people and maybe it's an hour too early, but a bottle of wine is opened anyway. Barry observes, delighted. From time to time he goes back to his cabin, then returns, watches the meal coming together, smells it, tastes a kale chip.

We talk about books and writers. I'm embarrassed to say here what I haven't read. At least with Gary, there was enough obscurity involved to avoid some embarrassment—*of course* I haven't read that nineteenth-century ethnobotanist—but the names I am hearing today are shamefully familiar. Some are Debra's favorites I've been hearing her talk about forever. J. M.

Coetzee's *Disgrace*. And I've long heard Barry extol the work of Jim Crace, but have read only one of his novels. I also forgot how much Debra loves Ian McEwan. It can be wonderful but also daunting to "discover" a writer with such a broad and deep oeuvre—*Do I really want to spend the rest of my life reading this writer?* Erin pauses in her cake-making and takes out her notebook, writes it all down. Some, Debra and I share: James Galvin's *The Meadow*, Harry Crews's memoir, *A Childhood*. Larry Brown's novel *Joe*.

The daylight is softening, four people now doing the work of one. As the long early-summer shadows fall, we're almost finished. The galettes are ready for the final baking, the cake is being frosted, the salmon rubbed, the gratin waiting in its heavy dish. Stephanie, Debra's second daughter, arrives, a box of fireworks, all big-smile dazzle and glamour, back from Mexico City and on her way to France. She and Amanda joke the way sisters do. It seems like just a moment ago I held them in the crook of each arm, carrying them across creeks in the Yaak.

The slabs of fish go on the grill. Stephanie comes out and stands in the dusk with me as the blue smoke seeps from beneath the lid. The summer evening is warm, and so dark now that all I can really see is her brilliant long hair and the horizontal white stripes on her dress. I think we make some small acknowledgment about our sorrow over the way things turned out for Elizabeth and me. Or maybe not. Maybe it's impossible to articulate, and instead we just stand there, feeling our long love for each other, and the knotted ache of loss, and say it without saying anything at all, while the sweet smoke of the fish washes over us.

*   *   *

I've been working off a crude but complicated recipe schedule, a homemade spreadsheet, in hopes that all the dishes might stand a better chance of being ready at the same time, and the oil- and butter-spattered notebook paper has served us well. We've worked backward from the desired dinnertime, seven-thirty, in order to avoid keeping Barry up too late. Only the elk is left to cook, and as Erin and Amanda and Stephanie are setting the table, I heat the iron skillet and drop the backstrap into it, searing it in butter and oil. A popping mist arises, and in those splendid juices I sauté the rehydrated morels, plump little butter-sponges that they are.

I carry the elk to the long table in the dining room and it sits there on a plate, steaming, a rolled-up core of muscle, waiting to offer us its explosion of taste. First, though, Barry wants to say a prayer. We hold hands around the table while he presents his graceful thank-yous. The joined current of us circulates around the table, and then we release one another's hands and behold the perfect meal.

Barry takes his ceremonial bite of elk, as do then the rest of us. He says he can taste the strength in it, the first red meat he's eaten in over a year. The two salmon are also delicious, and disappear quickly. The galettes are magnificent, a big hit. *We nailed it*, Erin will say later, and I'll know that it's true.

The advice unspools. One of Barry's concerns that evening: corporate ownership of media, and the need to work outside it. "It is the nature of most writers to have manners, but they must also have opinions," he says. "You must have drive." I remember being impressed by a book he did in 1991, about the legacy of Christopher Columbus, *The Rediscovery of North America*—an essay, really, but a statement, by its publication as a book, that the material was worthy of enduring; was more than doctor's-office reading. Barry wrote it at the height of his acclaim—right after his National Book Award–winning *Arctic Dreams*—yet published it with a small press, the University of Kentucky. Not the best business advice, perhaps, but the act resonated with me as I was beginning to write and publish books that were also intentionally noncommercial.

He also talks about how collaboration has helped his imagination, as when he did a children's book, *Crow and Weasel*, with the illustrator Tom Pohrt. Erin is rapt throughout, as if everything Barry is saying tonight is water in the desert of her fears and thirsts.

It's late, finally. Like a good guest who has excused himself to give his hosts some breathing space, time returns. Erin cuts her massive chocolate cake, and we serve it with a new round of wine. We agree it's a good time for Western writers, and all writers commited to social and environmental justice, to band together with a unified voice. We also agree it would be hard to pull off in these warp-speed days of fragmentation, and with so many of the elders aging (W. S. Merwin) or gone: Matthiessen, John Graves, and Welty, somehow long gone.

"I get what you are doing," Barry says. "I like it." He thanks us for the meal and, because it's later than we'd aimed for, he says his goodnights.

After he has gone to bed, as charged and stimulated as we are, the rest of us set about the remaining work: our mountain of dishes.

I failed at my marriage. I tried as hard as I could but failed nonetheless. And the fact that the standards were high does not diminish the heart-wrenching feeling of not reaching them. I recall several lines from Cormac McCarthy's novel *No Country for Old Men*, in which the small-town sheriff who prides himself on never taking shortcuts runs up against a battle he can't win: "He'd felt like this before but not in a long time and when he said that, then he knew what it was. It was defeat. It was being beaten. More bitter to him than death."

But in order for something to be a gamble, you have to be prepared to lose. If there was not an element of chance involved, it would be something else. I don't know what, exactly, but not life.

Wood rat that she is, Erin forgoes Debra's beautiful space and sleeps out on the porch under the pinpricks of stars that find their way down through the cedars, with the creek rushing past. In the morning, Debra insists on making us breakfast, and we in turn insist on getting out of their way as quickly as possible. There is little that is more injurious to a writer than the disruption of routine. The hard-sought flow is interrupted and one can sometimes spend days recapturing the mental preparedness that dissipates with a single conversation carried on one sentence too long.

One more cup of coffee, we tell them, and then we'll be gone. But if they feel despair at the loss of the invisible thing, they do not show it. Hugs, again, and then we're on the road once more, for the final leg to get Erin back to Ashland. As we draw closer, she points out the hills of her home, places where she's live-trapped—certain ridges where she has caught fishers, martens, skunks, flying squirrels, and weasels, and places where, earlier in the year, she hunted and found the morels.

Erin has spent so much time setting the animal traps with enough care that her quarry will not be injured. And she lines the inside of the box traps with moss so the flying squirrels will not succumb to hypothermia.

It's valuable for a writer to know something beyond the architecture of nouns and verbs, so she can then more easily traffic in metaphor. Knowing the logic of marten runways in the forest will help you write better sentences. Doug Peacock says that hunting is the act of organic intelligence that has most shaped us as a species.

When we arrive back in Ashland, Erin's husband, Pat, has a pizza waiting for us. We try to tell him how it was, but become lost immediately in a sea of adjectives. We keep using the word *intense*. Pat stares at both of us as if we're stoned. I can tell Erin just wants to go straight to bed and sleep for a week, but this homecoming is part of the journey too.

"May I take a picture?" I ask. I'm pleased to record the image of the two of them sitting shoulder to shoulder on the front steps of their home, an old house with a leaning picket fence, and furry Kiowa at their feet, as I once sat with Elizabeth for a hundred such pictures, with any of half a dozen of our dogs over the years.

In the old days I would have pushed on, ceaseless and indefatigable, but lately I've been experimenting with moderation, and so I've taken Pat and Erin up on their offer of a room. I sleep in Erin's office, awakening again at four a.m. and walking out to the empty car and pushing on, navigating the dark and empty neighborhood.

I've got thirteen or so hours to go—up over more mountains, across more high-plains desert, and then more mountains, more forest: winding my way home, where Lowry, back from college, is holding down the fort. There's a message from her on my voicemail, saying she has gotten me an early Father's Day present, a kitten, to keep me company when she goes back to school. I don't really like cats, but it's sweet that she doesn't want me to be alone.

I've already got two hundred miles behind me by the time the darkness begins to pale, the old miracle yet again. In that last light before dawn, when the road seems darker than the dim sky, a giant mountain lion sails across the road in two leaps, passing through the headlights like something imagined, here so briefly and then gone, as if it is not of this world.

ELEVEN

Tom McGuane, AKA Captain Berserko: Burning Down the House

D id we all not revel in Jeff Bridges's channeling of the Dude in *The Big Lebowski*? How we all pitied and yet envied his quixotic, weed-altered relationship to time. In this day and age the danger of overworking is far greater than that of under-working. While there are little eruptions of ambition in my psyche that urge me to get back to my desk for the real work— one novel left in my life, two, maybe three?—I'm proceeding with something akin to the same restlessness with which I be-gan as a writer, back in my twenties, pretending I still have all the time in the world.

I arrive in Spokane later in the day after leaving Erin's, and drop my rental at the airport before continuing on in my an-cient Subaru to Montana, to my secret cove in the woods. Bumping down the boulder-strewn, rutted driveway of home, past the dusk wildflowers, with the windows rolled down.

Home, where Lowry, and the pup Callie, and now a kitten are waiting. The snipe are making their winnowing sound over the marsh.

I want nothing more than to stop and get back to writing. But I'm going to be home for only a day: unpack, do laundry, repack, then keep heading east, to pick up Cristina in Missoula, then on to Bozeman, to collect Molly Antopol, who last visited Denis with me, and Skip Horack, another young writer friend whom I met at Stanford when he was teaching there with Molly. From Bozeman, the four of us will descend upon Tom and Laurie McGuane for what is becoming more of a party than an intimate dinner of counsel—the McGuanes have also invited a dozen or so of their friends and neighbors.

But if it has to be only a day at home, what a day it is. Falling asleep in my own bed. Awakening early, looking out the upstairs window at the sun stretching across the green of the marsh. Coffee. The wood floor familiar beneath my feet. Existing for a while in the fantasy that the road is not reaching, even now, to snatch me back up.

I sink deep into the perfect summer day. With school out, Lowry is doing survey work in the forest, but she's off today. She and I cook and eat a leisurely breakfast on the porch—morels, elk, fried eggs, more coffee—listening to the drumming of woodpeckers and the calls of ravens. Later in the afternoon, we ride our bikes to the trailhead that leads down to the lake, a perfect glowing blue eye in the middle of the forest. We walk through the forest under cover of lupine, so sweet-scented that the fragrance of it sticks to our clothes and skin like smoke, the blossoms burning the cool blue of a pilot flame, while bees maul and caress the flowers.

The lake water is cold. There's a bald eagle up in one of the giant cottonwoods; tree and eagle are reflected in the perfect bowl of the lake. As we swim, our wakes cleave the surface. The loons nesting at the far end of the lake yodel and howl. Now and again a tiny trout flips, rising to a midge or caddis fly.

Right now, mid-journey, midlife, I just want to shut down and rest. With half of my life having been knocked out from under me, it's starting to dawn on me that my initial impulse, *flight*, while understandable, might in the long run not be the best. It's a younger man's idea, one where stamina is not a factor. Tell me again why I'm going back on the road?

And yet it's great to see Cristina at the Missoula airport. She's as upbeat and enthusiastic as Erin and I have been angst-ridden. I'm buoyed by her energy—she's radiating *vacation*, not work—and I remember now being in my twenties and thinking, *I love writing*. I couldn't possibly possess that energy again—but it's fun to be around it and draw sustenance from it, to be pulled out of my funky dark-woods headspace.

We drive through the lengthening twilight, following the Blackfoot River for a while, and now I find myself excited to be back on the road. The old rivers of adrenaline return. As we drive, Cristina catches me up on her life. I haven't seen her for a few months. Although she is hard at work on a novella and hopes to someday make a living as a writer, for now she's taken a job teaching kids at the Quaker school where she went as a young girl. She asks me about Molly and Skip, who are both due in to Bozeman tomorrow, and I give the basics—Molly,

Jewish and raised in Brooklyn; Skip, an easygoing Southerner. We'll all have fun, I assure her.

The SUV I've rented at the airport the next day is, alas, tiny, like one of those cars you see in children's sandboxes. A tiny depth charge of anxiety flares in my solar plexus, but I snuff it out, and once we have gathered Molly and Skip, we roll on, grocery-laden, toward the McGuanes and their friends.

The highway is empty this far out into the prairie, and beyond the interstate every mile is new. Having not learned my lesson after the episode in the Alps, I have transcribed the directions from Tom in pencil onto the back of a tattered brown envelope. With no one else able to read my writing, I glance at it as we rattle down the gravel road, plumes of white dust rising from our passage, pebbles chinking against our undercarriage, and grasshoppers fanning away on either side of us toward the tall grass along a rushing creek. Mourning doves perch in the branches of cottonwoods, resting from the heat of the day. Tiny kestrels hover in the blue sky; harriers rise and fall, surfing waves and currents. The green light of beauty comes rushing into me like a great and terrible drug. My joy may be a little too desperate, but damn it, if one is to start critiquing happiness, what hope is there for anything?

I glance back at Skip, whose window is half down, the wind blowing his overgrown curls, and he's grinning like a dog, as if feeling that same delighted shimmering in the blood. Molly's toenails are a just-painted bright red—summer vacation—and I think she's thrilled to be between things, with her first book out in the world. Cristina? I can't tell. Perfectionist that she is, she might be at the edge of nervousness, thinking ahead to the meal we've promised.

When at last we arrive, Tom saunters out onto the long shady driveway. It feels like we're home. Speckled bird dogs gallop ahead of him in figure eights, and sleepy horses ease down the fence line to study us. Tom, craggy-handsome, looking easily a decade younger than his seventy-four years, calls the dogs to come back. They won't hear of it, are wild to be head-patted and belly-thumped.

I find myself remembering a letter Tom sent to me perhaps fifteen years earlier—Mary Katherine and Lowry would have been around five and eight—in which, responding to my inquiry about what he was up to, he wrote that his days were pretty much spent "blackening pages" and waiting, listening in vain for the sound of his children, who were grown, to come back down the driveway, home for a visit. A chill of loneliness broke over me, reading that, and I set the note aside and went out into the bright sun to play with the girls.

Tom has aged with grace. This cannot possibly be the same man who, in his late twenties and early thirties, down in Key West, reveling with Jim Harrison and Russell Chatham, was christened Captain Berserko by those who witnessed his antics. Something immense has happened in the intervening forty years. A life rescued by art. Maybe you don't have to go all the way to rock bottom. Maybe just way, way down is enough: and then, back up. Those Key West days were characterized by drugs, alcohol, sex, rock and roll, divorce, and fishing. It's astonishing—a testament to the vigor and luck of youth—that any of them survived, much less prospered. Tom stopped drinking in 1981, which helped. "It's true that I've had a life that's, shall we say, wild," he once told Will Blythe of those bygone days. "When I was in Hollywood, I took quite a lot of drugs, I drank an unnecessary amount. People think you're going to die, and that excites them." Tom had simply wanted, Blythe reports, "as the girls used to say in the romantic dramas, to live a little."

There's no real way to identify all that I love about his work. The early electricity of his novel *Panama*, about a delusional rock star adrift in Key West, the classic short stories in *To Skin a Cat*, the beauty of *An Outside Chance* and *Some Horses*—the latter two books collections of essays, which highlight McGuane's intellectual power and honesty as well as anything he's written. But mostly I just love him for how he's chosen to live his life.

Skip, like Laurie, Tom's wife, is from Mobile, Alabama, and the two of them are chatting about people they know, about streets and creeks and rivers, about fishing for sheepshead and crawfish, as if they are long-lost relatives.

"Chili!" Tom cries, when he hears about the meal. "Chili in June?" But he's pleased. He keeps looking at the door as if believing there might yet be more of us, an unending arrival of Merry Pranksters.

The McGuanes' kitchen is more than a kitchen; it's spacious and well lit, like a French farmhouse, reminding me of Peter and Maria's, and of David and Hugh's. All these similarities of elegance!

There's still a whole chunk of afternoon left, and Tom excuses himself to the river that runs just beyond us, some forty steps away. And do I imagine, as he retreats, that he's whistling? Such a jounce in his step. Oh, how much I want to be happy when I'm old!

Our group reconvenes. We've unloaded food everywhere, and we delegate, casting about for available pans and boilers in Laurie's neat kitchen, until even Laurie finally retreats, with a nervous but happy smile. She believes in us, against all odds.

The kitchen is ours. We talk, drink, laugh. My other chefs are young and energetic—garlic is being minced, jalapeños diced, tomatoes cleaved, cumin toasted in the skillet. The knives flash and blenders whirl. We have no concept of the time, but we trust that the food will be ready when it needs to be; that somehow, and just when we need to, we will all get to where we're going.

I burn the cumin but shake off this mishap and begin again. With oven space at a premium, Cristina finds a small toaster oven for her apple crumb. The turkey will take longest. When in trouble, simplify. I can do the turkey and trust all the others to do the rest.

Because we're a bit tight on time, when I go outside to the gas grill I turn it up all the way to preheat it as quickly as possible. It hasn't been used since the fall, having slept beneath several feet of snow, and is a little hinky in the lighting, but there's propane in the canister and—*whoompf*, fire! (I've brought a spare barrel of propane just in case. Like a keg of beer, the canister rolled around in the back of the SUV all the way here, clanging Skip in the neck and shoulder on sharp curves and bonking Molly in the head.) I've prepared a dry rub for the turkey—thyme, brown sugar, paprika—so all I have to do is coat the bird, stuff it with jalapeños and onions, and put it on the grill, which I do in short order.

Back in the kitchen there are always potatoes to be peeled, and more peppers to be cut for the double-baked jalapeño cornbread pudding. Cristina's multitasking, and Skip's got the chili bubbling: beans and elk and tomatoes and beer. Molly, meanwhile, has mastered the art of taking her own sweet time, stopping mid-dice to gesture with the knife, or to taste a bite of whatever she's working with—talking, visiting, laughing— and I'm deeply envious of her ability to enter an artificial reality, free of the ridiculous and self-applied constraints of time and perfectionism.

In my memory of what comes next, there is an explosion, one that rocks the sides of the house—a sonic blast. Laurie comes into the kitchen with a look of no small concern. She gestures to the window and asks, with urgency, "Is there supposed to be all that smoke?"

The air in the yard is as blue as that of a Civil War battlefield. Maybe it's not the turkey, I tell myself, searching desperately for some other possibility. A hired hand burning a trash pile? An early season wildfire? A nuclear bomb? There's no way one turkey could produce such an emission—perhaps there's something faulty with the old gas burners, or maybe the rubber hose is on fire and the whole canister of propane is about to blow.

I vault out of the kitchen and across the porch and into the yard, where blackened char and fragments of turkey flesh litter the green. The lid must have blown open, cast a spray of turkey shrapnel, then slammed shut again.

Chili, I think, with a strange calm, *at least we've got Skip's chili.*

The cooker is so hot it's glowing, and when I lift the lid with a piece of firewood I see one of the strangest sights I have seen in my life. It's a phenomenon, like the aurora borealis.

The turkey is not black, but gold. It is on fire, burning like a comet. Seeing it thus is like opening a treasure chest to behold the terrible, glorious rising of the sun: a molten, gurgling, flaming corona of beautiful yellow-gold fire in the shape of a turkey. It looks almost holy, like Jason and the Argonauts' golden fleece. There is so much fat on the fire, and inside that turkey, that it surely exceeds any known laws of thermodynamics. If I were to set a bird-size bucket of gasoline on fire, it could not burn with more gusto. It's an Olympic torch of a turkey, and there is no blackening, only the beautiful throbbing gold.

Maybe, somehow, I think, *it can still be salvaged.* I reach down to turn off the gas valve on the canister, but that supply was discontinued long ago when the rubber hose melted; the turkey is burning on its own now. From the edge of the deep blue smoke that's pooling in the yard, Skip comes rushing up with a bucket of water, but I ask him to wait. I still have hope.

Everyone else has gathered around, and now Laurie is howling, doubled over laughing—and then Cristina and Molly, who at first look uncertain, begin to laugh, and then we're all laughing, that utterly medicinal laughter where you laugh so long and uncontrollably that your sides begin to cramp and great sweet gusts of dopamine flood into every cell of your living, laughing self.

All the while the turkey continues to glow and pulse, and we laugh still harder, weeping. It's a weapon, something you'd put in a catapult now and lob over the castle walls.

Tom comes hurrying up the hill, still in his waders and holding his fly rod, and he cries out, "I saw the smoke from a mile away, I thought the house was on fire!"

Now we're laughing harder than ever—that silly, gasping cycle of heave and howl where the merest stirring of a breeze is enough to set off the chain reaction again, and it's only spurred on by watching Tom's incredulity at not only the shimmering glowball of turkey but also the sobbing band of monkeys that have taken over his home in the short time he's been gone. I have the thought that he's wondering if there are empty bottles of moonshine somewhere, or some strange and fast-acting drug imported from the Yaak, some fungus or spore, to have changed all of us so completely, and so fast. But the puzzle pieces come together quickly enough and now he's laughing too, and we simply cannot stop.

Somehow, like long-distance ocean swimmers dragging ourselves from the sea, we manage to pull ourselves together. I feel ten pounds lighter, cleansed. The turkey—smaller now, almost cute, save for the horrid blackness left behind, as the golden flame subsides—is gutterstubbing itself out, finally, and though the cycles of laughter continue to wash over us, the tide is going back out, and it's possible to believe that we might eventually be functional again. We stumble back inside, blinking in the bright sunlight, back into what Robert Penn Warren, at the end of *All the King's Men*, calls "the awful responsibility of Time." We're each reassessing the menu—how to feed so many from a single loaf, with no more supplies and no running into town—but there's also a greater clarity: we're still going to have a party, and with one less dish to worry about. Life has gotten a little simpler.

Once we're back at our posts in the kitchen, the facade of competence returns, though slowly. Butter simmers; a blender whirs. The air in the cabin is a little charged. Tom, energized by the mayhem, makes a quick tour through his home, inspecting the kitchen quickly for more potential trouble spots—whether out of true concern or a hope for more entertainment, I cannot quite be sure.

Now folks are driving up and wandering in, hugging, having arrived from not insignificant distances in this vast and still mostly unpeopled country. Some I know—the West is a small community. Gretel Ehrlich and her partner, longtime National Public Radio newscaster Neal Conan, followed by a man I haven't met, a neighbor of the McGuanes', Breon, who is an avid and intelligent reader, a bird hunter, and who has several bird dogs in his truck, including his great old dog Ranger, elderly and weak but still joyful.

In the green yard, with the sage hills fresh and the river running big and the sky so blue you want to drink it after the long winter, Ranger gallops for a few good moments, and yet there are stumbles, momentary humiliations, signs that Ranger's end is not far off. Breon watches Ranger carefully, and I watch Breon carefully, and my heart goes out to them. I like him immediately, and see why the McGuanes do. A kind man is a strong man.

The journalist Toby Thompson, from Billings, has arrived—where has time gone? As with Gretel, I haven't seen him in twenty years. I moved deeper into the Yaak, deeper into my stories. Then I became a father, and moved deeply into that. Now time has receded, leaving me in the bright daylight of new circumstances. One wants to squint and blink.

Over and over I keep turning this reality, as if trying to wear down its roughness and irregularity into a small stone that, when held in the palm of my hand, will finally fit.

More guests: Walter Kirn, and his partner, the journalist Amanda Fortini. Walter was married to Tom's daughter Maggie, and they have a son, Charlie, and a daughter, Mazie, who is several years younger than Lowry. Walter was edited and published by Gordon Lish while Walter was at Knopf, and has gone on to further success, with novels like *Up in the Air* and *Thumbsucker*, and a memoir, *Lost in the Meritocracy*. He's just published a nonfiction book about—well, you can't quite capture it in a few sentences, but it involves his agreeing to drive an acquaintance's aging dog across the country. The acquaintance has since been convicted of murder, which gives the book a typical Kirnish otherness. With his passion and energy, Walter puts me in mind of what Oscar Wilde might have been like, a raconteur who makes new connections at ultrahigh speed. He has an eye for disaster and listens keenly to the saga of the turkey, such that behind the jack-o'-lantern blaze of his eyes, it is easy to see him thinking, *Damn, I miss all the good stuff.*

The house is filled. People are settling in, talk flying back and forth. Just in time we send out a few hors d'oeuvres, which are inhaled. Meanwhile, despite the disruption of earlier in the day, all our other dishes are coming together. It's a party, rather than the intimate conversation studded with delicate and at times intense inquiries into the nature of our work that I had once envisioned—but what a party.

Tom, who has been sober almost four decades, is without a

drink, but possesses what is surely just as much gaiety as was ever present in days of yore, giving the impression that the mirth is surely what has sustained him, and those nearest to him, in the hard times. Skip asks Tom about the distance and the difference between those days and now—how one travels from being Captain Berserko to being a mainstream voice of America, publishing more stories in *The New Yorker*, for instance, during this current run than ever before.

Does something flicker in Tom, for a moment? He's so quick, so fluid—like Walter, really, with that high-octane wit—that his hesitation seems to mean something. "Well," he says, "becoming a grandfather helps," and leaves it at that.

As Breon and I talk about bird hunting, I overhear Tom telling Skip, Cristina, and Molly a story not from Key West, but from a little later in the timeline, the Paradise Valley days. It's about Russell Chatham, who, on the lam for one infraction or another, saw flashing lights behind him while driving late one night down the dark river road. Unable to afford capture, Russell pulled over into a snowdrift, leapt out of his car, and began running blindly through the snow and up a hill, like a crazed Dr. Zhivago, straining to remain free for one more day, long enough to apply at dawn the next brushstrokes to whatever masterpiece was in his mind. Stumbling over a boulder, he pitched face-first into the snow, breaking a leg in the process, and then sat up howling, only to watch the slow-moving blinking lights that belonged not to police or sheriff or any other gendarme, but instead the county snowplow, cruise past.

The painter had to gimp his way through the frozen dark back to the icy road, where his car was now stuck, and wait until daylight for the next passerby to hitch a ride to the hospital.

Another tale from the lively times: Russell and Tom were out driving around, somewhere near Chico, on that same river road, when from out of nowhere some ne'er-do-well came charging out with a crossbow and fired it at the side of their car. Russell, who was driving, never missed a beat, says Tom, but instead simply cried out, "Such is the plight of the artist in America!"

For all his robust health, Tom has not avoided the travails of aging. Two years ago he broke his kneecap while bird hunting. He had it reconstructed and kept going, hunting for a hundred days the following year. Then he fell again hunting, and this time broke his leg and was in a cast all autumn. He wrote to me with great joy near the end of December saying the cast was finally coming off and when it did he would throw it in the Yellowstone River and go fishing.

What a splendid paradox: a man whose idea of a perfect year is one in which he spends almost a third of it out in the field with his dogs, seeking Hungarian partridges, feathered buzz bombs that chortle and chitter in an adrenaline-inducing racket as they whir away, yet who was morose for a year, devastated, he says, when his pet parakeet died.

"I like having animals around me," he's said. "Horses, dogs, it doesn't matter. I don't like being alone." A further paradox: the man who lives, by his own design, down forty miles of dirt road, nestled in the willows and cottonwoods at the edge of a rushing river, with no other cabins or neighbors visible for miles in any direction, doesn't like to be alone. It occurs to me that, taken out of context, a piece of paper containing the checklist for the elements of greatness might, at the surface, appear not all that different from one containing the same checklist for batshit crazy: obsessive; solitary; able to hold two competing thoughts at the same time; reclusive; reads a lot, laughs often; generous to a fault.

With the meal concluded, we retire from the long dinner table and pull chairs into a big circle around the living room. Dogs pass between us, crawl up into our laps. Cristina has timed her apple crumb cake perfectly, and she's back and forth to the kitchen now, dolloping it with big spoonfuls of vanilla ice cream. The room falls into silent bliss, we're all eating like field hands. Cristina is praised to the high heavens. Night has descended. The conversation whirls around the circle, storytellers telling stories, stimulated by food and wine and company, and by the darkness outside. In the morning, every writer will awaken with the need to go back to the page, but tonight we're just telling stories the old-fashioned way, and it feels wonderful.

My favorite story? Tom's, of course. I've shared the story of being at my first book signing in France, paired with Jim Harrison, who is a demigod there. I sat at my table, largely alone, for two hours, smiling a ventriloquist's smile, while old Jim's line of devotees snaked out of the theater and onto the sidewalk and around the corner for a block. His fans brought him bottles of wine, chunks of devastatingly rich cheese, cured hams, and invitations to their chateaus. I watched him for two hours.

Tom laughs, says he had a similar experience when he was on a panel and book signing in Los Angeles with Michael Jackson, sitting shoulder to shoulder with him all afternoon and into the evening. Tom shakes his head even now, a wry wince, and I'm reminded of Sedaris's humility. They went out to dinner afterward, Tom says, some exclusive place where the hordes couldn't bother them. And again Tom found himself sitting next to Michael, who was being super quiet, retreating into that famed silo of shyness. There was a preternatural stillness at the table. Tom says he and Laurie could tell Michael knew he was supposed to be having a conversation with them, but just didn't know how to go about it. Then he tried, heroically, to rally. In desperation, Michael turned to them, Tom says, and blurted, "Y'all want to come over to my house?" Two long beats, then three, then four. "I've got a llama."

Tom is in a story groove. The hour is still respectable, somewhere closer to ten o'clock than to midnight, at that delicate spot where, having so much fun, the guests could open still more wine and sink down lower into their chairs and couches, entering the party glide. But an old poet learns, by long practice, to guard his moods. Departing in merriment is critical to a diplomatic leave-taking. Tom yawns, rises to his full height, and begins to excuse himself, reminding us he promised his bedtime would come early and he wouldn't be much of a reveler. And it's enough. We could carry on longer, but it's been rich and wonderful, and we're content to send Tom and Laurie off to bed. Toby is driving back to Billings, Walter and Amanda to Livingston; Gretel and Neal likewise. Breon will sleep in the camper shell on his truck with his dogs.

After everyone filters away, it's just us now, the four barbarians again. The kitchen is a wreck but we decide, in whispers, to wait till the morning, so as not to disturb Tom and Laurie's sleep. Blurry and happy, sated and buzzed, road-weary and lit-stuffed, we walk through the tall grass and moonlight to our guest cabin, a bunkhouse so far away we could fire cannons from the porch without disturbing our hosts. We're sleepwalking already but we stand on the porch in the steady wind, looking up at the stars. The sheaves of grass are blowing, and a rich scent gusts as though from between each blade—a remnant of the day's sun still hiding there. Then we go inside, each to our own bedroom, like bears heading off to hibernate.

Skip and I are up early, without alarm clocks. We make our way to the main house, back to the kitchen, where we work in careful silence, until everything is pristine again—as if devastation never visited. Slowly, our clan reassembles, rested and strong. We want to be on our way so as not to burden Tom and Laurie with the responsibility of hosting any part of yet another splendid summer day, but Tom does not appear eager to see us leave. He and Breon and Laurie drink cup after cup of good strong black coffee while the light pours through every window.

Instead of seeing us off, Tom takes us down and show us his writing space, a stone's long throw from the main house. It's a refurbished old homesteader's cabin made of big logs that are well chinked. As with the main house, it is filled with sunlight. It's so close to the river—perched just above it, at the rushing river's bend, with a cliff directly across—that we can sense the shudder of the river made by the rapids. A flagstone walkway leads around to the front, beneath the long drooping limbs of a summer-green willow. We pause, looking at the river, then pass through the double-paned glass French doors and into a world of books. The one-room cabin is all bookshelves, all of them filled with hardbacks. In the corner closest to the water is an old desk, and I note that to sit there Tom must turn his back on the river.

The desk contains only that which is necessary: a tablet, a pen, and three or four small stacks of manuscripts. An envelope or two. On the windowsills, a few talismans, slight physical anchors to the world above balancing the descent Tom makes each day into the spirit world. "My God," Skip breathes, "it's the best writing space ever," and *click*, another piece of the puzzle falls into place: they all have a place to work, clean and uncluttered. And looking around at the best writing space ever, I vow, upon my return home, to be better: to alphabetize my own big library, and to cleanse the hurly-burly of my own cabin at the edge of the placid marsh.

The cabin, like a musical instrument, has a memory. You can almost feel the echoes of certain sentences that were made here. We bask, drinking it in through every pore, and then we leave; as ever, taking more with us than we brought.

We're already packed up; we've loaded all our bags, our cardboard boxes of food and cookware, or so we think (farther down the road we'll discover we've left some things behind, and have inadvertently appropriated others). We go out onto the sunny lawn for a round of photographs, as if at a grand family reunion. And indeed, it's easy to imagine coming back with an even larger busload of young writers, such has been the pleasure and the depth of the hospitality.

For now, it's time to go. In the full-circle fashion that is his life these days, Tom escorts us out, past his hedgerows of wild roses, and follows us some distance down the driveway with all his dogs, walking beneath the shaded canopy of the old cottonwoods and waving, sending us on our way in the same manner in which he greeted us, smiling just as broadly, with the dogs galloping ahead of him.

Man, he's got his shit together, I think again. Who would ever, once upon a time, have thought?

TWELVE

Lorrie Moore, Fairy Godmother: The Road to the Corn Palace; or, The Trail of Ears

An hour after leaving Tom and Laurie's, the four of us find ourselves stopped at a crossroads in Big Timber, Montana, a dusty little near–ghost town, at high noon, paralyzed by indecision about whether we should turn back west. We have two days to get to Lorrie Moore's house, our next destination, in Madison, Wisconsin, some twelve hundred miles distant. We can undo some of our miles and drive back to Livingston, small but happening—Art Walk night—or we can continue eastward, pushing on toward Madison.

If we choose the latter, we'll have an extra night, something outside the itinerary. We could stop by the Little Bighorn Battlefield National Monument, one of the most haunting places I've ever been. We might also be able to swing by and see my friend Dan O'Brien, who, in addition to being a wonderful writer, is a falconer, and owns and runs a buffalo ranch in South Dakota. The image of the day grows in my mind: wandering the prairie with Dan's buffalo and his dogs working around us, watching him fly his falcon. Maybe a roast-buffalo dinner and some whiskey. A slumber party. But although I left a voice mail, I haven't heard back, so I'm reluctant to suggest something that could be a nonstarter. Another option is added: there appears to be a rodeo in Big Timber tonight. Yet no one's stirring. The townspeople, if there are any, remain hidden.

"Maybe we could stay at Tom and Laurie's again," Cristina says.

"Maybe we could live there," Skip suggests.

Back and forth we go, examining the richness of our options. We don't want to get to Madison too soon, and so we're just sitting at the crossroads in the gentle sun. In an overgrazed pasture, horses wander, swishing their tails and stirring dust. Now and again a car pulls up behind us, pauses, then drives slowly around. Our windows are down, and little blackflies are beginning to bite us. But after the bad winter, the sun feels good, and I am not keen to roll the windows up while we discuss and decide. Molly, who has had an entire winter of sweet California, is less enamored, swatting and fanning the air around her. I capitulate, rolling the windows up and turning on the air conditioner.

Already, in the hour's drive to Big Timber, we've had three separate incidents of luggage spillage, things sliding from the tightly stuffed hatch of the SUV into the crowded back seat, and there have been the first airy murmurings that it might be good to get a second rental car. *No*, I want to howl, *that's not how it's supposed to go!* I'm determined for this to have the vibe of a family vacation—one big happy on-the-road adventure.

To silence the budding dissent, I decide to tie some of our possessions on top of the SUV. With rope and bungee cords, I begin lashing a pile of stuff on top: my big rubberized duffel bag, Cristina's suitcase, a couple of old cardboard boxes of food and cookware, and a cooler holding various dry goods and produce. Skip and I perch on the running boards with the doors open, tossing ropes to each other, and the blackflies that have been hovering outside come pouring into the car. We hurry, crisscrossing and tightening down everything, while the sounds of swatting resume from those still within the car. Finished, we dive back in, close the doors, and continue our decision-making, or lack thereof.

To see what it might feel like to point the car back toward Livingston, I turn the car in a slow circle toward the west. But with a consensus still missing, I continue my arc until we are once again pointing toward the Dakotas. That choice, however, also lacks full buy-in, and so I make a second tight circle. It may be the threat of a third circle, and seasickness and mutiny, that leads Skip to say, "Aw, heck, we should probably head on to Madison."

It feels right to be leaving Big Timber and going forward, not backward. I don't know where we'll stay between here and there, but I've heard that the Corn Palace in South Dakota is better than some art walks—and, who knows, maybe Dan O'Brien will come in from the field this midsummer day, check his answering machine, call us back, and while he's at it, thaw some big buffalo steaks. As we thunder across a cattle guard on the ramp heading onto the interstate, there's a shifting on the roof—some mild readjustment—but we're already on the road, and, with no further sound, the situation seems to have resolved itself.

I relax immediately, made happy by the richness of the space ahead of us. I'm eager to get straight into lit talk with my passengers. I want to discuss Lorrie and her generation-changing use of the second-person point of view in her debut, the short-story collection *Self-Help*, published when she was twenty-eight. There's a desperate, last-chance immediacy to the point of view that shouts *Hear me*. It not only seduces the reader but includes the reader, almost violently. Has it really been over thirty years since this book appeared?

I'm admiring the green leaves of the roadside cottonwoods, and feeling my old ambivalence, excited about where I'm going but homesick about leaving Montana, when there is a great crumpling and a *whoosh*, after which food begins flying everywhere.

Much of the devastation is visible in my rearview mirror. In a slipstream whirlwind a gallon of milk tumbles through the air, moving in slow motion, and explodes like a bomb when it strikes the pavement. Sticks of butter and bags of apples, chunks of kale and whole peppers and onions, somersault backward like a juggler's attempt gone wrong. A steady sky-borne barrage of food twirls past our side windows too, ears of corn particularly, cartwheeling down the roadside embankment. The cooler itself skids behind us, discharging the last of its contents—peaches, no way can they be salvaged—and our feast is spread open to the blue sky.

I brake hard, pull crookedly to the shoulder of the interstate, and jump out, as does everyone else. We begin picking up our food, snatching it in big hurried armfuls, shoving whatever appears reusable back into the cooler, the lid of which is halfway up a tree, as if tornado-slung. The corn, with its thick husks, appears not much worse for wear, but I'm chagrined to see that the Tupperware of leftover chili did not fare as well.

We divide the food into two sacks, the salvageable and the lost. There's a bit of traffic and we're mindful of this as we police what is an eighty-foot stripe of litter along the previously immaculate Montana roadside. It's almost fun, like an Easter egg hunt.

"Where's the butter?" I ask. "I definitely saw the butter go past."

"We can get new butter," Molly says.

Now we pack and repack. The old cooler has no handles, which was why it was hard to tie down to begin with. A jar of honey broke, and a jar of huckleberry jam, which grieves me. Our hands are sticky. We attempt to wash them with little splashes from our water bottles, dry them with paper towels. Flecks of paper stick to the honey patches that remain. *Hang in there, folks, don't quit on me now. Who knows what Lorrie will say to us? Plus we're going to see the Corn Palace. And maybe— maybe—a buffalo.*

I had envisioned a quiet afternoon of contemplation at the Little Bighorn with my fellow scribes. Summer's first wildflowers, a hawk spinning in the sky. Always before, I've had the whole place to myself, or nearly, especially in that lonely little wedge of time right at dusk. I have all but promised a moving spiritual experience. But things are different today. We've arrived at the hallowed hilltop—unwitting as the general himself—on the 148th anniversary, which will be celebrated with a reenactment. There are cars everywhere, parking attendants shuffling people into roped-off overflow sections, buses, baby carriages, children wearing roller skates, and a bewildering phalanx of orange plastic cones.

The gridwork of unmarked ivory crosses, stretching in military column and row all the way down the hill, bespeaks the fodder of war. And now I see them, back in the few trees that have been planted near the visitor center, a handful of men in various stages of uniformed dress: the actors, preparing. We make a quick tour, uninspired. I point out one of my favorite markers: *Hevovetaso*—*"Little Whirlwind"*—*A Cheyenne warrior fell here on June 25, 1876, while defending the Cheyenne way of life.*

We drive on toward purpling skies. We begin to see antelope, ghostlike themselves, with their huge eyes and powerhouse sprinters' hearts, their sixty-miles-per-hour dashes an echo from the time when the North American cheetah, now extinct, hunted them.

We're satisfactorily in the middle of nowhere, heading toward Ekalaka, Montana, in the southeasternmost corner of the state, more than eight hundred miles from my home in the northwestern corner. The setting sun illuminates with painterly intensity the magnificent storm clouds toward which we've been driving all afternoon.

When Molly mentions that she's hungry, I tell her there might or might not be a bar in Ekalaka—I've never been there. It's still another fifty-odd miles. Cristina and Skip are hungry too. Might there be something closer? they want to know.

There isn't, and there may not be anything in Ekalaka, either. Efforts are made via smartphones to determine other routes that might lead us to restaurants, but there is no cell reception, only prairie and darkening sky.

"Look," I say, pointing upward through a window. "Venus."

We arrive at the Old Stand Bar, in Ekalaka, at exactly 9:02 p.m., in the last slice of dim blue ghost-light, but the bar is still open. A few motorcycles are parked out front and a sign advertises "showgirls" performing tomorrow night. Do they drive over from Billings, up from Rapid City? I can't help wondering. If so, do they carpool, or are they local? Is it a circuit, like the rodeo, or a traveling band?

The place is empty—the motorcycles, it turns out, are props—but while the kitchen is closed, the bar isn't. There are potato chips and beer. I return to the car, partly because the bar smells bad—a mix of Lysol and old cigarettes—and partly because I'm suddenly exhausted, and slump behind the steering wheel. The neon of the bar is isolate in the all-else darkness, my three friends the only ones inside. The wind, gusting now, shakes and rocks the SUV so that it feels as if I'm still traveling.

I awaken in the awful way of the catnapper, having blacked out and tumbled to the bottom of the sea in seconds, only to be jetted back up to the surface minutes later, resurrected by the sounds of merriment, my friends climbing back into the car. The wind is blowing still harder now, and lightning cleaves the dark. Raindrops the size of pollywogs splatter the windshield. I don't know where I am at first. The belly of the storm opens, gushing directly onto us—Skip and Molly and Cristina are wet from their short sprint to the car—and we spring into action, untying luggage from the top and shoving it back into the car.

It could be worse. It's actually exhilarating, standing on the slippery running board, drenched, fumbling in the darkness with rain-shrunken knots, groping for logic in the crisscrossings of bungee cords tangled like so many neural ganglia in a fraying brain. It's a great way to shake off the sleepiness, and then we're on the road again. It's late and we have no idea where we'll be staying, but we push on, united, refreshed: a band of hunters seeking stories.

It's still pouring when we pull into Rapid City, just after midnight. The worldwide web has indicated that the nearest available hotel room lies some eight hours away. We stop at one red-lit No Vacancy sign after another, pleading our case—seeking floor space in the lobby, a manger, anything.

"In a pinch, we can camp," I say, speaking loudly to be heard over the drumming on the roof. Badlands National Park lies just another hour farther on. Somewhere in the deep recesses of the car are a couple of tents and two or three sleeping bags. There's nothing left to do but drive on, into the slashing torrent. Damn the dark road, the lightning all around us like gated bars through which we seek passage.

We reach the national park and drive past the guard station, where no attendant is posted at this hour—and while the next year, as penance, I will buy the yearlong all-parks-all-the-time pass for sixty dollars, I don't have the money on this journey. "If we're up and out of here early enough," I tell my quieted passengers, "we won't have to pay the twenty." There's benumbed silence.

We drive, lost, wandering in the storm. It's a beautiful, phantasmagoric way to see the park, in the split-second illumination of lightning. A mesa here, a rock bluff there, a drenched jackrabbit bounding through the sage, its red eyes maddened. There's a sense that an enormous chasm lies close on either side of the winding road, which steams like a black snake. I have no idea where we are going, no idea how to get there. "We want to stay high," I say, "to avoid flash floods." From the back, more silence. A coiled tension.

We pass a large yellow road sign, reflective in the headlights. Beneath the illustration of a prairie dog standing up on its hind legs like a Tyrannosaurus rex are the words *Caution—Prairie Dogs Have Plague.*

Oh God, I think, *please don't let Molly see that sign.*

"What's that?" she says, from the back seat. "Plague?"

"I think it's a summer thing," I say. "Plus there won't be any of them out in the rain. They'll be down in their holes."

It's getting colder. The raindrops have lengthened into sharp sleet. I roll the window down to take in the smell of the crushed sage. We make two or three lightning-guided loops through the park. Certain arroyos and canyons, certain wind-lashed and time-beaten junipers, are starting to look familiar. From out of the endless dark another yellow prairie dog caution springs at us, unless it is the same one. There are no people anywhere, no silver Airstream campers, no bright tents. Finally I find a pull-off wide enough for us to drive a discreet distance off the main road—I do not want to be awakened by the spray of passing vehicles, nor by a park ranger drawing the fly back and inquiring, "Sir, do you have a permit?"

With the rain and sleet lessening, I get out and begin the slow excavation required to find the tents and sleeping bags. I know I put two tents into the car: my good one, and part of a second one. I find them and, moving quickly, spread them out like blankets for a 2:00 a.m. picnic. The second tent has mismatched poles, but I'm able to erect it high enough so that it at least looks like a tent, if someone had never seen a tent before. As long as the wind doesn't blow, it'll be okay. The sleeping-bag situation, however, is more dire—there are only two. Molly and Cristina sleep in the car with the bags. Skip and I wear every piece of clothing we have and lie down in our tents like dogs bedding on bare ground. It will be daylight soon enough.

I'm here to tell you: denial and its close cousin, compartmentalization, can be a fine thing. It feels good to lie down on the ground. Sure, it's cold and I'm shivering, but everyone's dry. We're all four resting. It reminds me of the flush of joy I'd get when the girls were young, and I'd go to bed late, having worked far into the night. I'd be tired, and I'd crawl into bed with Elizabeth, knowing all I needed to know in the world: that everyone I loved, everyone I was responsible for, was asleep and warm and dry. That all was well.

It's June and yet we awaken to snow, as if we have slept for six months. Skip is standing in the snow wearing his only coat. He has the look of a man who has been walking all night to stay warm. His pants are wet and his hands are shoved into his pockets and his shoulders are hunched in the way of the deeply cold. The sun is just up, orange-gold, and it's touching the tops of the grass that rises through the snow. The uppermost layer of snow is doing that diamond thing it does.

"There are buffalo down in the draw," Skip says quietly, and

I wonder how many times in the last ten thousand years that utterance has been spoken in this very spot.

We are perched on the edge of a cliff, and I walk over to the precipice with Skip and look down. There are a few trees, stipplings of sage and juniper. Several hundred yards away, four buffalo, looking warm in their heavy coats, trudge through the snow, stopping now and again to graze. Even at this distance they are bigger than anything else around them—trees, rocks, bushes—and their heads are enormous. How warm it must be under all that fur. It's a perfect morning to be a buffalo. Skip and I wake Cristina and Molly so they can see, too.

Afterward, we shake the snow from our tents. In the car, still damp and chilled, we crank up the heater and make our way out of the park in the early sunlight, before the arrival of any booth attendants. We point toward the sun, and soon enough I can feel the intangible quality of the West, that wildness, burning away. The fields are corn now, not grassland, and I have that uneasy feeling you get when you know you're making a mistake, heading in the wrong direction but powerless to change course. It's summer, for God's sake: why am I not in the Yaak? Only the Corn Palace can save us now, and we push on toward it like straggling penitents.

"We're almost there!" Skip says.

This is not at all true. We've got at least a solid ten hours to go to Madison.

Molly, no doubt sick of the smell of funky tent and the droplets of condensate dripping onto the back of her neck, says, "I just think we'd all be more comfortable if we had more space."

But I press on. The country of cornfields induces sleep. The infinite nothingness is hammer and anvil both, sky and earth.

Heads droop, and the mercy of sleep descends upon my passengers as if upon the poppy sniffers in Oz.

Signs begin advertising the Corn Palace a long way out. Driving through the humidity, one can almost sense the generations-thick density of yearning, the hour-by-hour anticipation of travelers drawing ever nearer. I don't know which is better: to awaken my passengers so they can participate in my excitement, or to roll all the way in through the castle gates and let them awaken in paradise, passing straight from one dream into another. I choose the latter, stirring them only when we are coasting into town, the streets and buildings of which possess a strange yellow hue, like the faded patina of daguerreotype. Even the sky is tinged with the butter-yellow of roasted corn.

We get out and wander the streets like children. The smell of popcorn and dust curls through the downtown, which resembles the movie set of a Western, complete with a boardwalk, a saloon with swinging doors, and hitching posts. The illusion is disturbed, however, by all the construction, with the roads ripped up as if in an archaeological dig. Strangely, we can't find the palace. Yellow painted footsteps on the faded red-brick road direct us toward the attraction, but we still cannot see it. A network of chain-link fences, designed to keep us out of the construction areas and guide us toward the palace, serves only to confuse us further; we career in circles, and finally must ask the other pilgrims for directions.

"It's just around the corner!" they say. "You're almost there!"

When at last we arrive, the Corn Palace is not as advertised. It's just an old high-school basketball gym converted into a retail outlet for plastic yellow key chains and candies of all kinds.

The non-corn themes include ceramic light fixtures of roly-poly bears, raccoons, and fawns gazing out from beneath their lampshades with looks of perpetual rascally endearment. Look at those eyelashes! It occurs to me that the only viable way to come here would be buzzed or even drunk or high.

I can't breathe. I do the quickest of laps, weaving between giant sweaty sun-warmed bodies wrapped tight in knit shirts and baring furry legs. Then I sprint back out into the bright yellow sunlight, sending out bat waves of despair, so frazzled that it doesn't even occur to me to text my mates. Outside, I lean against the corn-studded wall, pebbly with kernels, and overhear a teenage girl who's coming out tell her friend, "What it looks like on the outside is not what it's like on the inside."

Slowly, the palace disgorges my friends one by one. I can tell by their faces that they too dared to hope for some kind of transformative experience and have been disappointed. No such luck. It will now be up to Lorrie for that.

One thing we've decided for certain: we're not pushing on to Madison. There's no need to get in late at night, a day early, especially with no known lodging. As we barrel down the highway, Molly's working the phone again, looking for campsites or cabins next to lakes, the sort with recreational activities like horseshoes and volleyball. The sounds of the interstate will still be audible, I imagine, even after the children quiet down at bedtime. And if it's not raining, there will definitely be mosquitoes. But it will probably be raining.

Then I try to be positive. There might be the drum of a bullfrog. Or even if it does rain, we could get a jug of wine, sit in the lean-to, and play cards as we look out at the rain and the highway. Maybe eat some catfish. But it's too late. As if my sour mood has acted as some final, tiny titration to unleash the purple ocean above us, the bottom falls out, and we drive into a prairie downpour. Lightning strikes and the rain pounds so hard that even with the wipers on full blast the road becomes almost invisible: a carwash of a storm. Sheets of water plane across the highway, and our SUV shudders, leaving troughs and whitecaps in our wake.

"The mosquitoes will definitely not be out," I yell.

Cars are slowing to a crawl. I grip the wheel with both hands. Rivers surge against our undercarriage.

"No, we won't be needing a site after all, thank you," says Molly, who has been on hold with the campground attendant. She punches some more keys on her phone, and after perhaps ten minutes, with the storm lessening now to a sturdy drenching, she tells us she has secured a room at the Hilton in Minneapolis, some four hours away. "My treat," she says.

It's a suite—beds everywhere, a shower with hot water and clean towels. We unpack, adjust the air conditioning, and descend into a heavy sleep. And then the morning's upon us. There's no time to sit and eat a real breakfast. We have four hours still to Madison, groceries and libations to purchase, and the food to speed-prep beforehand at the apartment of Alexandra, a friend of Cristina's from her writing program who will join us for dinner. As is often the case, there's also a twist: Lorrie has texted to let me know that the acclaimed short-story writer and novelist Mary Gordon will be in town, visiting her.

We schlep back out, pile into the SUV, and mile by mile we tick our way toward the next extravaganza. (Molly, meanwhile, has reserved a rental car in Madison, and we'll need to detour to the airport for her and Skip to collect it.)

When we get to Madison, we pull into the first grocery store we see, a big-box establishment the size of a football stadium. Commando-style, we roll out with our hastily apportioned scraps of lists. Somehow it's already nearly five o'clock. Within sixty minutes we're out of the store and weaving through the clotted parking lot with our shopping carts. We shove bottles and bags into any crevice or pocket we can find. For now we just have to make it as far as the airport, where we'll offload Molly and Skip for their car, at which point our little SUV will expand, accordion-like, and we can all breathe again.

And yet I'm surprised by the emptiness I feel as Skip and Molly slide out at the Hertz station. Even though we'll see them again in fifteen minutes at Alexandra's, their absence feels abrupt, off-kilter.

We caravan the last distance to a row of weather-beaten apartments. It's hot and muggy, and dark shadows lengthen across the battered lawn. Alexandra greets us, seeming a little unsettled from the start by what must feel to her like a game-show urgency to the endeavor. After hauling in the groceries, we unfold the tattered recipe pages and get to work in what might be the tiniest kitchen ever—a doll's kitchen, with its miniature electric stove and, for backup, miniature microwave. But as we parse our ambitious menu, which includes a paella, we realize we're missing some critical elements. You can't substitute for garlic, tomatoes, or onions. Even if we left right now we would probably not arrive punctually, and so I text Lorrie pleading more time, which she and Mary are happy to accommodate. The new plan is for Cristina and Alexandra and me to finish preparing all we can without the missing ingredients, which will be provided by Skip and Molly when they meet us at Lorrie's. With that, we pop open some beers, roll up our sleeves, and lean in to our labors.

We pull up outside Lorrie's grand old home further into the night, in three different cars. We're *so* late. Still, we go up the walkway unencumbered, leaving the food in the cars for now, our hands empty as if to show we mean no harm. I feel like a trick-or-treater standing there at the door, waiting in the darkness.

By all rights Lorrie should be cross, or at least frosty, when she opens the door for us. I'm half expecting her to announce it's too late, that she's called it off, and I'm also fearing her incredible wit. But when the door does finally open, she's happy to see us, and I marvel again at the courage of these writers, welcoming our strange entourage, allowing their privacy, the oxygen on which great writers survive and prosper, to be breached for a night.

It takes time to be graceful, and often the social graces elude me. No sooner has Lorrie welcomed us into her home, shown us her kitchen, and introduced us to Mary, who's in a back room sipping wine, than I feel the need to pull myself away from this slow and happy welcoming, fifteen hundred miles and a couple of years in the making, and begin deploying the troops. The big house is darkened, and I feel more fully just how long Lorrie and Mary have both been waiting for us.

We have over a dozen big bags and boxes and a couple of coolers. We're tromping in and out to retrieve them, with each trip seeming to Lorrie, I'm sure, as if it'll be the last. Once again we lay out the little sheet of paper with our recipes. The paella's going to take a solid two and a half hours, with Alexandra and Cristina working hard to devein the shrimp and brown the chorizo. We open wine and Lorrie stays in the kitchen only long enough to visit a bit and take the temperature of the gig, which she quickly and accurately perceives as not conducive to relaxed conversation. She can't exactly be said to have fled, since she does have another guest to tend to, but she departs to the back porch with Skip and Molly in tow.

She used to have all her students over here, all the time—a long time ago, in this house, I attended such a party, and I remember the high energy, music and conversation, hors d'oeuvres on a big central table, beer and wine everywhere, and people shoulder to shoulder in every room: rotating groups of young people talking with animation about the stories of the day, and of past literary greats, until Lorrie, one of the last standing, had to shoo everyone away. This, like seemingly almost everything else, was twenty years ago now.

I chop the cilantro and scallions, dice some onions the way I like them, nice and tiny, and then, afraid I'm abandoning my hostess, I apologize to Cristina and Alexandra and leave the kitchen, heading out to the back porch myself. I've brought a new bottle of wine and take a seat between Skip and Molly, keen to get caught up. I'm amused to find that Skip has been unable to steer the conversation with quite the same savoir faire with which he engaged the McGuanes, for the conversation now is centered on babies.

Lorrie's for, Mary's against, with regard to a young female writer's career and development. Or maybe I've got it all backward and Mary's for and Lorrie more cautious in her counsel regarding the timing of having babies. Mary is visiting from

New York City, watching her grandchildren for her daughter, and needs to be back soon. We're lucky that New Yorkers are famed for late dinners, though in my experience no one eats a later dinner than Montanans in the summer, a side effect of the unbelievably long days of northern light.

There's rarely a good time to try to be in two places at once, but I go back to check on the chefs. The paella is coming along and they're doing fine, moving back and forth in the kitchen with the grace of trapeze artists, stirring skillets, sautéing, transferring pans to the oven and extracting others to cool. There's steam everywhere.

"I've got this," I tell them. "Just tell me what needs doing. Y'all go on back to the porch for a while and *listen*! It's what we're here for."

Both of them look dubious, but Cristina, after some thought, tells me to keep the heat turned low on everything and let it simmer. She tucks another bottle of wine under her arm and she and Alexandra hurry out to the party.

The kitchen is filled with the aroma of garlic, lemon, and white wine. I roll out the last of my pie dough, sprinkle the flour-and-sugar mixture over the rhubarb, and lay the second pie shell over the first, glaze it with egg wash, and fork-crimp its edges. I could do this in my sleep. A journeyman, alone in the kitchen, babysitting the meal. I can't help wondering how it's going out there. It feels good, knowing the meal is set up right, and the young writers are chatting with the older ones. After only a short while, however, Alexandra and Cristina come hurrying back in, their worry-meters so finely calibrated that it's as if they can sense me daydreaming—Cristina no doubt remembering the turkey at the McGuanes'.

More aromatics: mussels, scallops, and the sharp bite of ginger. The scent-scape is almost a meal in itself. My admiration for Cristina and Alexandra grows. Alexandra has pulled off the most amazing orzo, plump and soft and slippery with chicken broth. In an ideal world, I'd have brought some ruffed-grouse stock from the Yaak for the broth, but I didn't. Next time.

But there will be no next time. That, more than anything, has been my great lesson—that I am going to have to get better at saying goodbye. There's not always a second chance. What matters tonight is that we all got here, and that the orzo and paella are, in Cristina's estimation, *banger*, and that we're going home tomorrow.

The mind can hold only so many memories, so many experiences. I hope this will be one of them. We sit on the porch, finding space for our plates wherever we can, on various little tables, our wineglasses by our feet in the darkness. Candlelight casts shadows on our faces and catches the oily glint of the paella and outlines the shape of each of us. We eat and listen to the crickets in Lorrie's Midwestern backyard, the halfway point between the Rockies and Gotham.

No sooner am I mulling these happy, sleepy thoughts, and considering the commitment of these two women to a life of the mind, than Mary sets her bowl down and starts lamenting the tribulations of rent control in New York.

We are perched on the imaginary fault line between East and West, and like amateur anthropologists, we are hearing the first strains of dialect, descriptions of the mysterious territory that lies still farther on, as if a savage from over the mountains has wandered into the throw of light by our campfire and is telling us about her provenance. There is a place called New York and for over a century it has been the cultural fountainhead of literature in this country. The decentralized wellsprings of regionalism have fed the country's literature — Steinbeck in California, Faulkner in Oxford, Welty in Jackson, O'Connor in Milledgeville, Carver in the Pacific Northwest logging towns, and so on—but the distribution center has been New York, and the daily events of lives spent there are and always have been concerned with things such as rent control, trash removal, and new restaurants. Everything is history, everything is hurtling past, and we sit and listen, writers in America, every one of us.

Can greatness be about doggedness? I believe so. But without question, the sharpest edge of intelligence, an extraordinary intelligence, is another of its commonalities, mixing with that doggedness, and a quality that Lorrie and Mary share. Has the work itself made them smarter? Lorrie is brilliant, almost to the point where I wonder if it is a burden, as if she's so full of intelligence that if she moves too quickly, some of it sloshes out. When we relate to her the many miles it took to reach her, and get to the part about the corn flying off the roof, she nods without missing a beat and says, "Ah yes, the Trail of Ears."

Around midnight, Mary, our bonus guest, thanks us and rises to leave. We see her to the door and she swooshes into the night. It occurs to me that, with this kind of serendipity, were we to keep on traveling for another ten or fifteen years we might end up visiting a majority of American writers without even intending to. We slip back into our chairs to begin the post-feast chatting. It's so dark out on the porch, and for a moment, distracted by my pleasure, I have lost my edge, and the realization not just of how hard it is to go onto the page every morning and make something new in each sentence, but of how hard it is to keep that edge. To view the world always like a hawk.

We slump lower, drink more wine. Although Lorrie has kept her house in Madison, last year she left the University of Wisconsin, where she taught for nearly three decades, for a job at Vanderbilt. She has recently returned from her first year there, and I tell her how chagrined I am that Lowry *just* missed having her as a teacher. And perhaps in the spirit of the rent-control conversation, I find myself lamenting the cost of Wisconsin's out-of-state tuition, to which Lorrie responds, as if the answer should be obvious, "She can come live here. She can stay in my house, get a job, become a resident."

Holy shit, shades of Eudora Welty's lawn boy! The Lorrie and Lowry House! Lowry could hold down the fort while Lorrie's at Vanderbilt, and then whenever Lorrie comes home, she and Lowry could work in one-on-one workshop fashion, reading to each other, cooking together, talking about books, and everything else. A mentor and her mentee. Essentially, she's offering to adopt my youngest daughter. How often in life are we truly flabbergasted? All I can say, again, is *thank you.*

The night travels on without our noticing it. Lorrie puts some old records on the turntable—classic '70s stuff. The Stones. We're paella-stunned, barely daring to move, wanting to savor the night forever, even as it wheels around toward morning. Lorrie asks Cristina and Alexandra about their subject matters, their hopes for their writing. It's 2:00 a.m., then 3:00, and still we're sitting there. The music plays on quietly in the other room. No one wants to leave. We're enjoying the quiet depths of slow time and relaxed company. I look around at these four young writers, every one of them a generation behind Lorrie and me. Jim Harrison has written, "There is an intense similarity in people's biographies. It's our dreams and visions that separate us."

It's four in the morning and the young people are getting sleepy. At some point I wonder if we are going to see the sun come up in Lorrie's backyard. But it's time to go. It would be fine with me if we all just found couches and corners and napped like wild animals, but we have a room reserved already and a kitchenful of gear to hump out. Like boxers pummeled into the late rounds, we rise from the depths and begin the heart-tugging procedure of our goodbyes. As much fun as it's been, as wondrous as it's been, it's also the end of this leg of the journey—the moment I've been waiting for, without knowing it. How fitting that it comes in the home of one who is my same age, almost to the day; who has traveled the same territory along an entirely different path.

We embrace and begin the slow drift out, past the bouquet of bright yellow flowers on the center of the living room table, through the empty kitchen with its one overhead light burning. The bare countertops gleam. We work our way around to the front door and with the summer dawn not far off we stand on the threshold to the utter silence of this tree-lined neighborhood.

How can one be lonely and full at the same time? It is a rare and unusual feeling and for once I do not try to tamp it down or avoid it.

THIRTEEN

The Road Home

At the hotel with Skip and Molly, I nap for a couple of hours—Cristina went back to Alexandra's apartment in the last wee hours, and will catch her flight home from Wisconsin, as will Skip and Molly. I leave without waking them, rolling out in the early gray dawn, and while I won't make Montana by sunset, I'm hoping to at least cross the state line today, maybe by midnight.

It's two hours quicker to run the gauntlet through frack-land—to aim for North Dakota rather than South—but I choose the southern route again. Minnesota on that stretch is still corn, as it was on the way out here, and it allows me to turn my mind off and just drive. On my iPod, the Cranberries, Steve Earle, Lyle Lovett, Guy Clark. The residue in my brain is washing clean, as if I'm strapped to the car's grill and the wind is peeling away any complicating or extraneous thoughts, until all that remains is the elemental distillation of loneliness. I feel ready to write again.

I drive until the corn at last disappears, until the first green of summer hay fills my eyes. South Dakota. I'm still twelve hundred miles from home, but it feels like home. *West*.

As if only now having escaped some unnamable danger, I finally stop for a nap. I detour onto a gravel road and park beneath a giant cottonwood outside an abandoned church, with the prairie wind rocking the car. I know I shouldn't park beneath a cottonwood, the limbs of which are prone to fall, but I want the shade, and I hope to stay safe for the next half hour.

I nap, deliriously happy, and upon reawakening find that the wind has stopped. Cattle are lowing and mourning doves calling. On the gravel road in front of me an old guy strolls along with his daughter or granddaughter walking behind him.

In Mitchell I waltz into the Holiday Inn Express as if I'm a paying guest and case the free buffet. A banana and a bowl of Raisin Bran, some orange juice. I think I have enough money to get home. I have no idea where my next check is coming from.

From Mitchell, I detour due north, on up into North Dakota. Jamestown, nearing dusk. Strange clouds paint the sky. The wind's been out of the west all day. There are mobile homes everywhere, all for sale. What an oxymoron, *mobile* and *home*. For miles there have been silhouettes and billboards advertising a baby white buffalo. When I get to the exit I take the bait and turn off.

The place is as hokey as I knew it would be: a faux Old West town with a barn, a rail fence, a jail, a little museum, closed—it's just after seven. I imagine the old barbed wire and horseshoes that are inside it; the kerosene lanterns and rusted shovels. But I didn't want to see the old cattle brands anyway. I came for the white buffalo.

The other two cars in the lot are leaving. I park and walk past the blacksmith shop. It's all mine. Beyond the gravel parking area looms a giant papier-mâché buffalo, his crimson eyes bloodshot. He looks larger than the space shuttle; how does he hold up in this wind? Drawing closer, I see that a concrete shell has been poured over him. He looks wild, furious. It feels good to stand beneath him. This is a magnificent beast, even if he is made up. He comes from some place of truth.

I walk down toward a lower pasture, wondering where the white buffalo is. I see a few brown buffalo on the green hillside. A storm is hastening. Purple bulging clouds. The wind is roaring. I've decided it's a bullshit tourist trap—*Oh, he died last year,* or, *He's at the vet this week*—and then, on the hillside, emerging from a tangle of juniper, steps a fucking white buffalo.

Oh. My. God. He is a baby, a yearling.

Right from the beginning, there is an otherness that sets him apart from the rest. He is as beautiful and elegant as he is alien and other. For me he conjures one of those luminous desert plants with the bone-pale blossoms that open only at night. He trails the rest of the herd at a distance, the white ship of him drifting in the wind, and it's almost as if he's nervous to be out in the light like this, fading though it is. I walk along the fence, keeping pace across that distance—eighty, maybe a hundred yards—and then he works his way back into the juniper, as if the mere act of being visible was taxing him.

I go back to the car, cleansed and refreshed. I'm invigorated by the sheer absence of people, a feeling that carries me on into the night, all the rest of the way across the Dakotas. Eventually I grow sleepy again but push on for the Montana state line, hungry not just for home but for everything I have not yet seen. In these first few days after the summer solstice, there's very much the feeling that if I quicken my pace just a little, I can see it all. At last I cross the state line, leave the interstate, and pull into a small dark town. Giant mule deer wander the empty streets as if they are its sole residents. I park once more next to an old church, and again beneath a canopy of cottonwoods. Even in the night, I can tell by the sound of them that it's June. How much else do we know without knowing?

One of the best things about burning oneself down to the last nub of the wick is the quality of sleep into which one tumbles afterward, and that wavering line between the real world and the world of dreams in the final sinking down. As I begin to plunge, my last thought is a memory from long ago, back when I was just starting out. I was traveling with Elizabeth from Mississippi to Texas to visit my parents. We'd been driving all night, taking back roads without a map, just wandering south and west. At some point in the night, with the tracings of fireflies all around us, we'd ridden on a dilapidated ferry across a flood-swollen river. On the other side, when we could go no farther, I pulled down a sandy road back in a deep forest of pines. We were exhausted, and we each barely had time to lean our seats back before being sucked down to those waiting depths.

And at the bottom of that lake of sleep, I heard wolves, or coyotes, howling all around us, a whole pack of them baying and swarming either side of us. It seemed that the truck began to move again, driving forward of its own accord, the road still rolling forever, and the river of white sand beneath us possessing a current we could not resist, pulling us farther forward. I tried to come up from the bottom of the lake. I sat up and pumped the brakes. There were bright spotlights everywhere, and the swirling backs of wolves—or were they dogs?—visible out every window, and human voices behind the searchlights, voices in the darkness that I could not understand. They seemed to be hunting something. And then the lights, and the hounds, were moving on, we were not what they were searching for, the light was pulling away, and I was already falling back down again, could not stay awake or aloft any longer, if ever I had been.

We awoke at gray dawn to the songs of mockingbirds and courting cardinals and the two-note whistles of bobwhite quail; the florid May scents of loblolly, magnolia, honeysuckle, and wisteria. And etched into the white sand was a multitude of dog tracks from where the wild pack had passed by in the night, chasing whatever it was they were after, while we had remained behind, never quite waking, chasing sleep.

That a dream could be a dream and yet real life too—could even leave proof of its passage—was a revelation that I hope has not been lost on me. And here in Montana, back in the cradle of home, I am glad to call it to mind again, and to remember how those hounds went on—it was a dream—and yet how they had been there, too, as real as anything ever is or was.

FOURTEEN

Joyce Carol Oates, Badass

There are mentors you don't know are mentors: secret shadows. As a boy, in high school, I read Joyce Carol Oates's work, along with the other contemporary classics of the alabaster canon: Updike, Cheever, Welty, O'Connor. Back then it seemed (and this does not speak highly of the student I was) that these were the flavors of American lit: the Past, or the South, or the Northeast. And to me, Joyce Carol Oates was the Northeast.

It is of course this narrow-sightedness that each writer dreads—*Oh, she does those coming-of-age stories, doesn't she?* And the fact that Oates was so versatile—poetry, criticism, novels, essays, stories—and was, that damnable word, *prolific,* did not help matters. We couldn't be more different, and yet something pulled me to her.

Joyce has suggested we all meet at a restaurant she favors, a place called Two Sisters, not far from Princeton, New Jersey, where she lives and teaches. Cristina will drive from Philadelphia solo, I'll drive down in a rental car from Vermont, where I've been teaching at Bread Loaf, once the home of Robert Frost—red barns, rolling hayfields, birch and maple trees, brilliant white and mustard-colored clapboard farmhouses with green shutters.

The windows are down, the cold sky a rich blue. I've recently finished teaching a semester in the winter-gray dead cornfields of Indiana, during which I lived in an efficiency apartment with a bed the size of a matchbox, unable to even turn to my side without falling off. The apartment was across the street from a fraternity house and a highway upon the warped blacktop of which rattled 18-wheelers hell-bent for Chicago with the roar of ceaseless, frantic commerce. The stench of ethanol refineries, ever present, filled the cold winter fog.

I've been wanting to carve out time to return to writing fiction, which requires living in a dream, inhabiting a dream sometimes for years. A novel is a moon shot to another universe, and you can't get there if you awaken each morning and go to the computer to check your available bank balance, or if you are always glancing at the clock, hostage to the tyranny of time. "You've got to be obsessed." Matthiessen's words continue to ring true. How ironic that the most important words came to me on the first official day of the project. And still I keep searching, still I keep running.

It's with a mix of relief and disappointment that I pass through the green hills and small villages. I'm relieved I won't be cooking tonight—how stressed I would be, how *racing*, juggling specialized cookware, spice lists, much-folded and photo-copied pages of recipes, an ice chest, sacks of groceries, all of it against the clock. Instead, this time, I need only show up at an address in Hopewell, New Jersey, sit down, and focus on conversation. And yet I feel like I've been demoted, to let another chef do my work for me. I wanted to do something physical for her, something ceremonial beyond the unimaginative twenty-first-century gesture of picking up the damned tab. This restaurant meal feels like cutting corners. But at least Cristina and I will meet Joyce, and Dan Halpern, her editor. Cristina will get something from it, and I'm out of Indiana, where at least the people were nice, even if the country was a new level of grim.

Still, I wonder, what can I give Joyce, what can I do, if not cook for her? Worrying is such a bad habit, such a waste of brain sugar. Save it all for the page, I tell myself. Control what you can control. The world will provide the rest.

Hopewell is the sort of town the name would indicate, a snow globe of the affluent and the bucolic: groomed and manicured, tended. Leisure here seems to be a ferocious goal. When I park in the dappled late-day sunlight, so luscious it seems to be spread with a palette knife, I feel the delicious wildness of being in a new place: the thrill of the unknown. Everything around me is unfamiliar, as if I have parachuted into enemy territory. The young super-rich couples push their prams—I know they're super-rich because the men wear pastel-colored short-sleeved knit shirts, powder blue and pale pollen-dust yellow and pink, and because they glow with strange tans not available naturally this early in June. My senses are colliding, and I want a drink badly to dial things down, yet I do not want to meet Joyce and Dan with a buzz.

It's the restaurant hour. Again, I sniff the aroma of affluence as cafés begin spreading the linen tablecloths on their outdoor tables and, back in those kitchens, good oil and butter are heated in fine skillets. The smell of meat, and of seafood, fills the pretty street and like somnambulists awakened, people converge on the restaurants, tracking straight lines toward them. They're older folks, mostly—my age—and I feel a ridiculous jolt of envy: is this what their every evening is like, having someone else cook nice food for them? And then I realize it's not envy, but something even more unpalatable, hypocrisy: for soon I too will be standing in line, an impostor.

I feel like a wolverine in their midst. This is not my brand of leisure. It is not an agony, but neither is it a true pleasure. The street is remarkably silent, there is only the sound of a few slow-passing cars, and the scent of the restaurants, and the strange beauty of the early-evening canopy of green light, Hopperesque in its density. Each house is a perfect Victorian. American flags sprout chastely from most of the deep porches, which give off a slightly Southern vibe, except for the absence of the feral: no old couches, no dogs barking from behind chain-link fences, no ragged lawn mowers blowing crooked rings of acrid blue smoke.

Cristina passes by in her little red car, and I hurry down the sidewalk to greet her. We have not seen each other since the previous summer, at Lorrie Moore's house, and yet it doesn't feel as if a year's gone by; we've been in touch most weeks, as she continues to labor on her novella. How many revisions, in that time: twenty? thirty? But she's happy to see me, appears to bear no grudge for my never being satisfied. She's a glutton, really, for a work so ceaseless that it must seem like punishment. It's one reason I chose to mentor her. There are a lot of good young writers, but few who love the agony of rewriting.

Cristina is dressed to the nines. If you can't dare to dress up for going out to dinner with one of your heroes, when can you?

"I need a drink," I say, then realize how abrupt that must sound as a greeting.

Cristina, usually unflappable, looks a little startled, but is agreeable. First, however, she wants to show me the dessert she's made for Joyce, a beautiful Italian wedding cake, which she's transported in the back seat all the way from Philadelphia.

"It's gorgeous. She's going to love it," I tell her, even as I wonder why I didn't think of bringing something.

"It's my third try," Cristina allows. "I was up all night. The first two looked okay, but I'm happy with this one."

Three fucking cakes, on a Friday night before travel?

The restaurant is just opening its doors. We saunter inside to check it out. The pots in the kitchen glint. We catch glimpses of sous-chefs chopping away amid chatter and banter, their own energies ascending. It smells great already—our dear friend garlic—and I start to feel a bit better. It's such a lovely cool evening that we ask if we might stake our claim on the choice outside table, and when we explain there will be five of us—Joyce's husband, Charlie, is joining as well—we're told yes. It feels good to have secured the prime territory for Joyce.

We step back outside.

I have been where Cristina is now. There on the sidewalk I can remember it, and it stirs up dusty places in my mind, attic places. I remember the blood in my veins and arteries feeling incandescent at having discovered my talents and energies with the pen. I remember going out with George Plimpton and Susan Minot and Jamie Linville and Mark Richard for drinks along the Hudson, at dusk, and thinking, This is what I'm made to do, but how did I get into this magic slipstream, this current leading to my wild desire? And my answer to myself then was work, and luck.

During that first interview with Cristina, when we both agreed on "Death to cute," I told her she should read Joyce Carol Oates. And she did, voraciously. Later, when I asked her what she thought, Cristina, who described Joyce as a badass, listed her top reasons in bullet form:

- She writes dark shit that's still funny without trying to be funny.
- She writes complex, interesting women: mean, ugly, sick, violent women who are also moms, wives, daughters, etc.
- There are stories, scenes that stick with me so vividly it feels like maybe a nightmare I had that I can't shake: especially "In the Warehouse," where the little girl pushes her bully to her death, the blood spreading out around her, UGH, and same for "Mastiff," and also "The Story of the Stabbing."
- She doesn't stick to one genre, way of storytelling, subject matter.

So now we sit before the luminous white tablecloth, waiting for Cristina's No. 1 hero, and enjoy a glass of wine as we watch the perfect people pass by. We visit about which questions each of us will have for Joyce, though I have learned that a script is all but a waste of time. There is always a wild card.

And then Joyce appears, gliding down the sidewalk in entourage—with Charlie and Dan—and it is as if I am watching her with lenses of different magnifications. She looks ephemeral, drifting, and yet—blink again—she is moving briskly, with the authority of two bodyguards. She's wearing a long floating sheer summer dress—the word *chiffon* comes to mind—and a wide fancy straw hat that folds in different directions, a hat that is larger than she is by far. I am reminded almost of a young girl at a tea party, deliberate and careful in her movements.

Cristina greets her, holding her breath the way she sometimes does. Terror can be a wonderful thing.

Charlie, in casual slacks and a sweater, a tad rumpled, as befits a research neurologist, is affable and easygoing. He takes a seat next to Cristina. Dan, wearing a light sport coat that nevertheless manages to radiate casual, is tall and tanned, with a lion's mane of windswept silver hair and a Gallic nose. He takes his seat on the other side of Joyce, who is directly across the table from Cristina.

Cristina holds her hands in her lap, appears poised, but when you travel so many miles with someone and handle her rawest work, cutting sentences that should remain unsaid and demanding the ones not yet said, you know the truth. Such is the gonging of her heart that I wonder if Joyce and the others can hear it.

How many times in Joyce's life has she done this—another damned dinner, another damned public appearance? And yet she jumps right in, assuming the mantle of primary conversationalist, guest of honor—on stage, even if mildly, on this summer evening. It's work, but she leans into it with good cheer, a graceful bon vivant.

She can be dark on the page. I recall the Gillian Welch line about "a dark turn of mind," and I wonder: when one is dark on the page, does it free up space to be light in person? Because there's none of that darkness here. Joyce is talking about a movie she and Charlie watched the night before, *Patton*, with George C. Scott. Holy moly, 1970—I saw it as a kid. She liked it okay, she says; it was something she and Charlie could agree on.

"We cancel each other out," she says, "and usually end up on something in between—but this was quite good."

Cristina's still not breathing! Is she thinking, *I did not expect Joyce Carol Oates to start out talking about a World War II tank commander?* But somehow we're already sliding, like a river current, into another topic. Joyce is telling us about a conversation she moderated with one of her own heroes, Joan Didion, where Didion refused to address or even look at the audience, but kept her back turned toward them the whole time, so that Joyce was having to carry the evening, radiating graciousness. She was getting exasperated with Didion, who is a friend, because as the event went on and Joyce tried ever harder to pull Didion into engagement with the audience, Didion became ever more stubborn.

It sounds awesome—a high-powered battle of wills—and Joyce, even years later, is shaking her head and smiling, as if to say, "I finally met my match."

We order our meals and keep visiting, and into this pleasant, free-flowing conversation I try, perhaps clumsily, to slip a few interview questions. Joyce makes a face, and—is it my imagination?—shakes her head almost imperceptibly.

I inquire whether she knew Eudora Welty, and she says she did. And then I ask her that most predictable question in the world: Who were your influences? The names come loose and float over us like the petals of scattering cherry blossoms. Katherine Mansfield, Turgenev, Voorhies, Alexander Pope, Calvino, Russell Banks. Some I've read, others are known but not yet read. I have the urge to stop and pick them up and read them all, one by one.

I ask her about a few other writers. This is utterly uninteresting to her, but she plays along and asks if I know certain writers she knows. When she mentions Richard Ford, I ask if she's heard of his dead-rabbit-swerve philosophy—of how, if one is to review books, there's no sense in reviewing a book one doesn't like. It's akin to driving down the road and swerving the car in order to run over a rabbit.

Joyce is familiar with the quote and says she agrees, but it's clear to me she is not keen to do her thirteen thousandth literary interview over dinner. She prefers instead, and intends to have, a simple and pleasurable experience with new and old friends, and so I jettison my other lame questions to the bottom of a private sea.

It's different, being next to a great one—to hear the audible, steady breath of John Berger, and to see the sunlight entering his eerily translucent blue eyes; to hear his rich baritone. Different to witness the slightest hesitation in Sedaris before he speaks, to see the responses that travel at warp speed through his whirring mind, until, with a barely noticeable release of his body just before he speaks, he settles on the right one, having tossed out the others, and calmly delivers a witticism.

Joyce is engaged, and engaging. Where, I wonder, is the tortured artist who has produced the darkness of *We Were the Mulvaneys*, *The Gravedigger's Daughter*, and *Patricide*?

Dan's been listening, and turns the conversation toward me, asking about where I live—about the woods—and this leads him to tell a story about one of the only two times he's been outdoors. He and his family went to visit the writer and biologist Bernd Heinrich in deeply rural Maine, where, upon arriving midafternoon, all they could think about was fleeing the dark forest before sundown. When Heinrich answered their knock on the door, they were terrified they would be asked to stay for dinner, and pretty much told him, "Hello, but we need to be going now."

"I looked down at the steps to his cabin," Dan says, "and there were ants!

"Twice I have slept on the ground," he continues, as if recounting the worst hangovers of his life.

How I love the self-deprecation of the powerful, the graceful, the intelligent. This is the man who went to Morocco in his twenties—Cristina's age—not just to meet an elderly Paul Bowles, but to hang out with him, and become his publisher, in a new press he was starting, Ecco, still going strong almost fifty years later. The man who launched one of the greatest literary magazines, *Antaeus*. Who became a writer—a very good poet—himself.

I praise *Antaeus*—more than thirty years later I can remember the distinctive heft, gloss, font, and design of each issue (no work is ever wasted, no gesture toward quality ever truly disappears)—and I tell Dan what a formative element his quarterly was in my self-education: the idea, *literature*, made tangible in those thick volumes, held in both hands. Dan smiles, accepts the praise almost wordlessly—I think he says merely "Good," or, "I'm glad"—and I feel in that moment an intense satisfaction, almost as if I can see the moth dust of those old days, glory days, falling upon Cristina's shoulders.

Joyce, meanwhile, is enthralled by the saga of the ants. She turns to Dan and is asking questions of him—her editor for more than four decades—as if they've just met. "Danny! Were you a Boy Scout? Have you ever been camping?"

He tells another tale of having slept on the ground, which delights her.

"Oh, poor Danny!"

I want to ask Joyce about teaching, but deftly, gently, they keep asking me about myself—not, I think, as a defensive mechanism to avoid my own inquiry, but instead out of true curiosity. Joyce asks about my time in Indiana.

"It was awful," I admit, "but I'm on the other side now. The faculty was awesome—they kept me sane—but a lot of the students were, well, entitled."

"Where?" Dan asks, alert. There is a crispness to his question. I tell him the name and he smiles, laughs a small laugh, as if we're blood brothers. "I gave my first poetry reading there," he says, "my very first. It didn't go well. At the end, this old professor stood up in the back and began heckling me. The old guy told me I had no business writing poetry, that I was a terrible poet, and that I should quit, right then and there. My first reading," Dan says, still smiling. "Oh, he was a horrid old man."

Joyce is aghast. "Oh, Danny!" she cries again.

Dan just shakes his head. "I hadn't thought about that in a long time. I'm sorry to hear you had a rocky time. I'm glad you got out." He lifts a glass of wine in my direction.

The qualities that make Cristina such a good writer are honed so strong in her that they can occasionally cross over that knife-edge of strength, and into weakness. She can *focus*, almost obsessively. And so it is, with a sickening prescience—having stressed to her on all our journeys to please chronicle them—that I see the perfect storm rising, and rising quickly. Our meals last summer were with Lorrie Moore and Tom McGuane, where, especially in the rolling festivities with the latter, there was nonstop merriment and picture taking, both formal and informal. Cristina worked her big, fancy camera like a machine gunner. She might've taken a couple of hundred photos at that party.

With horror I see her reach down now to her bag beneath the table. No assassin ever moved more smoothly. I am powerless—there is barely time for me to even watch it, and she pulls out the giant camera like a rocket launcher.

The slow, single *snick* of the camera, mid-table, is deafening. A greater violence could not have occurred had Cristina reached into her handbag, pulled out a long-barreled pistol, and fired it into the sky.

Joyce freezes with a spoonful of soup lifted halfway to her mouth, her back bowed like a cat's, her eyes locked on Cristina's. "What are you doing?" she asks.

A tiny wisp of steam rises from the soup in the spoon. Time slows; my heart slows. *Thunk* one, *thunk* two, *thunk* three.

Joyce looks broken, and now Cristina looks broken. She

lowers the camera a little—though not all the way down, so that, still, she might lift it and begin firing again.

"That's just not right," Joyce says. "We're having dinner." And she looks down at her lap, as if she can no longer bear to stare directly at the violence she's just witnessed. She shakes her head, thinking, perhaps, *So much ugliness in the world.*

I feel like a bodyguard who saw the lift of the gun and who attempted to dive in front of the bullet but couldn't get there in time. "It's all my fault," I apologize. "I had asked Cristina to take pictures. I'm so sorry, it's totally my mistake." I can't tell whether Joyce can even hear me—her ears might be filled with underwater ocean-drumming outrage—and I say, "She brought you a cake."

For a second Joyce cuts her eyes at me. At the other end of the table, Dan and Charlie look away, as though studying the unseen arc of where Mars might be in a few hours. In that briefest cutting of Joyce's eyes I feel a tinge of the laser focus that just drilled Cristina, who is in a reverie, her eyes huge and glassy, all color having left her. She is like one hypnotized, so that if Joyce were to say to her, "Rise from the table and take your belongings and walk into the center of the street and stand there," I believe she would.

I apologize once more, and Joyce, as if fearing another ambush, stirs her soup. Dan and Charlie are still respectfully silent, holding the gravity of the faux pas. At last we begin to eat again, and to talk again.

It's true evening now. Out on the street there's a sudden backfire.

The violence and volume of the sound are incongruous with all the baby strollers and the quiet sidewalk conversations of other diners, and Joyce starts ever so slightly, then says, "It's just a car," speaking as one would to calm a child.

The air is chilling with the sun down. Little lights, as though for the holidays, blink on at the various restaurants, including ours. The night could go on forever. It begins to seem that the camera's snout, which lies dormant in its bag beneath the table, is miles away.

Now and again, as the darkness deepens, I'm reminded of how tiny Joyce is. No one would use the word *frail*, but *delicate*, I think, *vulnerable*. A breeze stirs over us. Joyce, in her gauzy summer dress, appears to shrink beneath it, and I know suddenly, wonderfully, what to do.

I excuse myself, get up and leave the restaurant, and run back to my nearby car, where my zip-up fleece rests in the front seat. The night is now so cold I would put it on myself, but at least I'm wearing a long-sleeved shirt, whereas Joyce's arms and shoulders are bare. It is a great pleasure to hurry back to the restaurant and offer her the fleece, a great pleasure to drape it over her shoulders. I'm a little terrified, self-conscious of my Texan-ness, of my old-mannered chauvinism, which I thought I'd unlearned. But that worry dissolves when I see how relieved Joyce is as I assure her I have no plans tonight for the sweater. She folds herself into it, and I feel a flash from the past; she's the size my daughters were as young teens.

I did not stay up all night baking a ricotta cake in triplicate. I did not prepare an overlong list of interview questions, did not read each of Joyce's seventy-plus books (a book a year beginning when she was a toddler?). And yet the world paused long enough for me to do something for the cold great writer sitting at her table by candlelight in the north wind. Joyce leans back into the conversation, reinvigorated and reanimated, a badass indeed.

"Pain, in the proper context, is something other than pain," Joyce has written, in *On Boxing*. Her father was a devotee of the sweet science, and it impresses me, how much of the warrior's ethos informs her. "The punishment—to the body, the brain, the spirit—a man must endure to become even a moderately good boxer is inconceivable to most of us whose idea of personal risk is largely ego-related or emotional."

Her prose makes it clear that she loves the struggle, the hand-to-hand combat of writing, in which laziness is the enemy, in which shortcuts tempt the writer.

Cristina is picking at her food, listening. I wish the camera incident had gone otherwise, and that Cristina was conversing with Joyce about boxing, about fathers and gyms, about long-distance running, another activity shared by the women. And yet, to paraphrase one of the more famous poets of my generation, you don't always get what you ask for, but you almost always get what you need.

"What makes a good editor?" I ask Joyce, with my typical suddenness.

The abruptness works, though: both Joyce and Dan, despite the earlier distaste for talking lit, answer simultaneously, and with verve, "Less is more!"

At first, I think they're reiterating the advice that my first editor, the great Carol Houck Smith, gave me—the Hemingwayesque idea of the iceberg, where the writer labors to keep the bulk of the story buried beneath the surface, with as few words as possible forming the part that juts above. But now they're joking and yet not joking, talking about a hands-off, trust-the-writer ethos. And because I rely so much on editors to help me cut the overflow, I'm intrigued, and want to ask more, but time is no longer on my side. Somehow, despite my best efforts to sustain it, the dinner is ending.

More people are walking past on the sidewalk now: old people, powerful people. An endowed professor at one Ivy League school or another passes by; an art historian. They're all heading back to their homes and cars.

Living in the woods as I have for the last thirty years, and being broke for most of those years, I have come to assume that mine is the default condition for much of America. And I believe that is the case; I have read the inarguable demographics of the vanishing middle class. Yet there are also pockets of extreme comfort. And we're in one, Cristina and I, if but for a few minutes more, waiting on the carriage to return, to take us back to where we came from, back to who we are.

Joyce glances at her purse. After we rise to leave, we shake hands and embrace. Joyce and Charlie and Dan tell us to come back and visit, perhaps in New York. "Maybe we can cook!" I say, and they do not flinch, but instead tell us it sounds like a fun idea, and they seem to mean it.

Rather than walking away with them, Cristina and I stand there and watch them leave, and I realize, in the cool breeze, that Joyce—Joyce Carol Oates—still has my favorite old sweater. What do I do? She'll wear it home, but then, thinking it's expendable because it's so old and worn, she'll give it to Goodwill. I'm shocked by my miserliness: for I had been carrying on about how much I wanted to give her something, and the world accommodated that wish. I know that I have to let her go with the sweater and be satisfied I have kept one of my mentors warm.

But then Joyce turns and comes hurrying back down the sidewalk, the gray sweater folded neatly over her arm, carrying it as she would a coyote pelt, or a dead fish. She's gracious, grateful, annoyed at herself, apologetic, and then she vanishes back into the night with Charlie and Dan.

"Are you all right?" I ask Cristina, when Joyce is out of earshot. "Holy shit, how are you doing?"

"I'm a little shaky," she says. "But I'll be okay."

We take when we mean to give, and we receive, sometimes, when we least expect it. I look back down the dark sidewalk, the empty street, in the direction Joyce went—back into her incredibly full and productive life—and I know sharply that although I am in the middle, I am ready to move forward into the last stage, toward the end.

FIFTEEN

Terry Tempest Williams, Red-Rock Solid

There's almost no reason we should be best friends, other than that we've had the same mentor, Doug Peacock, and that we share a love for the West, including the strange state of Utah, where we both went to college. Terry was trained as a natural historian, and I a wildlife biologist. As I've mentioned, the world first pulled us together at Edward Abbey's memorial, near Moab. The second time I met her was at a dinner party in the Tetons for various Western writers. I closed a car door on her writing hand and broke her thumb.

She works in the exact opposite fashion of me. I'm a grinder, showing up for work every day, seating myself at the desk, and wearing down the paths into the subconscious—not getting up to leave until something has happened, good or bad. Some days the wellsprings are dry, but I go down to them anyway, hoping, because sometimes you find it.

Terry, on the other hand, disappears from her writing for weeks, even months, at a time, fully engaged with whatever cause or opportunity life brings her way. The world demands her time, savages her reservoir of it, and she rarely says no. Visiting President Obama or meeting with Bishop Tutu, traveling to Northern Ireland and Rwanda to talk about reconciliation and spirituality. Despite her middle name, she works from a place of greatest calm, of candle-flame centeredness. When she writes, there is nothing else in the world. I've never known anyone with such focus, or ferocity.

She's best known for her memoir, *Refuge: An Unnatural History of Family and Place*, but as with few other writers, each new work travels to surprising places: art history, national parks policy, Africa, the Galápagos, prairie dogs. In this wide-ranging curiosity, she reminds me of John Berger. She is a frequent participant in civil disobedience and direct action. She is the person who most typifies the phrase *force of nature*. She's won just about every award in the world, and has changed countless lives for the better with her wisdom, passion, and generosity of spirit.

To the outer world, she is like a saint. It's fun to tease her about this. "Nobody can even have lunch with Terry without crying," Doug Peacock says, bemused and admiring—but it's also true.

She and her husband, Brooke, have a successful marriage of forty-two years. They met in a bookstore—how romantic and geeky is that? Terry was working the counter, and Brooke, with his then girlfriend, buying a stack of field guides to Western birds. Brooke's girlfriend was complaining about his choice in reading material, and Terry, ringing the books up, looked across the counter with her ice-blue eyes, said, "I *love* these reading choices," and that was that.

Tempest. Occasionally, chaos does attend her, as if drawn toward her calm. When she and her family were camping in Glacier National Park several years ago, a wildfire swept in, forcing them to flee the stone chalet where they were staying and run for their lives, down the backside of the mountain and into a creek, with embers settling over them like scorched stars. She was in New York on 9/11, and at the Boston Marathon, watching her nephew run, on the day of the bombing.

The red-rock desert of southern Utah is her beloved home. Terry has dedicated her life to fighting for its wilderness, but she does so much more. She is also a citizen of the world. She will spend weeks preparing each talk or lecture, then scrap her notes as she approaches the podium and speak extemporaneously, reducing audiences to tears, then raising them to standing ovations. She is at once elegant and earthy.

One icy, foggy December she was the keynote speaker for the Montana Wilderness Association's annual banquet, and I picked her up at the airport, out in the agricultural lands north of Kalispell. On our way, in the center of the six-lane highway to Glacier National Park, lay a car-struck bird, feathers still fluttering from the windblast of each passing car and truck.

"A Hungarian partridge!" I cried. "A gift from above!"

Terry was wearing a long black dress and jewelry, but I made a U-turn, drove down that double-wide center turning lane, and instructed her to open her door as we passed and snatch it up. In the cold weather, and when their individual feathers are still ruffling like they do when the bird has not been dead long, they're all right to salvage. (I was already dreaming of how delicious it would be, one of the best-eating game birds.) And as if she'd been doing it all her life, Terry opened her door, leaned out, and scooped up that plump little bird on the fly, with me slowing only enough to facilitate the pickup.

Just like that, the bird was in my old Subaru, still warm, almost as if it was unharmed there in Terry's hand, with each feather a miracle, mahogany and russet and mustard, taupe and amber, earth-colored for camouflage yet also somehow as singular and flamboyant as a parrot.

We rode into town and checked into the Garden Wall, a little Victorian bed-and-breakfast, where, the next morning, in cold sunlight, wearing fleece, we sat on the front steps and plucked that beautiful bird. Its feathers swirled around us and clung to our jackets. When we had the bird plump and ready, our hosts took it and said they would fix it for us for dinner, which they did, complete with finely diced garlic and onions, a jalapeño, and an olive oil, huckleberry, and balsamic vinaigrette reduction. They grilled it perfectly, and with the snow falling outside we ate it on fine china, with a bottle of ruby-colored Beaujolais. By the time we checked out a couple of days later, one of our hosts had tied each of us a beautiful tiny fly with the hackle feathers of the Hun's downy legs.

So much has changed, of course. Terry knew Elizabeth well, and was witness to our dissolution. But enough time has passed that the scars, while still scars, are starting to be accommodated. I know how to deal with the pain when it returns; I know, too, that it will pass on, like a cloud, and that ever so slowly other things will become visible at its edges.

Mary Katherine, my older daughter, has been coming home as much as she can. She has enlisted me to be a board member on a campaign she's running, at the ripe old age of twenty-four, to create medical-research centers in California and Montana. She travels to Australia and Switzerland to give presentations and interview Nobel Prize–winning scientists. She sits down to lunches and dinners with ex-presidents, mayors, senators, governors, ambassadors. She works eighty hours a week some weeks, as I once did.

Lowry is home again in the Yaak this summer, following a life of the mind, a life of literature, supporting her studies as a student of environmental writing and general nonfiction at Middlebury, where she decided to transfer after her freshman year. (Not to be, I'm afraid, her adventure house-sitting for Lorrie Moore.) She's the best reader I've ever come across, reading more patiently and deeply than I do: curling up in the overstuffed chair by the window, with the marsh beyond, and spending hours in paradise, while we trade off cooking and I shovel more books at her. Hoagland, Welty, McKibben. After so much loss and grief—such failure—I feel like I'm getting my feet back under me, helped by those I helped for so long, my own children.

Terry, who has known both of the girls since birth, wants to see Lowry before she heads back east to Vermont, and so, having spent weeks planning this meal, Low and I head south, to the cottage that Terry and Brooke keep near the Grand Tetons.

Lowry and I share driving duties en route to Jackson Hole, with me typing while she takes her turn. The car is stuffed with backpacks and gear—after cooking for Terry, Low and I will go into Wyoming's Wind Rivers on an ambitious backpacking trip we've been planning for years—as well as ice chests, skillets and pots, pie dishes, and groceries for the meal with Terry. (Brooke, alas, is down in Utah.) After the long trip, Lowry will return home for a few days, then rocket back out to Vermont. The big house will be empty again. There are stirrings in my mind, men and women made of clay becoming slowly animated in the landscape of the novel I want to write, the one I've been making notes on for fifteen years. I can feel them churning around, way down there in the mud, the late-summer sun awakening them. It feels good.

In Dillon, several hours out from Terry's, we stop at the famed taco bus for huevos rancheros and green chile enchiladas. We reach Jackson Hole, and the Tetons, ten minutes ahead of schedule. The peaks above are magnetic. I don't mean metaphorically. You can feel their mass tugging you as the moon must feel the pull of the earth. The flecks of pyrite, hornblende, mica, and zinc glitter. The ice caps soothe the air around them.

When we pull up in Terry's driveway, she's on the porch, wearing a long black dress and turquoise necklace, the picture of elegance in the cool green bower of her and Brooke's cottage, which their family has owned since long before Jackson Hole became Jackson Hole. Aspen leaves flutter and quake. Mule deer emerge from the cooling shadows and into the darkening green of the meadows.

Terry envelops us in a hug, seeming as strong as ever. This is a woman who for the last several years has lived with the everyday presence of a bleeding brain, a meningioma, which induces a stroke-like response in her body every time the lesions burst. Numbness, then partial paralysis of limbs, speech difficulty, migraine, cognitive fuzziness—in short, everything that could conspire against a writer. Surgery is one possibility, but such a high-risk procedure that she's opted against it, and instead just keeps living one day at a time. The surgery could render her a happy vegetable, the doctors say; she would still be able to take delight in the world, but would have no capacity for memory. This could still come to pass, even without the surgery, as a result of the disease itself. Living in the moment was a skill she possessed before her diagnosis, and one that she practiced better than anyone I've met, but now she does this more than ever.

Her writing has gotten even better. I don't think it's necessarily due to any neurological alteration, though there has been one curious side effect: as if less able to traffic in clichés, her brain's wiring for idioms and colloquialisms appears to have gone completely FIGMO, so that when she means to say something like "It's no skin off my nose," she'll say instead "It's no shit on my knees." It's delightful—and, knowing her so well, I understand exactly what she means.

Two chairs sit on the porch and a single newspaper, the *New York Times*, on a wicker table, unread but plump and waiting. We pass inside, into a home that is neither spartan nor over-appointed. A small kitchen, a small dining area—with the house and its corners ceding to the central living area, adorned by a long leather couch, bookshelves, and a stone fireplace.

Before unpacking—before we even open the Cowgirl Creamery blue cheese, the oily green and black olives, the Raincoast crackers, and the rosemary butter and sourdough baguettes—we go out to the back porch in the late-day sun with a bottle of cold sparkling wine. We sit in the thin sun and catch up for over an hour, while cooking time slips away, guaranteeing us a late dinner. It is a delicious squandering. A moose, dark as chocolate, wanders past, browsing the willows.

Lowry and I string a hammock for Terry and insist she lie in it and read while we begin making the meal. And she tries; she reads for about ten minutes, but then comes back inside for more talk.

With our ingredients spread across every available space, we begin stacking things in tiers of two and three. Lowry's unflappable, simultaneously preparing the salad—figs, goat cheese, basil, arugula, pumpkin seeds, and a vinaigrette—along with her homemade black pepper and lime gingersnaps (perfected even further since our trip to see Sedaris), which she'll use to make ice-cream sandwiches. As if that weren't enough, she's also assembling the galettes: baking the sweet potatoes, rolling out and cutting the rough puff pastry dough into squares, brushing it with oil, mincing the jalapeños, and toasting the pumpkin seeds. All while I stand in the kitchen staring at the pile of dough with which I'll make a double crust.

I've made hundreds of pies, but tonight I feel I'm moving in slow motion. My brain won't let go of my instinct and desire, which is to relax and visit with Terry, who is perched on the other side of the bar. All I have to do is bake a crust, pour Yaak huckleberries in it, cover it with a latticed crust, and be done. At the last minute I'll salt and pepper the elk tenderloin, throw it into the iron skillet with some Yaak morels, and sear it.

The galettes don't bake long. Soon their parchment-thin laminae are browning and it's time to fire up the meat, which is seasoned only with kosher salt and cracked black pepper, all it needs. I stir-fry the morels quickly in butter, caramelizing them. The weight of the meat, and the sound of it in the heated skillet, tells you how long it will take for it to be done just right. There's also a smell the peppercorns make when the elk is ready. At this point, you want to slice and eat it immediately. (The veteran of a thousand such dinners, Lowry knows this, and is bringing the dishes to the table as Terry lights the candles.)

This is the meal of my dreams. The house is a universe of scent: not just morels and butter and seared elk but also the holiday aroma of baked sweet potatoes. The pie, meanwhile, is in the oven, and the hint of vanilla that Low put in the gingersnaps wafts through the air. We hold hands, Terry says thank you, and the three of us sit down to a great feast of the earth: potatoes, wild meat, wild mushrooms and greens, with wild berries awaiting. Terry all but roars at the first bite of elk.

It's been a year to the day since she and I last saw each other, and we make an agreement not ever to let more than a year pass. Terry asks us each what was the best thing that happened in the last year. Low's and my best was a horse-packing trip to British Columbia's Muskwa-Kechika Management Area, just a month earlier.

Terry's lowlight, her meningioma, is obvious. Not far behind that, being persecuted by her former employer, the University of Utah, for her environmental activism. Her highlight was having her father and Brooke accompany her on the tour for her latest book, *The Hour of Land*, her personal, idiosyncratic, and political journey through a dozen of America's national parks. It was the first time either of them has done that.

Her biggest surprise was becoming the owner of two oil-and-gas leases, as a counterintuitive means of continuing her work to stop drilling on public lands. She and Brooke and her father started their own energy company, with leases they had secured but which the government is trying to take back from them, given that their definition of *energy production* differs from the state of Utah's. They intend not to drill for hydrocarbons, but rather to use the lands for natural-history field trips and exploration. A different kind of energy. Litigation against them appears inevitable.

"The job of the poet is to remain indignant," Terry says.

It's remarkable, how much food we've eaten. It's so good that we can't stop. We're stuffed, but the pie and the gingersnaps remain. Terry and I lean back in our chairs, beyond sated, while Low scoops vanilla-bean ice cream onto her snaps, sprinkles it with lavender sea salt, then pours the thinnest drizzle of black-pepper simple syrup over the ice cream before pressing the cookies and ice cream into sandwiches. I get up and cut wedges of hot huckleberry pie, each round and sweet berry having been picked by hand in the backcountry just a few days ago specifically for this pie.

After dessert, we sit in the candlelight, delirious with happiness. Terry wants to play dress-up. "Let's blow out the windows and have a fashion show," she says. Her request seems to make perfect sense. We snuff out the dinner candles and go into the living room. She's come across a beautiful long maroon velvet dress she wants Lowry to try on. It's ankle-length, with a flamboyant belt and padded shoulders, totally Parisian, and Lowry wears it elegantly.

For me, Terry finds a soft buckskin blazer—a Halloween prop?—and it's great fun to model it as if I were Natty Bumpo.

Coupled with the fantastic meal, it feels like the best therapy ever. It's like we're all seven years old again. Low is so radiant in the maroon dress that Terry gives it to her. The two of them are taking silly photos, which they'll post to social media. The evening stretches to the other side of midnight. Terry insists on getting Low's guest room just right, plumping the pillows, then arranging and rearranging my spot on the couch, fooling with different variations of sheets and blankets. "Are you comfortable? Are you *sure?*"

All the while, time slips away; as if we are made of time, and as if our lives are defined not by the balance of equinox and solstice, but instead by the ebbing away of time.

Breakfast: huckleberry pie, purple in the high-altitude morning sunlight, gingersnaps, vanilla-bean ice cream, black coffee. Terry and I sit quietly, with the awareness of more than half a lifetime's friendship between us unspoken. I am reluctant to leave but the day is stirring, and we must go out into the world. Terry has work to do on an op-ed for *The Los Angeles Times* about national parks, and Lowry and I have miles to go to reach the Wind Rivers.

We embrace, after which Lowry and I load our car with all the cooking gear amid the camping gear, and pull away. I worry sometimes that Terry is traveling too much, waking up in too many different hotel rooms. The thing we most wish for her we cannot give. The more famous and revered she becomes, the more she gives, and the harder it gets for her. The physical as well as emotional and spiritual toil accrues. I feel both fortunate and guilty to be going off into the woods for a week. Maybe in the fall things will slow down for her. Or if not the fall, then the winter. She'll write again. It's forming in her, even as she waits for it, gracefully.

What I know most of all is that I'm lucky. Other than Terry and I both loving the woods with the ferocity of a wolverine, we couldn't be more different. And yet I couldn't wish for a better friend.

SIXTEEN

Mississippi Ghosts

The plan for finishing up the project is to meet in Mississippi for the Conference of the Book, held in Oxford each spring. Initially, all of the mentees, including Molly and Skip, were to be down there, but in the end only Cristina can make it. She and I will cook for some of the Mississippians who were there for me at the very beginning, nearly thirty-five years ago now: Richard and Lisa Howorth, the founders and owners of Square Books; Lyn Roberts, the longtime store manager; and Lyn's husband, Doug. Along with Square Books, the other bookstore that taught me how to write was Lemuria, down in Jackson, and I will visit the gang there as well.

Lowry and a writer friend of hers, Katy, the one for whom I suspected Lowry of pilfering Sedaris's linen napkin, will join us. Katy, who's finishing up at Barnard and has already had a story published, does a good job of hiding her wicked and sometimes slightly dark if tender wit behind her serious demeanor. She's quiet, always listening and watching, and is the best thing a young writer can be: hungry.

My hope was also to make a meal for Elizabeth, who is living down in Mississippi now, and to honor her contribution to my writing journey. That part is not to be, as Elizabeth's brother, who hasn't seen Lowry since she was little, lives in Birmingham, and the weekend of the conference will be the only time for Lowry to see her uncle. But she and Katy and Elizabeth will join Cristina and me for evenings in Oxford and Jackson on either side of the weekend, with a visit to Birmingham sandwiched in between. Meanwhile I'll be staying at Doug and Lyn's lovely rambling farmhouse in Taylor, just outside Oxford. Afterward Lowry and Katy will continue south to New Orleans, then west toward Texas, on their own literary journey, which will eventually lead them back to Montana.

Mississippi is thick with ghosts, of writers especially. Faulkner and Welty and Richard Wright, Shelby Foote and Lewis Nordan, Willie Morris and Barry Hannah and Larry Brown. It has crossed my mind that given the state's propensity as a ghost-making factory, a writer who finds him- or herself in Mississippi might do well not to linger. It may be wiser to absorb the swamp ether of melancholia, passion, and occasional insanity that rises from the soil and the bayous and the furrowed delta, but then leave before being claimed oneself.

Grief is a ghost too. The divorce wasn't what I wanted. It's taken me a long time to shoulder my share of the blame. I tried my hardest to save the marriage and it wasn't enough. They say not to use the word *failure* in these instances. They say to get on with your life. Perhaps we are all ghosts, even in the waking. It can sometimes seem that even in the broad light of high noon we are all merely hurrying through the fumes.

It's hard being back here—I recall my first date with Elizabeth, lunch at a park in Jackson in the springtime. Winter-dried leaves skittered past and the cold blue sky above was like the mother lode of hope and ambition. So what if she was the most beautiful girl in Mississippi? She was already dying to get out, she just hadn't quite realized it yet. I was twenty-two, she was twenty-one.

I worked in the office with her mother, Janie. Elizabeth was a free spirit, doing part-time drafting work. Elizabeth's brother was fifteen years younger, and Janie a single parent. I took her little brother camping and fishing. I had my pilot's license and took him flying too. Janie was a bit of a free spirit herself, letting her youngest go up in a plane with me all over the green state of Mississippi. Once, flying low, near the Alabama line, we passed over some feral chickens roaming a field next to a little gravel airstrip. We landed, put one of the stragglers in a cardboard box, got back in the plane, and took off with a white chicken in the cockpit. Chicken at five thousand feet, then ten thousand. We flew all day, thinking we'd take it home to keep as a pet, but decided against it and in the end returned it to its flock. "The years went by," wrote John Prine, "like sweet little days, with babies crying pork chops and Beaujolais."

Elizabeth said she liked BLTs. I told her I did too, that I ate them all the time. A fib. I brought my microwave to the park with us, with an extension cord. She said she liked tennis, and I said I did too, the truth this time. We played a few games in that silly wind, with our whole lives before us, and then I plugged the microwave into an outlet at the base of a light pole and cooked the bacon. I cut up the tomato, spread the mayo, added the lettuce, and we ate hot, fresh sandwiches in the sun, with the tips of our fingers glistening and those crisp leaves blowing past.

Her approval did not come easily and I wanted to please her. I still do, I realize, and always will. I have this fantasy where we become friends again. I remember how Russell, the painter, said his ex-wife was his best friend now, that he called her every day. Not the stuff of fairy-tale romance, but sweet and, toward the end of a life, who cares for style points? I try to operate as if each day is all there is.

Before my event at the conference, Cristina and I meet up with Lowry and Katy at William Faulkner's home, Rowan Oak, which I've never visited despite the years in Mississippi in my youth. I haven't seen Lowry since Christmas, and I haven't ever seen her as an adult in the South. It's strange and new, glimpsing her there among all the old oaks and the trellises of Spanish moss. It takes me back thirty-five years, for in certain moments she looks just like her mother. Sometimes it can feel as if time is nothing more than a fabrication of man.

It's midafternoon, hot and bright on the lawn, shady and cool beneath the canopy of oaks. The house embodies the word *relic*. There is a palpable sense of the despair, the alcoholism, the depression that once existed here, and walking along the warped red-brick walkway, you do not have a hard time imagining that it was this force, radiating upward, that knocked those bricks asunder. Lowry says it's easy to picture him sitting under any of the great old trees, drinking the day, and—unavoidably—his life away.

Then she mentions to me that her mom is going to join us at Rowan Oak.

"Oh good," I say, and I mean it. I haven't seen Elizabeth since the last meeting—the cleaving, the apportionment—six weeks ago. The day the papers were finally signed was, fittingly, a cold and windy one. I examine that scar briefly, then refocus.

We go inside. The house is as I imagined—it reminds me of my grandmother Robson's home; it's even painted, it seems, from the same bucket of cool blue-gray paint. More ghosts. I remember the girls running through that old house. What must Grandmother Robson have thought? Our older daughter, Mary Katherine, is the namesake of her daughter, my mother, who did not live to see her granddaughters, and Lowry is my grandmother's namesake. I remember the girls crawling like puppies into the lap of their great-grandmother, a woman born in 1898, one year after Faulkner himself.

The inside of Rowan Oak—empty and static, ghost-gutted by all the visitations, lacking the bouncing vitality of lives in disrepair, in love, in hope and ambition—is only mildly interesting. Absent the keen attention to the sentences, the keen attention to his daughter, the keen attention to the bottle, there is little to see. Faulkner used to ride south to Taylor, eight or so miles away, and water his horse at the fountain. *That* is what I'd like to see. If he was still alive for us to cook for him, I think we'd grill him a whole pig. "Every time I see a pig, I tip my hat," Grandfather Bass used to say.

When the four of us exit, it feels good to be back outside. Redbirds call and swoop, streaks of bloodshot song through the trees. Lowry and Katy are wondering where Elizabeth is—

we have to be at the courthouse for my talk soon—and I see her before they do, a long way off, walking through the trees. Those old neural pathways will never go away. More than thirty years of keen attention to another's movements leave their mark.

She makes her way toward us. My old synapses are sending and receiving signals—*Greet her, be observant, what might she need or desire?*—and then I remember that she no longer requires my attention. There can be something even more sorrowful than ghosts, which is the separation of the living.

We all look around at Rowan Oak, chat briefly—and then, in a moment that saddens me disproportionately, we go our awkward ways in three separate cars: Elizabeth in one, Lowry and Katy in another, and Cristina and me in the third. What was once a family unit, with the ever-present pleasure of duty and watchfulness, is now a roving pack. Not strangers, but every bit as separate. And I do what I have been doing for four years now, and what I suppose I will keep on doing, as one must do with any grave injury, which is simply to push forward.

We park near the square and walk the rest of the way, through the same country we walked when we were young. The same sunlight, the same sidewalks—every footstep the same as it was when we were in love. No ghostliness now, nothing bittersweet, just pain. We walk past things that recall our old lives—black-and-tan hounds in that spring sunlight, preposterously young couples with children in strollers—and past the bookstore where I became the writer I am, and up the steps to the courthouse with minutes to spare before it is time for me to speak.

We slide into the pews as if arriving at a friend's wedding.

Richard Howorth, not only the owner of Square Books but also the former mayor, gives a lovely introduction, and then I go up and talk about how I came to writing. How the two bookstores told me what to read, hand-selling me my curriculum over the years. I talk about Mississippi's ghosts, not just Faulkner and Miss Welty, but the new ones—Barry Hannah and my dear friend Larry Brown, a longtime firefighter before he was a writer, who died much too young, a heart attack at age fifty-three that shocked and devastated us all. I talk about how my daughters supported my writing. I speak of Elizabeth's helpful critical standards—never shy about saying something sucked when it did, which was often—and, of course, about Richard and his huge heart. How he survived the crash of the publishing industry and, after that, the Great Recession: hard times through which the community kept him and Lisa going. I give a few writing tips, then say my thank-yous and am finished, and the conference is over for another year.

For old times' sake we walk over to City Grocery, one of the best bars in America. Up the steep rickety steps, past the friendly bouncer, and into the great shoulder-to-shoulder friendliness of the place, music and conversation, shouting into one another's ears. When I step to the bar to order cold beers, there's a picture of Larry Brown on the mirror behind the taps, and I tell the bartender we were friends. The man standing in line behind me, a blue-collar guy still in his work clothes, taps me on the shoulder and says that Larry was a dear friend of his and he's glad to hear me say Larry's name.

When we finish our drinks, the five of us head to Taylor Grocery, the catfish place where Elizabeth and I used to go with Larry and his wife, Mary Annie, and sometimes with

Barry and his wife, Susan, after readings or signings. A crowded place out in the country with the best fried catfish in Mississippi. Ghosts chest-high, and all a traveler can do is lean in. I'm glad for Lowry and Katy and Cristina to be seeing the past, and particularly glad for Lowry, since this is where she came from before she was here.

At the cash register, there's another picture of Larry, and when I ask the waitress if she knew him, she tells me she's really good friends with his family. I'd forgotten how social he was. He'd carouse till midnight or later, go home, play his guitar, write letters, then settle into work, writing until just before dawn. Sometimes there was work that needed doing—a field to plant, a tree to saw up. An airport to get to, a place to give a reading. Leaning forward. But writing was the best thing. The sole purpose of all the other work was just to buy time to be still for a moment and write.

We walk out into the night. Elizabeth, knowing my hearing is declining, asks if I can hear the frogs. I can. Again, there's that walking-on-broken-glass feeling—three different cars in the parking lot. Doug and Lyn's house is just across the road from the restaurant. Elizabeth, Lowry, and Katy go over there while I shuttle Cristina back to her hotel in Oxford, then head back to Doug and Lyn's, where everyone is still up, chatting. Too many years have passed. We don't keep them up long, but it's a great comfort to be back in their beautiful old house.

Then Elizabeth leaves to drive back to her house and Lowry and Katy go into Doug and Lyn's big front bedroom. Meanwhile, in the guest cabin, which doubles as the library, the room of ten thousand books, all the way to the top of the twelve-foot ceiling, with sliding librarian's ladders, I roll out my sleeping bag and sink into the depths, with tens of millions of words latticing the sky above me, encircling me. These are the new days.

With all the close shaves and command-performance meals, it's great to have a whole day to shop for food, and to cook for friends with no pressure. It's like floating on your back in the middle of a mountain lake on a summer afternoon. I meet Cristina in town, and we saunter over to the bookstore, where I sign some stock—hundreds of books—as I've done often in the past. The first time I expressed dismay at Richard's habitual big buy—"What if you can't sell them all?" I asked—he said not to worry, he'd sell them, even if it took twenty or thirty years. And it's true; he did, and always has.

Cristina buys a bag full of books, including Larry's great novel *Joe*. The gas station where we stop has farm-fresh eggs, and next to the cans of Starbucks espressos and Yoohoo, the Gatorade and Red Bull, are bottles of milk from Billy Ray Brown's dairy, just down the road. I buy a paper bag of peanuts and we make our way north of town, to the farmers market, where Cristina's astounded and delighted to find meats she can't find even in Philadelphia. "There's got to be an Italian around here somewhere," she says. A run to Albertson's for the cheaper stuff, then to the liquor store and back to Taylor, where Doug is waiting for us.

Doug, an attentive sous-chef, stirs the filling for the coconut cream pie, careful not to scald it, while I work on the dough. The developing scents of Cristina's family-recipe pasta suffuse the room—garlic sautéing on one burner, tomatoes on another, spices being added. What a marvelous afternoon, what a marvelous kitchen. There are two big gas ranges side by side, and Doug jokes that this should be required, that it's a marriage saver. I smile and tell myself to ignore the hurt. It's too great a day.

When Lyn gets home from work and walks in to the homey smell of steaming pasta and just-made red sauce, the veal and beef and pork patties Cristina has made, her face radiates. It's a hearty meal, suitable for ditchdiggers—and with plenty of bread to make sure not a drop of sauce is wasted. Then Doug and Lyn's daughter, Cecile, wanders in, followed by their neighbor Elizabeth Dollarhide, and then Richard and Lisa, looking spry and festive despite this being about their tenth night in a row of socializing.

We carry our plates out through the screen porch into the guest cottage, into the Great Room of books where I slept the night before, and sit at the long table with tall candles and old family silverware. Lisa, never one to beat around the bush, looks over at me, and at the beautiful food, and says, "I wish Elizabeth was here."

"Me too," I say. "I really do."

It feels good to have said it—to have gotten it out, clean and honest—so that now we can proceed without its lurking under the surface. We dig in, pass plates. Cristina appears happy, having successfully fed a boatload of her elders. Her new Mississippi tribe. Lisa, particularly, is delighted to welcome her in. It turns out they both have relatives back in some little village in Italy. The food reminds Lisa exactly of her way-back.

After a while, we exhaust ourselves, unable to eat any more, but with plenty of capacity for the stories that keep spooling out. No small number of them involve the most recent triumvirate of Oxford's hard-drinking writers—Larry, Barry, and Willie Morris, a Mississippian who returned home after a stint of many years in New York, including as the youngest ever editor of *Harper's* magazine, where he published Norman Mailer and William Styron, among others. Barry in particular loved the Howorths and their children. The three young Howorths were fascinated by his electric bent of mind and followed him everywhere like ducklings. One day, Lisa got a call from a neighbor who didn't know this, saying, "Lisa, I think I just saw Barry Hannah going into the woods with your children." Another time Richard and Lisa received a call from Barry when he was out carousing with Willie, saying he was too drunk to drive but that someone needed to get Willie and take him to the hospital right away because his eyes were yellow.

As for Larry, he often ended up staying at the Howorths' after a night on the town. He would wander over and crash in the guest bedroom. Or not sleep, but just stay up. One gray morning, the Howorths' youngest, Bebe, came to Lisa very concerned and said, "Momma, Larry Brown's out by the woodshed, and he's just staring at the wall."

I love how they tell these stories—not just in the buttery rich Southern accent of my youth, but with the graceful tag-team elegance of the long-married: Richard and Lisa, Doug and Lyn. Willie died years ago, and after that Barry stopped drinking, though he too is gone now, from a heart attack, like Larry. After decades of turbulence, a calm has settled over the land, pooling like silver fog.

* * *

We've been offered indefinite lodging, but guests, like fish, are good for only two days. I'm up early the next morning, working, and then it's daylight, time for pie and coffee, hugs, then the road. Cristina has to fly back to Philadelphia, while I will push on farther south, into the truer heart of my own ghosts: Jackson, where I'll meet up again with Lowry, Katy, and Elizabeth. Because we have some time and it's Cristina's first trip south, we decide to drive toward the Mississippi, into the Delta—the heart of what was once the black-soiled center of the economic engine that made the United States a financial powerhouse. Where each spring the great river that cleaves the country into east and west flooded and deposited a great bounty of nutrients, resettling a garden of Eden, and where almost anything could grow, cotton especially. Later on there would be a great cost, but beneath that broad plain of suffering and injustice, music and literature arose. Of course Cristina should see that landscape. As a writer, as an American.

It always surprises me how close Oxford is to the Delta. After just a few miles, we're descending; the hills are less rumpled, and then they're gone. We're tracking due west, through forests and fields, and the world is increasingly made up of Big Agriculture—a civilization of giants, with sprayers and tillers and seeders towering far above the little tractors and plows of my youth.

Clarksdale. Highway 61. We drive north toward Memphis, past all the casinos, past the tract-home subdivisions that have sprung up in satellite clusters, and into the airport. I drop Cristina off and she goes on her way, back to her life and her writing, and I feel a little as I did when I'd drop my daughters off at school.

Afterward I travel on, wandering back downriver through the Delta, little towns with all their used-car lots, still fraught with poverty, now as then.

The following day in Jackson, at Lemuria, Johnny Evans, the owner, is as happy to see me as if I've come back from the dead. There's a pack of young store clerks well practiced in the process of handing me books to sign, opening them to the flyleaf, taking them from me, then putting them back in their boxes. We blow through a few hundred books in a matter of minutes.

John tells me that over at the Eudora Welty house, where my reading is to be held, they're hoping to be able to give me a private tour. I have to laugh. Thirty-plus years, aiming to get into her house, even her backyard; I've definitely taken the long way around.

Lowry and Katy meet me at the bookstore, John gifts us with T-shirts and bandannas, and Lowry hands me my birthday present, a beautiful watercolor of the two of us climbing a mountain in the Yaak at sunrise or sunset. I'd forgotten it was my birthday today—I'm fifty-eight, born in '58. Then I've got to dash to catch the tour, and will see Low and Katy and Elizabeth at the reading.

I park out front of Miss Welty's old house and walk right on up the walkway as if she's been expecting me, has invited me in for tea. One of the docents, Bridget, takes me into the house. I've got only ten or fifteen minutes.

For some reason, Miss Welty seems more present here than Faulkner does at Rowan Oak. Maybe the house hasn't been as over-visited; maybe the spines of her books, and the molecules of scent in her cabinets, have not yet been burnished into nothing. You can tell she's gone, but it doesn't feel like she's been gone long. And in truth she has been dead only fifteen years, compared with Faulkner's more than half-a-century absence. There's something of Miss Welty still here, some spirit or essence.

I wander from room to room with Bridget's guidance. I try to remember everything I see. The Persian carpet, the books left on her coffee-table as they were when she was living. Her record player in its fine mahogany case—how she loved music! (I think of her classic story "Powerhouse," about a virtuoso musician.) The stairwell, going straight up, which she writes about in *One Writer's Beginnings*. The portrait of her father. Her sunlit kitchen, so identical to Grandmother Robson's. The porcelain corrugations of the countertop's built-in drying rack: an unspoken ethos from those days, perhaps, when cooking was less artistic expression and more family sustenance. You cooked and you cleaned up; you did not leave the dishes for later. You finished what you started.

How I want to run my hands over things. I want to open the kitchen cabinets, where I feel certain I'll find the same comforting robin's-egg blue Fiestaware of my youth. Earlier, I spied a literary journal I'd had a story in thirty years ago—did she read it?—but museum rules prevent me from picking it up and thumbing to it. I can only try to drink it in, all at once, and then hold it for as long as possible.

Minutes are melting away. Bridget shows me the hole in the kitchen wall where there used to be the chimney pipe for a wood-burning stove. Miss Welty once grew exasperated over the rejection of a manuscript and started a chimney fire when she burned the manuscript. The house was almost lost. A couple of weeks later, a letter arrived from an editor asking for the manuscript. She had to write it again.

There's not time to go into the backyard, but at the back of a long downhill slope Bridget points out a little shed resembling a clubhouse. "She called that Passion Parlor," Bridget says, with a hint of pride at Miss Welty's impishness. We tend to think of her as a spinster, forgetting that she too was young.

Upstairs, quickly, her bedroom, pristine, as if the life it belongs to has yet to be lived, and then her writing room, the sunroom, facing out over Pinehurst Street and Belhaven College. "She always wrote with her back to the window," Bridget says. This gives me a pause of sadness, a momentary judgment—what would it have hurt, in the long run, to face the window? This from a woman who said that all serious daring starts from within. And yet McGuane too writes with his back to the river. And John Berger's son, Yves, paints with his back to Mont Blanc.

I'm two minutes late. I leave the house with some hesitation—though it's not hard to imagine Miss Welty being grateful to have it returned to her after closing hours. I hurry across the lawn to the museum, where people are still heading inside, dressed nicely, in that way I forgot young Southern professionals will still do, so different from the Missoula informality I'm used to. Esteem for Miss Welty, for entering her space—an acknowledgment that even though she's gone, she's still here.

The museum is an intimate reading space, an elegant old house with folding chairs. Every seat is taken, and people are standing too, spilling into other rooms where I cannot see them, nor can they see me. This fills me with an extra sense of responsibility, speaking to people I cannot see, almost as if I'm speaking into the future. They love their stories in Mississippi, and I love them for that.

Inside are people I haven't seen in thirty years, my old Sierra Club friends, river-paddling buddies who kept me sane in those first years when, having just gained the West for the first time in my young life by attending college in Utah, I had to give it back up for a while, returning to the South after school for seven long, wonderful years. My writing apprenticeship. And alongside these do-gooder, wilderness-loving anarchists, my old-school oil-field wildcatters, staunch conservatives. How strange to have the two elements of my Mississippi days in one house, all here together. They were never officially at war, but in their individual lives each side possessed a sensibility that wasn't compatible with the other, despite their living under the same sky, in the same town, shopping in the same stores, breathing the same air. I would like to believe a story, and time, can facilitate the unification of such friction and resistance.

I finish reading my story—I never tire of that ancient act, the oral tradition—and then I answer questions for a long time. It feels good to be able to acknowledge Elizabeth's emotional support for the stories, despite our differences that widened rather than narrowed over time. A lot of the audience's questions are about writing, some are about reading, and some, as they should be, are about Miss Welty. These folks knew her well; their stories still possess the beautiful dust of the living.

Afterward, walking down the steps away from the now-darkened old house and into the spring night, I remember that when I used to do triathlons and marathons, I trained in this neighborhood, ran all up and down these bulging hills. The red Yazoo clay, named for the nearby river, which feeds into the Mississippi, is stretched drum-tight across the dome of an old volcano. People tend to forget that in these parts there is a fault line to rival the San Andreas: the New Madrid Fault, which as recently as a century ago shifted in such a fashion as to reverse the flow of the Mississippi itself, sending its current south to north, from the Delta up toward its source, as if time itself, for a few days at least, had decided to run backward.

As opposed to Oxford, we will consolidate to one car to go out to dinner. First, however, Elizabeth needs to get something from her car—a tiny brownie cupcake, baked by our friend Corrine, with a single candle in it, which, once all four of us are in my car, she lights. They sing "Happy Birthday," and I start the car. The evening edition of National Public Radio is airing an interview with me about my story collection, and we listen to it with some horror and fascination.

"Did you have a cold?" Elizabeth asks. "That doesn't even sound like your voice."

It feels good to laugh. "No," I say, "it's just me." Several years older now than when we were last truly together.

Meanwhile, it's the eve of the Republican primary in Mississippi. Donald Trump, a name I have never before typed, is in town, agitating the citizenry, and Lowry, fascinated by the bizarro quality of this cultural shipwreck, wants to check out the rally, notebook in hand. Elizabeth, however, is hungry, ready to go eat at the Mayflower, one of our haunts. It's a tricky piece of business, mediating between two strong-willed women. Elizabeth and I decide to place a time limit on the rally exploration—we'll just buzz out there and gawk. For some unclear reason of irony, Lowry wants a poster. Then we'll blast back out.

But by the time we get there, it's already over. The legions are walking out in a dejected overflow—the candidate arrived, spoke for a few minutes, then dashed away—and now we are caught in the mother of all traffic jams. As the subdued pilgrims head back to their vehicles, Lowry and Katy get out of the car and walk past them, searching for discarded signs and posters.

This is nothing more than a fever, I think, as the people pass by. *Look, it is already fading.*

Downtown Jackson is eerie, empty. We pose for pictures beneath the swirling loops of red and green and blue neon outside the Mayflower, then step inside. We order our favorite, soft-shell crab—fried and broiled both, since we can't decide. The waitress is chatty and exuberant despite its being the end of a long day. She can tell we're happy about something, maybe celebrating, and offers to take our picture. We're sitting against a wall mirror, so the waitress with the camera is in the picture, as is a lesser, second representation of us. It's a great picture, like something taken fifty or sixty years ago, a happy family of four, nuclear as hell.

And what is the difference, really, between what the camera shows, and what is? This evening, right now, we are happy, no less so for its being a complicated happiness. If things both are and are not as they seem, isn't that almost always the case? We are hard-wired to develop plans and to chart paths; yet whether it's a recipe or a life, surely some of the greatest pleasures come from veering away from how we thought a thing should be and into the freedom of that which was previously unimagined but is here now. The only thing you can do, at the beginning of each day, is work with what you have.

We finish our meal but keep talking until at last we realize it's closing time, a fact from which we've been shielded by the kindness of our waitress, who has left us untroubled and is folding napkins and tablecloths at another booth. We thank her, pay, and step out of the restaurant into the night. Already the kitchen workers are sitting in their aprons on a bench, smoking. We walk to our car, and I can feel the edges of something eroding, as when surf foam stretches in, reaching. I will need to drive everyone back to their cars, but first we tour the vacant streets, the skyscrapers rising up into the mist. We show Lowry and Katy the Federal Building, with its worn steps. I remember going into the post office every day on my lunch break to mail out one terrible manuscript after another. We show them the old capitol, where I would go to write on those lunch breaks, and then, just a few blocks away, the old house where I lived, 826 North Street, and, just behind that, Elizabeth's, on Jefferson—or rather where that grand old house used to be. It has been torn down—a long time ago, from the look of things.

We describe for Lowry and Katy the time the circus passed through town after midnight, with all the animals walking down State Street on their way from the Coliseum to their train, illegal as hell. We heard them from my house—the elephants trumpeting—and went out and followed them for a while, in the wake of their shadows as they sought the darkest streets, headed to the train yard.

We drive on, back to Miss Welty's house. It is not yet extraordinarily late, but it feels that way. Everyone is sleeping. It staggers me to realize that I used to live in a city. There's Kiefer's, where we used to get the best gyros, and there are the tennis courts in the park where I once made those BLTs for Elizabeth.

I stop to let them out at their cars, and when we trade hugs, it takes all my powers of denial and self-deception—all my talents for make-believe and imagination—to live in the feeling that we are not drifters, unraveled. That we still hold, and forever will, some larger unity.

In the morning, breakfast at Janie's, just as we used to do, sitting on her back porch listening to redbirds. The same breakfast as a thousand others taken here: Community coffee, oven-baked bacon gleaming, small mounds of grits with butter and black pepper, two poached eggs with black pepper, and half an English muffin. We chat amiably about the Trump weirdness, about springtime, as if our lives have not been blown apart; as if, having never done this before, we are not at a loss as to how to revise them. Where, if they exist, are the points for reattachment?

My flight back to Montana doesn't depart until midafternoon. There are still more than a few ghosts left unexhausted, and in typical fashion I want it all. We'll drive out on the Natchez Trace, again rolling in three vehicles, then leave two at a roadside pullout. Prior to meeting them at Janie's, I stopped by the grocery store to get some picnic treats, including a cold Coke in a bottle, to which Elizabeth and I were once addicted—and crackers, smoked cheeses, apples, hummus. We won't have time to visit the farmhouse where I lived and wrote, twenty or so miles south of Jackson, but we can make it out to the farm where Elizabeth lived—Mrs. Ferris's farm—south of Vicksburg. The Big Black River. The old general store with the "F. L. or W. B. Yates" signage. Two brothers co-owned it, and clearly neither wanted top billing. On past sharecropper William Appleton's farm.

It occurs to me that to do this right—to stir up all the ghosts—you would almost have to go back and live your whole life. There's no time for that. There's barely time for the remembering.

But it's a glorious spring day, sunny with a chill breeze out of the north, and the meadows are ripe green from all the rain. We drive slow through dappled sun, the windows rolled down: back in time. Back beneath the long drooping trellises of Spanish moss, and the slick black-tar road of the Natchez Trace, on which Elizabeth and I rode our bikes many evenings.

Down the steep hill leading to Mrs. Ferris's sprawling farm—across the bridge and into the dazzling light. Past the old empty house where I found the two black-and-tan hounds, abandoned, not even weaned yet. I carried them to Elizabeth's house, where we fed them, raised them. Homer and Ann, we named them. They traveled with us to Montana, became Montana hounds. Mary Katherine and then Lowry were born, and these hounds licked both girls, who played with them and came to love them too.

There's time to show the girls Mrs. Ferris's big house on the hill, where she had tea and a big lunch every day, usually alone, at a long elegant table that looked out over the rolling hills. She was vibrant into her nineties. Still, everything is finite, and we're dealing now with minutes rather than hours. We do not have time to show Lowry and Katy the lake down in the woods where we swam on hot summer days. The Lake of Peace, I called it—a lake not unlike the one in which Anne Stanton and Jack Burden swam in *All the King's Men*. Nor is there time to show them the waterfall, strange for this country—a twelve-foot drop, like something in Hawaii. There's no time to do anything but go past Vicksburg National Military Park, with its steep hills, where so much blood was shed, now a forest of spooky, ancient oaks with small clearings in which the battles must have raged fiercest. In shadow and sun, with the glint of the river far below, it's a landscape that looks, strangely, like peace.

I think Lowry knows how much in love her parents were.

There is time—twenty minutes, by my calculation—to do what we set out to do: picnic. We leave the river-bottom country—Elizabeth has her hand out the window, is looking at the green fields—and cross the river. After a while, I pass a weedy gravel road, the turnoff to which is covered with pine straw, suggesting it has not been traveled in a long time. There's definitely a "Good Man Is Hard to Find" vibe to the lane, and we joke about that. We pull in and drive far enough not to be visible from the road, then get out and walk farther, through a narrowing lane of greenbrier tangles.

We emerge into a meadow, a rolling valley of green in which a tractor rests, and settle at its edge, in the bright sun, and I begin spreading crackers with different cheeses, and hummus, and handing them out. It feels exactly as it did when we were starting out—countless such picnics with our daughters, deep in the forest, and the great simple pleasure of providing.

We share the Coke, and then the four of us split a couple of Larry Brown ales, a gift from Richard and Lisa. I have a bar of fancy chocolate and pass out little squares, which we savor with the beer. Then we spread our jackets behind us and stretch out, falling away from one another like flower petals from the stem. We close our eyes and do not quite nap, but float for a short while in sun-soaked bliss, and I try to be both aware and unaware of the minutes.

I hear a car on the gravel. I hear it drive up and park behind our shiny little rental with its Illinois license plates. A door opens and closes, then a man comes walking down the lane. We sit up, one by one. He's maybe a few years older than I am, blinking a little. He looks more stupefied by our presence than displeased.

He asks our names—never a good sign, skipping the *how-are-you*s and *nice-weather-we're-having*s. I give him our first names, as if making introductions, and ask after his.

Jack, he says.

"I guess this is your field, isn't it?" Elizabeth says, and I'm happy to let her do the talking. She tells Jack about Mrs. Ferris, who of course he knows, and he does the math: anyone who was a friend of that grand old lady is not a drug-running cartel of hoodlums or mob leaders down from Chicago.

He seems more puzzled by the anachronistic quality of our repose than by the act of our trespassing, as if he's gazing half a century into the past, and he continues to study us, knowing he should be cross, yet also somehow wanting to approve. "I guess y'all can finish your picnic," he says finally.

"Thank you," I tell him. "We won't be long."

*   *   *

As we sit at the edge of the field I do not know that in less than three weeks, the one who started it all for me, Jim Harrison, will die from a heart attack on a Saturday night, seated at his desk, working on a poem. A poet's death. A journey that began with a death, Peter's, will end with one; and this is of course precisely the reason I have carried these young people with me, to visit these living ghosts, and to tear open the bread, and soak it in the gravy. "Death steals everything except our stories," Jim once wrote.

I will not resort to the hoary pronouncement that in every death there is a beginning. While this is as true as the sun's rising, it is just as true that some things go away and do not come back. We are not much practiced at sitting with, and holding, loss. Would I have even been a writer, a fiction writer, had I not read Jim—had I not read that first page of "Legends," so long ago now? I don't know. I know only that I have never been through such a season of ghosts.

We drive back up the Trace to where the other cars are parked, and again we scatter like quail: Elizabeth back to her winter home in north Mississippi, Lowry and Katy down to New Orleans. I in turn hurry east to Jackson, and the airport, where afternoon thunderstorms and spring tornadoes will shut down air travel for half a day. I'll end up taking a late-night flight to Houston, skirting beneath the belly of the torrents, and then a red-eye back to Montana, floating the whole way through black storm clouds ripped open every several seconds by beautiful spiderwebs of lightning.

Back to work. Back to Montana in springtime, a Montana little different than it was three years ago, when I began this long journey. Work, as it always has, awaits. I took a three-year leave of absence—to some extent, pursued the writing degree I never had. I fed my ghosts, helped nurture them a while longer, as I in turn slumbered, as if within a chrysalis. Not neglecting my writing, but waiting. Meditating, I think, on hunger.

And when I finally awakened—when the last bite was eaten, and the last of the dishes cleared and washed, and the candles snuffed out—what I awakened to was not so much a different world with different sensibilities, but instead the same old world in a different season. Autumn, you'd have to say, even though here in Montana it is the edge of spring, as all that is old waits to start anew.

Alone, my first day back home, I will make a fried-oyster po'boy. Thinking about Jim, I will eat a honey-chicken biscuit for breakfast with thick warm rosemary-and-black-pepper cream gravy clotted with slow-roasted dark chicken meat, the biscuits dense yet delicate. I'll top it with clover honey and— hell yes—a fried egg so rich its yolk is the color of a tangerine. A slice of French toast on the side, some maple bacon, and brandy-butter syrup, macadamia nuts, and mascarpone spread on top. For lunch, a lamb potpie, and a bowl of potato-leek cream soup.

Then I will go up into the steep blue mountains and hike for hours, with the view of my valley below—in which hardly anyone lives, and now one fewer, my wife—climbing so high that the valley looks as it must from an airplane. I possess no ailments yet, other than of the heart. I'm still as strong and durable as I ever was, able to pour food into the furnace of my body and ramble all day, uphill and under a load. At what day and hour I'll cross the boundary into old age, I don't know. But I'm not yet old. Others, all around me, are falling off the map, but not me.

When you have been away for a long time from a thing you love, it feels good to get back to it. It feels good to sink into it, invisible, as if down into a cloak of darkness, where time stops, and there is only the beat of your heart, and the next word, and the next.

Acknowledgments

First and foremost, I'm extraordinarily grateful to the writers and their families who welcomed me into their homes and lives over the past several years. A kitchen can be a sacred place and to allow me and my merry band of chefs and travelers to spill and sprawl into a previously immaculate space, with matches, cigarette lighters, alcohol, and meat, seems a great act of trust and generosity. I'm grateful also to the mentors and heroes—and there were many—who entertained my request to come cook for them but who demurred, with grace. How I would have loved to visit and cook for all of them, but I cannot fault their suspicion or reticence, their prudence—their survival skills. There's no way I would have said yes to this project and its requests, had I been on the receiving end. Time matters to a writer as much as imagination; time *is* imagination. Vital also is routine and stability. Over time, said Thoreau, an old poet learns to guard his or her moods and emotions as carefully as a cat watches a mouse in the corner. And this, too, paraphrased from Flaubert: Be daily and routine in one's regular life so that one may be violent and original in one's work. Midnight paella for eight really doesn't figure into either of these directives, and the older the writer, the more fiercely the clock ticks. So again, I'm grateful to all my mentors, whether I was able to visit them or not. Some were delightfully blunt in saying *No, but thank you*; others, like Mary Oliver, heartbreakingly gracious, stating, "The me of ten years ago would have leapt at this project," but she needed now to conserve her remaining time.

I'm grateful also to my mentees, who, like me and my mentors, juggled their work lives, families, weddings, and other special projects, including their own creative work, to travel the world to hunt down and cook for the greats while the greats were still among us. Most notably and steadily, Erin Halcomb and Cristina Perachio, but also Molly Antopol, Skip Horack, Katy Lee, Jessie Grossman, Alexandra Delacourt, Caroline Keys, and Lowry Bass.

Others who assisted in the seemingly unmanageable logistics include Ben George, who provided me with introductions and contacts, my agent David Evans, who helped with edits and wiring money to me on the road, Yves Berger and his family, Marc Trivier and Daniel, Mrs. Ferris and her sons Bill and Gray and daughter and son-in-law. Hester and Jim Magnuson in Mississippi, as well as the Eudora Welty House, Doug and Lyn Roberts, Johnny Evans, Richard & Co. I'm grateful to Elizabeth Garriga and Ron Ellis for publicity assistance. The staff and faculty and students at the University of Southern Maine's Stonecoast MFA program were supportive, as was the English Department at Montana State University, where I worked as writer in residence. Mandy Hansen and Brady Banks helped enormously in this regard, as did Brady and Katy Lee and Jessie Grossman with typing and editing. I'm grateful to the editors and publications that have published excerpts from these sojourns—*Mountain Magazine, Narrative*, the *Georgia Review*, and *Black Warrior Review*—and to Dan and Carol Sullivan of Mustang Café in Livingston for innumerable bison rocks with which to travel. Deepest appreciation goes to chefs Tom Douglas and Gordon Hamersley and Tim and Joanne Linehan and Elizabeth Hughes Bass, as well as my beloved daughters, Mary Katherine and Lowry, who encouraged me to start cooking in the first place, as well as to Jessie Grossman, a true kitchen magician.

I'm grateful to the hundreds of editors and publishers who have fed me their time and knowledge over the years—most steadily, the late Sam Lawrence, Nicole Angeloro, the late Harry Foster, and the late Carol Houck Smith.

I'm also grateful to the mountains of the Yaak Valley, which produced so much of the food I was able to serve my writing heroes. For more information on how you can help protect this splendid wild country from its many imminent threats, please contact the Yaak Valley Forest Council (yaakvalley.org and info@yaakvalley.org).

I'm grateful to Ben George and Cynthia Saad for editing assistance, to copyeditor Allan Fallow, to production editor Pamela Marshall, to Allison J. Warner for the book's design, and to Lowry Bass for the "EAT" photo. It was hard being gone from home so much, on the road so much, and I will appreciate always the support of those who took care of me when the road tried to get the better of me.

About the Author

Rick Bass, the author of thirty books, won the Story Prize for his collection *For a Little While* and was a finalist for the National Book Critics Circle Award for his memoir *Why I Came West*. His work has appeared in *The New Yorker*, *The Atlantic*, *Esquire*, and *The Paris Review*, among many other publications, and has been anthologized numerous times in *The Best American Short Stories*. Bass has won multiple O. Henry Awards and Pushcart Prizes, as well as NEA and Guggenheim fellowships. He lives in Montana's Yaak Valley, where he is a founding board member of the Yaak Valley Forest Council.